ADVANCING METHODOLOGIES OF CONDUCTING LITERATURE REVIEW IN MANAGEMENT DOMAIN

REVIEW OF MANAGEMENT LITERATURE

Series Editor: Sudhir Rana

Review of Management Literature is a multi-disciplinary series presenting unique and ground-breaking literature reviews and examinations of new and emerging trends in research across the management discipline and beyond.

Examining broad disciplinary areas including new research developments in fields including Marketing, Operations Management, Finance, International Business, and HRM, as well as well as more focused studies on the big data and gamification in management literature, the series also explores practical research guidance with titles examining methodologies for conducting literature reviews in management domain.

Supported by a highly reputable editorial board from across the globe, the series will be an essential research resource to access and interpret cutting edge global developments from across the management discipline.

VOLUMES IN THIS SERIES

REVIEW OF MANAGEMENT LITERATURE
VOLUME 2

ADVANCING METHODOLOGIES OF CONDUCTING LITERATURE REVIEW IN MANAGEMENT DOMAIN

EDITED BY

SUDHIR RANA
Gulf Medical University, UAE

JAGROOP SINGH
Gulf Medical University, UAE

AND

SAKSHI KATHURIA
Fortune Institute of International Business (FIIB), India

United Kingdom – North America – Japan
India – Malaysia – China

Emerald Publishing Limited
Emerald Publishing, Floor 5, Northspring, 21-23 Wellington Street, Leeds LS1 4DL

First edition 2024

Reprints and permissions service
Contact: www.copyright.com

British Library Cataloguing in Publication Data
A catalogue record for this book is available from the British Library

ISBN: 978-1-80262-372-7 (Print)
ISBN: 978-1-80262-371-0 (Online)
ISBN: 978-1-80262-373-4 (Epub)

ISSN: 2754-5865 (Series)

INVESTOR IN PEOPLE

We dedicate this volume to all the academicians, scholars, and thought leaders who are going to expand the body of knowledge by utilizing literature review methodologies.

CONTENTS

LIST OF FIGURES

LIST OF TABLES

ABOUT THE CONTRIBUTORS

Aakanksha Uppal is an avid academician and research professional, having 171 years of Experience. She has a doctorate and also holds two Master's Degrees, one is in Business Economics with specialization in Economics and Human Resource and the second one is in commerce. Her areas of teaching and research interests are human resource management, organization behavior, compensation management, etc. She is presently working as an Assistant Professor at Symbiosis Law School, Noida, constituent of Symbiosis International University, Pune. She is also the QIC coordinator at Symbiosis Law School, Noida. She is a keen researcher who keeps herself involved in doing good research and has written more than 25 research papers for conferences and Scopus indexed journals.

Alex Anlesinya (PhD, University of Ghana) is a multiple award-winning researcher, experienced lecturer/management trainer with extensive consulting experience. He is a Lecturer in HRM and Organisational Behaviour at De Montfort University, Leicester, England; and Associate Editor of Review of Business Management (RBGN). He has consulted for several institutions in Ghana. Alex received Best Paper Awards from several prestigious organisations including Emerald Publishing Limited; Wiley; Sage/FIIB Business Review; and was also valedictorian. Alex researches at the intersection of work, human resources and sustainability, specifically, talent management, sustainable HRM, decent work, CSR strategy, and grand societal challenges. He has published severally in high impact journals and presented in top international conferences.

Amna Farrukh is an Assistant Professor in the School of Management, FAST, NUCES, Pakistan. She has completed her PhD in Engineering Management from Massey University, Auckland, New Zealand. Her research focuses on the environmental sustainability issues of manufacturing organizations in a developed and developing economy. She has conducted research on the environmental sustainability issues of the packaging industry in New Zealand and Pakistan to address the increasing environmental problems of plastic waste in these regions. She is passionate about promoting research in the areas of operations and business management, sustainability, environmental management, circular economy, lean six sigma, total quality management, supply chain management, and organizational theories.

Anubha Srivastava is an Assistant Professor in the management department at I.T.S Ghaziabad. She has been associated with the institution as faculty member since 2017. She is also the coordinator of the BBA program. She has extensive teaching experience spanning 11 years. Dr Anubha completed her PhD at Dr. A.P.J. Abdul

Kalam Technical University, Lucknow. She earned an MBA (International Business) and a Gold Medal from the honorable governor while studying at Bundelkhand University in Jhansi. Her research interests are in the area of marketing, digital marketing, and electronic banking, ranging from theory to design to implementation. She has two patents in her name and has collaborated actively with researchers in several other disciplines of management, particularly consumer behavioral studies in several areas of management.

Aymen Sajjad is a Senior Lecturer in Sustainability and Business Management at the School of Management, Massey Business School, Massey University, New Zealand. Aymen's research focuses on sustainability issues that confront organizations and societies including sustainable supply chain management, business sustainability, corporate social responsibility, United Nations sustainable development goals, and sustainable business strategy. He is an Associate Editor of Corporate Governance: The International Journal of Business in Society, FIIB Business Review, and The International Journal of Sustainable Society. He is also an active member of the Sustainability and Corporate Social Responsibility Research Group at Massey Business School.

Ellen Pittman (PhD) is a Research Fellow at the University of Melbourne and also Managing Director at Amfractus Consulting, a boutique consulting firm based in Melbourne, Australia. Working between academia and consulting, Ellen specializes in organizational performance analysis and culture change in the health and human services, public administration, not-for-profit, and higher education sectors. Her doctoral studies culminated in the development of the novel "hive model for high performance cultures" – a biomimetic management model based on the principles of complex adaptive systems theory. She is particularly interested in research and theory that can be readily translated into real-world benefit. During the early days of the coronavirus (COVID-19) pandemic, Ellen provided strategic policy advice to the Victorian Department of Health, and she has previously led large-scale change and reform programs, including the application of "lean thinking" for hospital process improvement.

Hussain G. Rammal is a Professor of International Business at the Adelaide Business School, the University of Adelaide, Australia. He is the founding Editor of the *Emerging Issues in International Business and Global Strategy* book series, coeditor-in-chief of the *Review of International Business and Strategy* journal, the Real Impact Editor (Oceania) for the *Journal of Knowledge Management*, and Associate Editor of *Business & Society* journal. Hussain's current research interests include the internationalization of services firms (trade in services), the transfer of knowledge across the inter- and intra-MNE networks, global talent management, international business negotiations, and faith & religiosity in business.

Jagroop Singh is an Assistant Professor for Operations Management (Supply Chain, QT, and Production) at the College of Healthcare Management and Economics, Gulf Medical University, Ajman (UAE). He earned his PhD degree with Financial Assistantship (Scholarship) from the Government of India under

Technical Education Quality Improvement Program (TEQIP-II). He worked as a postdoctorate researcher with Putra Business School (AACSB Accredited), Universiti of Putra, Malaysia. He has contributed to the society through his teaching and research commitments for the last 10 years.

Dr Jagroop Singh has published in journals of International repute (ABDC/Scopus/SSCI), and serves as a reviewer for various international journals. He is also managing editorial responsibilities with SCOPUS indexed Emerald series "Review of Management Literature".

Monu Pandey Mishra holds an MBA in HR from School of Inspired Leadership, Gurgaon, India. She has done her graduation and postgraduation from Banaras Hindu University and Allahabad University in India. She has more than 10 years of experience in industries such as healthcare, education, IT, and manufacturing and is the founder and Chief People Officer at Digital Musketeers, a digital transformation consultancy company. She has published in peer reviewed SCOPUS indexed journals. Her expertise includes but is not limited to change management, gender diversity management, and stress management. She is lifestyle coach and career guide for reputed schools and colleges in India.

Rahul Dhiman received his PhD from National Institute of Technology, Hamirpur (HP), Government of India and Master's in Business Administration (MBA) in Finance and Marketing. Presently, he is working as an Assistant Professor in Department of Business Management at Dr. YS Parmar University of Horticulture and Forestry, a state University, Solan (HP), India. Dr Dhiman is in the reviewer board of many prestigious international journals and has several Scopus and ABDC papers in international journals of repute published by Taylor and Francis, Springer, Elsevier, Sage, Emerald, etc. He has presented papers at several international conferences across reputed public and private universities. Dr Dhiman has also visited a few European nations for teaching and research collaborations.

Rahul Pratap Singh Kaurav is an Associate Professor at FORE School of Management (FSM), New Delhi. Here he is responsible for teaching, training, research, and consultancy. His teaching and research interests include marketing management, services marketing, research methodology, marketing research, and marketing analytics. He is a professionally acquired trainer for quantitative and qualitative research software and into the training of Bibliometric Analysis, SPSS, Jamovi, MAXQDA, and NVIVO. He has been associated with the Taylor's University, Malaysia, BITS-Pilani, and University of Liverpool, UK, as an adjunct faculty.

Rajni is currently a doctoral student (SRF) in the Department of Management Studies in Bikaner Technical University (state university), Rajasthan. She qualified UGC-NET (JRF) in December 2019 and attained AIR-2. She has around 2.5 years of teaching experience and 2 years of industry experience. She has expertise in some of the data analysis tools like SPSS, AMOS, SMARTPLS, and Vosviewer. She has attended various international and national FDP's/workshops/seminar/webinar/conferences and has few publications including Scopus indexed. Her research interests center around Quality of work life and workplace spirituality and Organization Citizenship Behavior.

Sakshi Kathuria is an Assistant Professor in the Marketing Area at Fortune Institute of International Business (FIIB), India. Her current research focus spans social media, sustainability, and Industry 4.0 in the context of emerging economies. Her work has been published in leading journals such as Business Strategy and the Environment, Journal of Public Affairs, Technology in Society, and International Journal of Entrepreneurial Behavior & Research. She is also Managing Editor of Emerald Book Series "Review of Management Literature".

Samuel Ato Dadzie is a Senior Lecturer in the Business Management Department, Ghana, Management Institute of Ghana, and Public Administration department. He holds a PhD in International business from Vaasa University, Finland. He had earned a Master of Arts (MA) degree in International Business from Wolverhampton University, UK. His research interests are in international business, in particular foreign direct investment to emerging markets; strategies for entering and post-entry into African markets. In these areas, he has published in reputable international academic journals such as Journal of Transnational Management, Thunderbird International Business Review, and the International Journal of Emerging Markets. "Benchmarking: An International Journal, Journal of Strategic Marketing, and presented papers at several international conferences".

Shalini Sahni is an Independent Researcher and is a founder of Koach Scholar. She has over 15 years of experience in academia and corporate. She is an internationally certified PPA Thomas and Emotional Quotient trainer. She has also conducted MDPs for companies like Parle G and Mancer Consulting. She has published papers in the ABDC category, Scopus, and WOS-indexed journals. She has taught papers like research methodology, performance management, and organizational development. She has conducted training on different research methods using various statistical softwares like NVIVO, VOSViewer, Biblioshiny, SPSS, and AMOS. Her areas of interest include human resource management, organizational behavior, conflict resolution in teams, organizational justice, and workplace diversity issues.

Sudhir Rana is an Associate Professor of Marketing and Strategy and Program Director at the College of Healthcare Management and Economics, Gulf Medical University, UAE. He has set in high standards in academics and research. He has published research articles in the Journal of Business Research, Journal of Consumer Behaviour, International Journal of Emerging Markets, The TQM Journal, Benchmarking, and Journal of Promotion Management among others. He is Editor-in-Chief of FIIB Business Review, Coeditor-in-Chief of South Asian Journal of Marketing, and Editor of two series Advances in Emerging Markets and Business Operations (Taylor and Francis) and Review of Management Literature (Emerald).

Vimal Srivastava is a practicing CSR and Sustainability expert having more than 15 years of experience. He is presently associated with Mahindra & Mahindra Ltd and did his PhD in the area of CSR and sustainability. Considering equal importance to both research and industry practices, he has published various research papers in International Journals and his research areas are CSR, strategy, employee engagement, and sustainability.

Vinaytosh Mishra is an Associate Professor for Healthcare Management (Management, Digital Health, and Heath Analytics) at the College of Healthcare Management and Economics, Gulf Medical University, Ajman (UAE). He has more than 15 years of experience in industries like Healthcare, EdTech, Finance, and Information Technology. He has successfully filled out a patent for a device for the early detection of diabetes using nail fold capillaroscopy and serves as domain expert for AI implementation in healthcare for Al Habtoor Bikal.ai. He is also a mentor for leading business incubators in India and UAE. He has published in journals of international repute (ABDC/Scopus/SSCI) and served as an editorial board member of reputed journals such as Hospital Topics, Frontiers in Digital Health, and Abhigyan.

FOREWORD

It is our pleasure to introduce the second volume in the series "Review of Management Literature". This volume focuses on literature review (LR) methodologies. Over our respective careers, we read, write, and review manuscripts, and many of us (editors) write decision letters on business management research contributions. In every case, we expect and like to see the extent to which the contribution at an individual level and the volume as a package offer a distinguished contribution/s. As knowledge and research writing impactful literature review papers continue to grow, the majority of scholars still struggle to understand the standard protocols and structures of LR papers. One of the dominant reasons is a lack of a common template and checklist that they can follow while writing their LR papers. Hence, it is pertinent to explore literature review methodologies further. This volume includes eight contributions explaining different LR methodologies. The distinguished contribution of this volume is looking to simplify the guidelines on conducting various LR studies utilizing Bibliometric, Critical, technology-based, PRISMA, and realist reviews. Additionally, the volume explains the POWER framework with empirical evidence and suggestions to write a review paper. The implications of this volume are important for scholarly communities in general and specific to those who read, write, review, and make decisions on literature review papers. This volume concretely broadens the debate on the science and methods behind LR studies.

This volume is important for both early as well as mature career scholars in exploring the ways of conducting LR studies. At the same time, we alert the authors not to showcase a few approaches just because it is important to have an approach in LR studies; instead, we motivate them to learn LR methodologies and opt for the approaches and frameworks judiciously.

This volume introduces both general guiding principles as well as specific frameworks for business management and social science scholars. We hope that this volume will foster learning and motivate more LR contributions in the business management field.

We are highly thankful to all the authors and reviewers for their valuable contributions in making this volume a useful project. And thanks to editor colleagues who agreed to spare their time and valuable knowledge in making the exclusive POWER framework introduced in this volume.

We thank all the members from the Emerald publishing team for helping us throughout this project. We highly appreciate their consistent efforts to the series Review of Management Literature.

Your suggestions and comments on this volume are warmly welcomed.

PARAMETERS AND DECISION ELEMENTS OF WRITING EFFECTIVE LITERATURE REVIEW PAPERS: EMPIRICAL EVIDENCE FROM MULTIPLE STAKEHOLDERS ON POWER FRAMEWORK

Sudhir Rana, Jagroop Singh and Sakshi Kathuria

ABSTRACT

The study responds to the common concerns of authors, reviewers, and editors on writing and publishing high-quality literature review (LR) studies. First, we evolved the background and decision elements on the five parameters of a quality LR paper: Planning, Operationalizing, Writing, Embedding, and Reflecting (POWER), from the editorials and guiding literature. Statistical procedure and refinement of 256 responses from writers, reviewers, and editors revealed 37 decision elements. Finally, a multicriteria-decision-making approach was applied to the detailed responses from the lead editors of ABDC, Scopus, ABS, and WoS journals, and 31 decision elements were found strong enough to represent these five parameters on the quality of LR studies. All five parameters are found important to be considered. However, a high priority is suggested for embedding (the results coming out of the review) and operationalizing (the process of conducting the review), whereas reflection, writing, and planning of LR papers still remain important. The purpose of the POWER framework is to overcome the challenges and decision dilemmas faced by writers and decision-makers. The POWER framework acts as a guiding tool to conduct LR studies in general and business management scholars in specific ways. In addition, this study provides a checklist (Table 6) and template (Appendix A1) of a quality LR study to its stakeholders.

Advancing Methodologies of Conducting Literature Review in Management Domain
Review of Management Literature, Volume 2, 1–25
Copyright © 2024 Sudhir Rana, Jagroop Singh and Sakshi Kathuria
Published under exclusive licence by Emerald Publishing Limited
ISSN: 2754-5865/doi:10.1108/S2754-586520230000002001

Keywords: Literature review; POWER; review design; review style; review method; writing review

1. INTRODUCTION

Numerous researchers have emphasized the crucial role of literature review (LR) papers in scholarly research. These papers hold an important position in research. There are many studies available on how to craft a well-structured and effective LR paper (Bodolica & Spraggon, 2018; Fan et al., 2022; Lim et al., 2022; Patriotta, 2020; Paul & Criado, 2020; Paul et al. 2021, 2023; Snyder, 2019; Tranfield et al., 2003; Whittemore & Knafl, 2005). To summarize these studies, four aspects are critical for scholars to write, review, and read the LR papers: (1) publication outlets that publish LR papers – so that you decide where to read from and where to target to publish (2) LR methods – so that you opt for the most appropriate method while performing the review, (3) type of review performed – to understand which review type is appropriate in which condition, and (4) LR frameworks – to bring quality and refinement to the review results.

Coming to the first aspect related to publication outlets, both readers and authors need to consider the publication outlets that exclusively publish LR papers. For example, the *Academy of Management Review*, *Management Review Quarterly*, *Review of Management Literature*, and *International Journal of Management Reviews*, to name some. With regular reading and engagement with LR papers on these publication outlets, research scholars gain valuable knowledge in their domains and identify possible areas for future research. Also, these outlets are multi-disciplined, so every researcher can expect something published that is closely related to their domain. Scholars who are interested in doing an LR will find unique elements, ways of presentation, and methods incorporated in these papers. Because these publication outlets focus exclusively on LR, their editorial team and reviewers also keep on building more knowledge on LR. Hence, subjectivity reduces, and quality work occurs in these publication outlets.

Moving to the second aspect of LR methods, there are two types of methods for LR: quantitative and qualitative. Also, literature can be handled manually or with the help of any tool. It can be a quantitative method such as meta-analysis or qualitative such as systematic literature review (SLR) or mixed-method combines both of these and uses text analysis or other analytical techniques such as regression analysis or correlation analysis on the previous literature.

Considering the third aspect, understanding the types of the LR is important. Often, scholars struggle to understand what type of LR they are doing and what protocols they should follow. An understanding of LR methods and types can be gained by reading Tranfield et al. (2003), Xiao and Watson (2019), Paul and Barari (2022), and Lim et al. (2022).

The fourth aspect relates to the frameworks, which are highly important in conducting LR papers. Often, LR methods are misunderstood and mixed with the LR frameworks. However, these two are different. Frameworks set the process of shortlisting, screening, and reviewing the collected samples. A recent study by Paul et al. (2023) summarizes the frameworks for writing SLRs. The available and mostly used frameworks include (1) antecedents, decisions, and outcomes (ADO) by Paul and Benito (2018); (2) theory, context, characteristics, and methodology (TCCM) by Paul and Rosado-Serrano (2019); (3) PRISMA – preferred reporting items for systematic reviews and meta-analyses by Shamseer et al. (2015), and (4) 6W (who, when, where, what, why, and how) framework by Callahan (2014), and recently 6 steps and 14 decisions by Sauer and Seuring (2023). The following question arises:

Why existing frameworks are insufficient or not suitable to conduct literature review studies in business management and social science domains?

PRISMA framework is one of the most preferred frameworks in LR papers. The framework was developed keeping in mind the research published in medical journals. The framework primarily focuses on the reporting of reviews evaluating the effects of interventions with objectives other than evaluating interventions (e.g., evaluating etiology, prevalence, diagnosis, or prognosis). Surprisingly, over a period of time, we see that almost every second paper claims the use of PRISMA and misuses the citation of PRISMA to bring authentication to their LR work, without knowing the full elements and the checklist of this framework. The PRISMA-P checklist contains 17 items (with 26 sub-items) considered to be essential and minimum components of a systematic review or meta-analysis protocol (Moher et al., 2009; Shamseer et al., 2015). The PRISMA framework advises PICO (participants, interventions, comparators, and outcomes) approach, which may not reflect in the majority of research papers published in the business management and social science domains today because we are nowadays theory focused. In our papers, we always like to see the new enhancement or development toward theories and concepts. Considering the needs and nature of research publications in business management and social science areas, ADO and TCCM frameworks were adopted. But, as recently reported by Paul et al. (2023), the available frameworks have some limitations, and hence, authors need to make more careful decisions related to novelty and contribution, structuring, and enhancing future research scope.

In this study, we strengthen the previous LR frameworks by (1) consolidating the important criteria and elements of conducting LR papers from the existing frameworks and literature; (2) empirically testing these elements by collecting responses from experienced scholars, reviewers, and editors; and (3) further diving deep and prioritizing these elements by using a multicriteria decision-making (MCDM) approach from editors of high-quality journals (details are given in the research methodology section).

Elements collected from the literature are categorized under five categories: planning (P), operationalizing (O), writing (W), embedding/evaluating (E), and reflection (R), that is, POWER. In the previous version of the POWER framework (in the first volume of Review of Management Literature), we collected arguments and the need to have a framework that is not perspective-based but has scientific rigor.

2. BACKGROUND AND ARGUMENTS ON
POWER FRAMEWORK

The existing frameworks (TCCM, ADO, PRISMA/PICO, 6W, etc.) come with their own strengths and challenges. The existing frameworks are more skimmed toward authors' perspectives. Something largely missing in these frameworks is: on which criteria and elements are LR papers evaluated by the reviewers and editors? What do decision-makers and readers like to see in the LR papers?

To answer these questions, we need to understand the challenges and expectations from both scholars/writers of LR papers and decision-makers on these papers (reviewers and editors). Many of these frameworks suggest some common and some unique points for scholars. Something that looks common across almost all the frameworks is emphasizing what, why, and how? However, literature also suggests emphasizing the other important elements such as structure (Fisch & Block, 2018; Palmatier et al., 2018), solving complex and fragmented bodies of knowledge (Patriotta, 2020), developing evidences (Tranfield et al., 2003), balancing breadth and depth (Fisch & Block, 2018). This brings a lot of subjectivity to both LR writers and evaluators. Hence, a complete, consolidated, and comprehensive picture would make the job of both readers and evaluators easy.

Second, the knowledge about these guiding elements of conducting LR papers is fragmented into several papers. Hence, it requires presenting a consolidated and summarized view. And to overcome the opinion conflicts, a framework based on empirical evidence would be more inclusive and scientific.

The reason authors and reviewers of LR papers often struggle with how they bring merit and meaningful arguments to their LR papers may be because of common templates and structures clearly guiding LR papers. And therefore, LR papers are judged based on the perspectives of the evaluators (reviewers) instead of having a scientific evaluation based on the set criteria. Considering the limitations of the available frameworks and having a more inclusive and scientific approach, first, we collected the arguments and criteria from the previous studies/ frameworks and then performed statistical refinement as well as prioritization on these elements by using a MCDM. Taking the base from previous version of POWER framework by Rana et al. (2022), we reviewed the previous studies to re-organize the POWER framework elements.

The POWER framework is based on three criteria:

(1) Editorials that guide LR writers (Table 1).
(2) Frameworks and studies that guide how to conduct LR papers impactfully.
(3) Consolidated the important elements and tested them empirically with responses from the authors, reviewers, and editors.

The major elements of an impactful LR are summarized in five measures, that is, planning, operationalization, writing, embedding, and reflecting POWER. Being inclusive and based on scientific procedure, the POWER framework is expected to be a more fit framework for business management and social science scholars in

Table 1. A Review on Suggestions From the Editorials/Notes.

Year	Editors	Title of the Editorial/ Note	Journal	Critical Points	Suggestions
2002	Webster and Watson	Analyzing the past to prepare for the future: Writing a literature review	*MIS Quarterly*	Key concepts Identifying the literature Structure of the review Tone and language Theoretical development Discussion and conclusion	Writers should understand what is expected from a review paper.
2014	Callahan	Writing literature reviews: A reprise and update	*Human Resource Development Review*	Who When Where How What Why Concise Clear Critical Convincing Contributive	Six W's of literature review methods and five C's of literature review characteristics to be checked properly.
2018	Palmatier et al.	Review articles: Purpose, process, and structure	*Journal of the Academy of Marketing Science*	Topic formulation Study design Sampling Data collection Data analysis Reporting	It is important to understand the rigor, depth, structure, and process of literature review papers.
2018	Fisch and Block	Six tips for your (systematic) literature review in business and management research	*Management Review Quarterly*	Motivation and questions Systematic way Balance between breadth and depth Meaningful conclusions Coherent article structure	It is better to have some experience in the field because the interpretation of the results is subjective and by no means trivial.
2020	Patriotta	Writing impactful review articles	*Journal of Management Studies*	Comprehensive presentation Theory building Sense making Sense giving	Developing theory through review articles requires ongoing interactions of reading and writing, sense-making and sense-giving, consumption, and production in search of interpretation.

(Continued)

Table 1. (Continued)

Year	Editors	Title of the Editorial/ Note	Journal	Critical Points	Suggestions
2021	Paul et al.	Writing an impactful review article: What do we know and what do we need to know?	*Journal of Business Research*	Reconcile conflicting findings Suggest new directions Reference to methodology, theory, constructs, and context	It is important to understand the type and methods of review articles.
2023	Kunisch et al.	Using review articles to address societal grand challenges	*International Journal of Management Reviews*	Clarifying key concepts Advancing theory Revealing assumptions, ideologies, and values Scrutinizing trustworthiness and generalizability Guiding research practices Enabling new research methods Consolidating knowledge for practice and policymaking Reflecting on utilization of knowledge Translating and contextualizing existing knowledge	Review papers should reflect on three related roles in addressing societal grand challenge: (1) advancing theoretical knowledge, (2) advancing methodological knowledge, and (3) advancing practical knowledge.
2023	Ketchen and Craighead	What constitutes an excellent literature review? Summarize, synthesize, conceptualize, and energize	*Journal of Business Logistics*	Need for the review Feasibility Coherence Future research Quality in every aspect Summary and synthesis Conceptual diagram	Four key interrelated steps are necessary: (1) Take stock of the puzzle pieces are present, (2) put these pieces together that fit synthesize, (3) figure out what the overall picture should look like, and (4) create a wish list of future puzzles to be solved.

conducting impactful LR studies, as well as bring a holistic approach between evaluators and writers to understanding what is important from a common point of view. The measures of the POWER framework are discussed next.

2.1 Planning the Review

Planning is an important phase of any project. A few critical decision aspects that we encountered for the planning phase were, how important the topic and area are that you are going to review. Who are your team members, and do they have adequate knowledge and experience of domain and LR methods? What time frame are you going to study, and why is reviewing this time frame important? Checking the feasibility of having an adequate number of papers (minimum 50) that fit your evaluation and quality criteria. While planning, you can see whether or not there is a scope for establishing future research areas (FRA) on this theme and how long that can survive and remain important. What are the driving objectives and questions supporting you to conduct this review?

2.2 Operationalizing

While operationalizing the concepts to conduct the review study, it is important to think properly about the method of review (qualitative, qualitative, or mixed method). The quality of documents gets collected only when authors navigate the search to reputed databases and libraries because review results depend on the quality of the documents reviewed. Hence, it is important to select the database and libraries carefully. It is suggested that business scholars prefer their search from two primary indexes – Web of Science and Scopus. Because these indexing platforms are used as standard quality databases, authors and academic institutions consider the journals, books, and conferences indexed of them as a "quality publication." Also, while refining the selection, you can choose to select journal quality lists. For business scholars, two lists (a) the Academic Guide by the Chartered Association of Business Schools (CABS) and journal quality list by the Australian Business Dean's Councils (ABDC) are considered more important than others. However, one should give proper justifications and reasons for choosing the database and quality list to narrow down the documents included for review. At this stage, it is also important to think that how you are going to operationalize the review results and propose a conceptual diagram and prepositions. Are you going to reveal the possible independent, dependent, mediating, and moderating variables from the review? If yes, the method and review results should have mutual coordination.

2.3 Writing

Remember that writing is an art, but publishing is a business. The paper that we write undergoes different stages. Impressing gatekeepers (reviewers and editors) is the first job to get it published and attract readers to read and cite it (Rana et al., 2022).

However, writing is very subjective and depends on the knowledge and experience of the writers. But, something important for LR writers is to have the art of clarifying key concepts, the art of presenting the paper comprehensively and concisely, and finally, the art of integrating the concepts, methods, top journals, influencing papers in the field, and FRA. Do not give a chance to the reviewers and editors to be a proofreader of your paper; hence, make sure that the paper is free of grammatical errors. The writing should be clear, critical, and contributive. Also, researchers should be highly careful about tables and figures. Tables and diagrams should be able to provide more detailed information. Remember that the quality of the information is more important than having a large number of tables and figures in the paper. Table 1 reports the suggestions for planning and conducting LR-based studies.

2.4 Embedding/Evaluating

Research in social science and management is more perspective-driven than content-driven. Hence, it becomes highly important how the writer/s interprets the findings and tie these with past, present, and future actions. Something that is important to evaluate and include in the LR papers is advancements taking place in the concepts and theories you are reviewing. The assumptions and questions that you are answering in the review should be properly evaluated. Simplify and bridge the conflicting arguments. Every editor and reviewer likes to see something new and important; hence, it is important to highlight the new knowledge that your proposed review paper is adding to the literature. Researchers' own perspectives, experience, and knowledge must reflect on making the review paper relevant to the readers (simply, you must try hard to include the information in a way that it becomes important for the readers to think about why it is important to read your review paper rather than reading several other papers that you are reviewing and summarizing).

2.5 Reflecting

Reflecting back and forward both are important. It is important to reflect the unique and important knowledge gained from the review, which gaps this review bridged, and which research questions are still mysteries to be solved. Make sure that the review paper has something for all types of readers. Have offerings for industry practitioners on advancing their practices, and for scholars to have a rich and relevant future research agenda. Make sure your future research agenda is organized in a minimum of four microareas, cite and discuss important studies related to these areas. Do not forget to acknowledge what you have not considered including in the review and why. You have not included something has two interpretations: (1) it is not so important, and that's why you have not included it, so why should others work on it? (2) it requires a different method or different skillset to explore more upon something that you left out. So be clear and authentic. The future research agenda is one central objective of the LR papers. So, it should be included carefully.

3. RESEARCH METHODOLOGY

3.1 Survey Items

After carefully reading the previous editorials and papers, we included 43 items in the questionnaire. These items are extracted from the editorials given in Table 1 and previous studies by Paul et al. (2023), Lim et al. (2022), Paul, Merchant, et al. (2021), Xiao and Watson (2019), Tranfield et al. (2003), and Post et al. (2020). The meaning duplications were carefully checked. The designed questionnaire was sent to eight LR experts for the evaluation of face and content validity. Based on their feedback, several modifications were made in terms of language and the placement of items.

3.2 Respondents' Selection Criteria

Responses must be collected from those who have adequate knowledge and experience in writing, reviewing, and evaluating the LR papers. Therefore, we decided to consider the responses from those respondents who have authored a minimum of two LR papers. A special email campaign and personal requests were made to the editors and authors of reputed journals (especially those who have substantially published LR papers) to submit their responses. An email request and snowballing were made to include more editors in the survey. A total of 256 responses were found suitable and met the set criteria that are taken forward for further evaluation. Table 2 summarizes the respondent's characteristics.

4. RESULTS AND DISCUSSION

4.1 Exploratory Factor Analysis

As the number of parameters for the POWER framework was predetermined, an exploratory factor analysis (EFA) was used on 43 items to get an initial idea about construct validity. It also compares their loading on the construct they are supposed to measure to their loading on other scales. Maximum likelihood estimation with ProMax rotation was performed. Table 3 reports the results of EFA.

4.1.1 Homogeneity and Sampling Adequacy

Homogeneity and sampling adequacy of respondents' data are prerequisites for factor analysis. Both of these measures ensure the appropriateness of data. Homogeneity and adequacy were checked using Barlett's test (BT) of sphericity and Kaiser–Meyer–Olkin (KMO), respectively. BT values were found to be significant, that is, less than 0.05 (Hair et al., 2015). Further, KMO values above 0.50 confirmed the appropriateness of constructs for factor analysis (Kaiser, 1974; Pituch & Stevens, 2016). All KMO values were found to be above the minimum cut-off value, as shown in Table 3.

Table 2. Respondent's Characteristics.

Criteria	Labels	Percentage
Number of literature review published in their career	2 to >5	59.6
	5 to >10	18.9
	More than 10	21.5
Number of literature review papers reviewed	0 to >10	43
	10 to >20	28.5
	20 to >30	10.5
	30 to >50	6.5
	Above 50	11.5
Number of countries included in the response	26	
Research domain	Marketing, HRM, finance, international business, information technology, business analytics, healthcare management, operations management, tourism management, operations research, entrepreneurship, technology management, disaster management, general management, economics, strategic management, family business, CSR, sustainability, educational management, agricultural economics, communication, organizational behavior, innovation and design, corporate governance, Islamic management, etc.	

Source: Survey data.

4.1.2 Reliability Analysis

Reliability reflects internal consistency using Cronbach's alpha. According to Nunnally (1978), alpha values of 0.60 are considerable, and the values above 0.70 can be considered adequate. As can be seen in Table 3, alpha values of the parameters (factors) are in the range of 0.80–0.90, that is, well above the threshold value. Hence, it exhibits that summated that POWER parameters have good psychometric properties.

4.1.3 Convergent Validity

Convergent validity measures the convergence between the individual items measuring the same constructs. Convergent validity compares item loading on the construct they are supposed to measure to their loading on other scales. For convergent validity, factor loadings, and eigenvalues should exceed the critical values of 0.4 (for sample size more than 200) and 1, respectively, (Hair et al., 2015). In the first run, six items, P7, P9, O5, O7, W12, and E1, were deleted due to existing cross-loadings (Table 4). Thus, only 37 items were carried to the next level of purification. In the second run, the pattern matrix was clean, and all

Table 3. Exploratory Factor Analysis: Assessment Values.

Parameter/Decision Elements		Factor Loadings	Cronbach's Alpha	KMO	Eigenvalue
Planning (P)			0.809	0.823	3.303
How important is the topic and area taken for review	P1	0.640			
Importance of identifying the key concepts before starting the review work	P2	0.747			
Role of questions behind the LR paper	P3	0.605			
Supporting the need for (this) further LR on the topic if reviews on the same topic exist	P4	0.660			
Checking the feasibility of conducting the review before starting work on it	P5	0.554			
How important is authors' (writer's) experience and knowledge in writing LR papers	P6	0.585			
Importance of time frame in the LR	P8	0.535			
Operationalizing (O)			0.835	0.740	3.029
Importance of a study design (type of the review, i.e., systematic, structured, and bibliometric)	O1	0.762			
Importance of the right literature source (selection of the database to collect literature, i.e., Scopus, WoS, EBSCO, and ProQuest)	O2	0.724			
Importance of sampling (inclusion and exclusion criteria)	O3	0.642			
Importance of the data analysis (analysis techniques such as bibliometric, VOS viewer, meta-analysis, leximancer, text analysis)	O4	0.720			
Importance of having a conceptual diagram (developing prepositions and showing a relationship among the variables considered for review) in the review paper	O6	0.708			
Writing (W)			0.921	0.932	6.175
Importance of balancing breadth and depth of the topic (how important it is to deep dive into the detailing while writing an LR paper)	W1	0.724			
Importance of clarifying key concepts	W2	0.652			
Importance of explaining, simplifying, and contextualizing the existing knowledge	W3	0.722			
Importance of comprehensive and concise presentation of the LR	W4	0.683			
Importance of sensemaking and sense giving (is it important to express the reading understanding in a way that it makes sense for the scholars in the field)	W5	0.710			
Importance of actual language (grammatical, tenses, syntax, and clarity of the language)	W6	0.707			
Importance of style of the language (critical, argumentative, and scientific expression)	W7	0.776			
Importance of coherence between all the sections (all the sections should relate to each other)	W8	0.689			
Importance of way of integrating variables and concepts in thoughts behind the LR (the art of integrating and debating on the concepts,	W9	0.734			

(Continued)

Table 3. *(Continued)*

Parameter/Decision Elements		Factor Loadings	Cronbach's Alpha	KMO	Eigenvalue
methods, top journals, influencing authors, future research areas, etc.)					
Importance of tables and figures in the LR papers	W10	0.750			
Importance of clear, critical, convincing, and contributive writing	W11	0.760			
Embedding/Evaluating (E)			0.889	0.885	3.894
The importance of properly reporting/presenting the results of the review	E2	0.749			
Importance of advancing or developing theory in the LR papers	E3	0.729			
Importance of identifying all assumptions, ideologies, and values	E4	0.656			
How important is it for the review paper to develop new knowledge?	E5	0.878			
Importance of debating and including arguments from writers' own reading perspectives and interpretations	E6	0.748			
Importance of elucidating and simplifying the critical and conflicting arguments/concepts	E7	0.797			
Reflection (R)			0.900	0.911	4.777
Importance of having unique and novel conclusions coming out from the review	R1	0.714			
Importance of scrutinizing the trustworthiness and generalizability of the unique arguments, relationships, and concepts introduced in the LR (is it important to show their generalizability)	R2	0.791			
Importance for the review to identify gaps in the existing literature	R3	0.875			
Importance of providing guidance on future research areas	R4	0.748			
Importance of revealing and enabling new research methods in the field	R5	0.597			
Importance of consolidating knowledge for practice and policy making	R6	0.854			
Importance of writers' reflection on utilization of knowledge (is it important to give an implementation plan in the LR papers)	R7	0.633			
Importance of summary and synthesis arguments in the discussion and conclusion	R8	0.633			

Source: Survey data.

Abbreviation: LR, literature review.

required parameter values were above the acceptable limit. All other results are reported in Table 3.

4.2 Delphi Technique

Factor reduction techniques offered some factors with more than seven items. In 1956, a pioneer cognitive psychologist George A. Miller suggested that the

Table 4. Items Excluded During Factor Analysis.

Decision Elements	
Role of motivation for literature review paper	P7
Importance of only using latest literature	P9
Importance of a coherent and logical article structure	O5
Importance of including sections in the review (such as introduction, need and background, review method, review results, future research agenda, conclusion, and implication)	O7
How important is it to reconcile, identify, or justify conflicting findings?	W12
Importance of adding writers' own definitions to the concepts, exploring new variables, and proposing new relationships	E1

Source: Survey Data.

average human short-term memory has a limited capacity of around seven. Thus, he proposed the "7 ± 2" principle, referred to as "Miller's magic number." Considering the outcome of factor analysis, the Delphi technique is used to achieve "Miller's magic number" to ensure better cognition and outcome (Saaty & Ozdemir, 2003). Three rounds of Delphi were run with five experts for writing (W) and reflecting (R).

The role of experts is highly important for the Delphi technique. Whom we state as an expert is slightly difficult (especially distinguishing between those who teach LR subject to doctorate programs or provide training, or those who have written N number of papers in X category journals, or the editors of the journals). Because this study aims at LR authors and scholars for writing research papers, decision markers on the LR papers are considered experts in the study. For this first, we set that an editor from ABDC-B, ABS-2, Scopus Q1/Q2, or SSCI Q1/Q2 (at least one from these indexing and rankings) would be the most appropriate respondent as an expert. The reason is that these editors handle a large number of manuscripts on routine, and they come from a rich publishing background. Most of these editors also play the role of reviewers in a similar level of journals. Hence, the lead/main editors, or the editors who handle only the LR section of the journal, were contracted with the sample details of the questionnaire, and a personal request for an e-meeting was made for a better understanding. We were lucky to have eight experts for this study.

After three rounds, a point of saturation was achieved. Out of 11, 7 decision elements were obtained for writing (discarded W1, W2, W5, and W8). For reflection, six out of eight decision elements were retained by excluding R2 and R5. A total of 31 decision elements under five POWER parameters were carried forward for the next stage of analysis.

4.3 Analytical Hierarchy Process

MCDM techniques are valuable tools for making informed decisions in complex situations. They allow for the consideration of multiple criteria and preferences, enabling a comprehensive evaluation of alternatives. In this study, with 31 decision elements obtained after factor reduction, it is important to explore the priorities of LR constituents through a multicriteria analysis.

The analytic hierarchy process (AHP), introduced by Saaty (1988), is a popular MCDM tool known for its effectiveness in solving complicated and unstructured problems (Mishra & Singh, 2022; Saaty, 1988; Singh et al., 2019). It takes into account interactions and correlations among different factors. AHP is widely applicable due to its simplicity, flexibility, and consistent approach. It excels at decomposing complex problems into hierarchical terms and producing priority weights.

To determine the influential parameters and decision elements for LR, a three-level hierarchical structure was created based on Saaty's guidelines. Five second-level parameters and 31 decision elements were identified. In the AHP framework, priority refers to the relative importance or influence of an element compared to another parameter positioned above it in the hierarchy (Fig. 1). The POWER framework has five dimensions: planning, operationalizing/organizing, writing, embedding, and reflecting.

To prioritize parameters (factors) and decision elements, Saaty's nine-point scale (Table 5) was used. Experts were selected through purposive sampling technique (Eshtaiwi et al., 2018) to evaluate these parameters and decision elements. Previous studies by Kamaruzzaman et al. (2018) determined that a small group of experts (8–11) with appropriate knowledge and experience is preferable over a "cold-called" large sample of respondents. Therefore, a group of eight experts, well versed in the subject matter, possessing substantial experience in LR, well versed with the editorial process, was considered adequate to assess the parameters and decision elements.

Each expert was requested to mention his/her judgments w.r.t. each parameter and contribution to this study. The consistency ratio (CR) is employed to affirm the use of parameters or decision elements in decision-making (Crowe et al., 1998). Table 6 shows the CR for the AHP hierarchy. As obtained CR is below 0.20, the degree of consistency is considered acceptable (Yadav & Sharma, 2016).

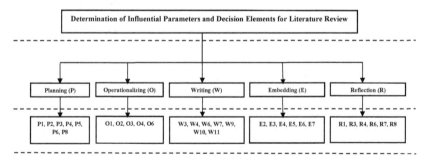

Fig. 1.   A Hierarchy Model of POWER LR Framework.

Table 5. Saatys Nine-Point Scale.

Scale	Judgments of Preferences
1	Equal importance
3	Moderate importance of one over the other
5	Essential or strong importance
7	Very strong or demonstrated importance
9	Extreme or absolute importance
2,4,6,8	Intermediate values between the two adjacent judgments

Source: Saaty (1988).

4.3.1 Detail of Local Weights POWER Framework Elements and Their Constituent Items

The parameter with the highest weight and rank is "embedding" (0.329), indicating its significant importance in the LR. "Operationalizing" (0.225) and "reflection" (0.189) hold the second and third ranks, respectively, while "writing" (0.181) takes the fourth position. Lastly, "planning" is ranked fifth with the lowest weight (0.076). Overall, the rankings and weights justify the significance and contribution of each parameter in the LR, providing a clearer understanding of their relative importance in the LR process.

In the initial phase of planning, "questions behind LR" holds the highest weight (0.271) and rank. Formulating clear and relevant questions helps guide the review and contributes significantly to the overall outcome. "Feasibility of conducting the review" takes the second rank with a weight of 0.223, showing that parameters such as available resources, time constraints, and access to relevant information play a significant role in determining the feasibility of conducting the review. The next important decision element emerges as "justification of further review (LR on the topic exists)" with a weight of 0.175. This indicates that the presence of existing LRs on the topic is considered in the LR writing. Together, these top three decision elements make up 67% of local weights, highlighting important considerations while planning an LR.

While operationalizing, proper sampling techniques are crucial to ensure the reliability and validity of the study's findings, as reflected in "sampling criteria" (0.318), emerging a top-ranked decision element. Furthermore, "data analysis" (0.231) and "study design" (0.223) emerged as important considerations. This suggests appropriate data analysis methods contribute to the accurate interpretation and meaningful insights. Also, the overall design of the study, including its structure and methodology.

To write an LR, "way of integrating variables and concepts in thoughts" holds the highest position (0.273), suggesting a well-integrated review reflects a deep understanding of the subject matter and contributes to the overall quality of the review. In addition, "clear, critical, convincing, and contributive language" takes the second rank with a weight of 0.185. This indicates that the language used should effectively convey the author's ideas and arguments. "Translating and

Table 6. AHP Priority Weights and Ranks for POWER Parameters and Their Constituent Decision Elements.

Parameter/Decision Elements		Local Weights	Local Rank	Global Weights	Global Rank
Planning		0.076	5	0.076	5
Operationalizing		0.225	2	0.225	2
Writing		0.181	4	0.181	4
Embedding		0.329	1	0.329	1
Reflection		0.189	3	0.189	3
Planning		CI = 0.25, RI = 1.32, CR = 0.19 for $n = 7$			
Topic and area of review	P1	0.150	4	0.011	26
Identifying key concepts	P2	0.069	5	0.005	29
Questions behind LR	P3	0.271	1	0.021	20
Justification of further review (LR on topic exists)	P4	0.175	3	0.013	24
Feasibility of conducting the review	P5	0.223	2	0.017	22
Influence of scholar's (writers') experience and knowledge	P6	0.064	6	0.005	30
Time frame in the LR	P8	0.049	7	0.004	31
Operationalizing		CI = 0.17, RI = 1.08, CR = 0.16 for $n = 5$			
Review study design	O1	0.223	3	0.050	6
Right source for LR	O2	0.185	4	0.042	11
Sampling criteria (inclusion and exclusion)	O3	0.318	1	0.072	2
Data analysis (review and analysis technique)	O4	0.231	2	0.052	4
Conceptual diagram	O6	0.043	5	0.010	28
Writing		CI = 0.17, RI = 1.32, CR = 0.13 for $n = 7$			
Translating and contextualizing existing knowledge	W3	0.172	3	0.031	15
Comprehensive and concise presentation	W4	0.108	5	0.019	21
Actual language (grammar, syntax, and clarity)	W6	0.068	6	0.012	25
Importance of style of language (critical, argumentative, and scientific expression)	W7	0.137	4	0.025	17
Way of integrating variables and concepts in thoughts	W9	0.273	1	0.049	7

Clear, critical, convincing, and contributive language	W10	0.185	2	0.033	14
Tables and figures	W11	0.057	7	0.010	27
Embedding		$CI = 0.20$, $RI = 1.22$, $CR = 0.16$ for $n = 6$			
Proper reporting/presentation of the results of the review	E2	0.272	1	0.089	1
Advancing or developing theory in the LR papers	E3	0.131	5	0.043	10
Identifying all assumptions, ideologies, and values	E4	0.157	3	0.052	5
Developing new knowledge	E5	0.091	6	0.030	16
Debating and including arguments from writers' own reading, perspectives, and interpretations	E6	0.144	4	0.047	8
Elucidating and simplifying the critical and conflicting arguments/concepts	E7	0.205	2	0.068	3
Reflection		$CI = 0.20$, $RI = 0.1.22$, $CR = 0.16$ for $n = 6$			
A unique and novel conclusion coming out from the review	R1	0.130	4	0.025	18
Identifying gaps in the existing literature	R3	0.130	4	0.025	18
Providing guidance on future research areas	R4	0.205	2	0.039	12
Consolidating knowledge for practice and policymaking	R6	0.246	1	0.046	9
Writers' reflection on utilization of knowledge	R7	0.084	6	0.016	23
Summary and synthesis of arguments in the discussion and conclusion	R8	0.205	2	0.039	12

Source: Authors' analysis of the expert's responses.

Abbreviation: LR, literature review.

contextualizing existing knowledge" (0.172) is also significant. It involves presenting information in a way that is accessible and relevant to the research topic and objectives. "Importance of style of language (critical, argumentative, and scientific expression)" (0.137) and "comprehensive and concise presentation" (0.108) are considered important. Thus, the review should demonstrate a scholarly approach and engage in critical analysis; at the same instance, it should cover relevant information without being excessively lengthy or redundant. "Tables and figures" (0.057) seem to have a relatively smaller impact on the overall writing, but they may still be valued.

Under embedding, "proper reporting/presentation of the results of the review" (0.272) enhances the credibility and usefulness of the article. "Elucidating and simplifying the critical and conflicting arguments/concepts" (0.205) to make the review more accessible to readers by simplifying and explaining intricate or contradictory ideas is the second most important consideration. "Identifying all assumptions, ideologies, and values" holds a weight of 0.157 and is ranked third. It helps readers understand the contextual biases and perspectives that may influence the interpretation and understanding of the research. "Debating and including arguments from writers' own reading perspectives and interpretations" (0.144) and "advancing or developing theory in the literature review papers" (0.131) were also close contenders. This means theory building by presenting and discussing different viewpoints, arguments, and interpretations. This decision element enriches the LR with diverse perspectives.

Toward the end to reflect, "consolidating knowledge for practice and policy-making" holds the highest weight (0.246) and is ranked first. This decision element is crucial because it makes an LR a valuable resource for practitioners and policymakers, enabling evidence-based decision-making. "Summary and synthesis of arguments in the discussion and conclusion" is ranked second with a weight of 0.205 in order to enhance the understanding and impact of the review, enabling readers to grasp the main points effectively. "Providing guidance for future research areas" shares the same weight of 0.205. By identifying areas that require further investigation and suggesting potential research avenues, it ensures that the LR contributes to the advancement of knowledge and fills existing gaps. "A unique and novel conclusion coming out from the review" (R1) and "identifying gaps in the existing literature" both hold a weight of 0.130 and are ranked fourth. A unique conclusion demonstrates the value of the review by presenting new insights, while identifying gaps highlights the need for further research and provides opportunities for future studies. "Writers' reflection on the utilization of knowledge" (0.084) is not considered of similar importance.

4.3.2 Detail of Global Weights for Constituent Items of Power Framework Decision Elements
The results indicate the relative importance of different decision elements in conducting an LR. Proper reporting and presentation of the results hold the highest weight (0.089), indicating the importance of clear and concise reporting of the review findings. The sampling criteria hold the second rank (0.072), emphasizing the

importance of a well-defined and appropriate sample selection. The third rank is assigned to elucidating and simplifying critical and conflicting arguments and concepts (0.068), indicating the importance of a clear and concise presentation of complex ideas. The fourth and fifth ranks are assigned to data analysis (0.052) and identifying all assumptions, ideologies, and values (0.052), respectively.

The study design holds the sixth rank (0.050), emphasizing the importance of a well-designed and executed study. The way of integrating variables and concepts in thoughts holds the seventh rank (0.049), indicating the importance of coherence and consistency in presenting and integrating ideas. Debating and including arguments from writers' own reading perspectives and interpretations hold the eighth rank (0.047), indicating the importance of a critical review and discussion of the literature.

Consolidating knowledge for practice and policy-making holds the ninth rank (0.046), indicating the importance of the LR's practical implications. Finally, advancing or developing theory in the LR papers holds the tenth rank (0.043), indicating the least weightage assigned to this decision element.

Overall, the above results provide the top 10 elements offering valuable insights regarding their importance when conducting an LR. By considering and addressing these decision elements, researchers can enhance the quality, impact, and practical relevance of their LR studies.

4.3.2.1 Some More Important Questions. One common question that authors generally ask is how many papers should be included in the review study. As specified by Paul, Merchant, et al. (2021), we also asked this question to our respondents. Based on the responses and feedback, we found that a review paper must include reviewing a minimum of 40–50 papers. Yet, the number will vary keeping the review design, inclusion/exclusion criteria, and scope of review in mind. Another important question that bounces around scholars' minds is the length of the LR papers. Many authors believe that the length of LR papers should be higher than empirical papers. However, the length of LR papers depends on the review methodology and insightful outcomes. We asked this question in the survey and found that the majority of the respondents suggested that, in general, the study has a word count between 8,000 and 12,000 words. However, the word count limit is a major criterion for the publication outlets. Hence, word count should be used judiciously. Third, an important question arises: who should write an LR paper, the early-career researchers or experienced researchers. We found that the knowledge and experience of the scholars play an extremely significant role in LR papers. Hence, if an early-career scholar is motivated to write an LR paper, it is better to collaborate with an experienced scholar who helps in bringing a better interpretation of the results and bringing different perspectives from the literature. Fourth, the majority of the LR manuscripts get rejected because they fail to express their contribution, lack of proper structure, repeat the tables and figures in the text, no careful selection of the journal, have high ambitions, etc. Therefore, the authors of LR paper must go beyond just reporting the previous literature. Most of the rejections come because authors focus more on reporting the literature instead of impactful inferences from the literature. Finally, 80% of respondents believe that LR papers are more time-consuming and hence, authors need to keep patience and do a consistent effort on.

5. CONCLUSION

The five elements of the POWER framework fill the gap in the literature by offering a holistic view of both authors and decision-makers. The five parameters (planning, operationalizing, writing, embedding, and reflecting) of the POWER framework are refined through various steps and procedures. Finally, 31 decision elements related to these five parameters are found suitable for writing and evaluating the merits of an impactful LR study. The study contributes multifold to the body of knowledge on LR. The knowledge on how to conduct an impactful LR paper is scattered in the literature. Most of these papers were based on the authors' own experiences and knowledge, but empirical evidence was missing. Also, the majority of the authors in business management and social sciences have been using the citations of available frameworks without checking the suitability, depth, and standard elements. The concerns on why LR papers get rejected were not centrally discussed; hence, a holistic perspective of authors, reviewers, and editors was not available under one umbrella. Hence, the present study helps in solving the raised issues. First, we analyzed why business management and social science scholars/reviewers, and editors need another framework for conducting LR. We gathered impactful elements and standards from the available frameworks and literature. The need for the POWER framework was well taken and appreciated (thanks to the respondents; we heard a lot of appreciation and comments in the open space) by the stakeholders.

6. IMPLICATIONS

6.1 Implications for Scholars

The POWER framework will help scholars to write impactful LR studies. Evaluate their study and prevent rejections. Scholars can evaluate their decision to write an LR paper before starting, during the process, and finally by contributing value to the publication outlets and readers.

First, the authors should look at the checklist of the POWER framework, that is, five parameters and 31 decision elements (Table 5). Before undertaking the LR work, the author or team of authors should think about and debate the implementation of these 31 decision elements. An evaluation of the shortcomings, challenges, and strength areas will help the authors understand how much they can achieve from these items and will help them prepare their path forward. If the criteria match 90%, they are on the right track. Otherwise, you need to rethink before you execute the project. This will also give them sufficient time to identify and fulfill their gaps.

The template (Appendix A1) given in the study will help in organizing the study in a better way. The do's and don'ts related to each section will help in making a clear decision while developing the paper.

To bring more weight and self-evaluation to your manuscript, you can submit the checklist as an appendix in the cover letter. So that editors can see that you have completely matched the desired parameters.

6.2 Extension of POWER Framework – Future Research Agenda

The POWER framework can be further expanded by adding more perspectives and decision elements that are specific to other subject areas such as humanities, engineering, medical science, etc. A more specific framework can be proposed on the nature and review methodology, such as POWER for qualitative review methods and quantitative review methods. A cluster-wise comparison can be done between the old and new frameworks to see what got changed and why. Scholars can look deeper into the framework to explore which decision elements and parameters suit a particular stream of management research, such as HRM, marketing, operations, IB, strategy, finance, economics, etc.

6.3 Implications for Decision Makers and Publishers

Implications for reviewers and editors: As a decision-maker, we aim to make quality research available to our readers. And therefore, the peer review process aims to improve the manuscript by getting opinions and feedback from experts. Being a subject expert on one side, you are expected to write constructive criticism and give suggestions to improve the manuscript further. The parameters and decision variables of the POWER framework help in spotting the missing gaps easily, and also you can put forward the feedback point by point. You may like to use the given checklist as a review and evaluation form for the LR manuscript.

6.4 Implications for the Publishers

It is important to spread good knowledge about the importance and relevance of LR papers in the larger academic community. Hence, the POWER framework acts as an easy LR training tool. Also, during this study, we found that there are not enough publication outlets that welcome LR papers as warmly as empirical papers. The LR publication outlets and papers have yet to capitalize on their value. Hence, there is a chance of promoting LR papers and publication outlets. More training programs and exclusive campaigns can be run through the LR papers. Information and framework can act as a food for thought for these campaigns and training programs.

REFERENCES

Bodolica, V., & Spraggon, M. (2018). An end-to-end process of writing and publishing influential literature review articles: Do's and don'ts. *Management Decision, 56*(11), 2472–2486.

Callahan, J. L. (2014). Writing literature reviews: A reprise and update. *Human Resource Development Review, 13*(3), 271–275.

Crowe, T. J., Noble, J. S., & Machimada, J. S. (1998). Multi-attribute analysis of ISO 9000 registration using AHP. *International Journal of Quality & Reliability Management, 15*(2), 205–222.

Eshtaiwi, M., Badi, I., Abdulshahed, A., & Erkan, T. E. (2018). Determination of key performance indicators for measuring airport success: A case study in Libya. *Journal of Air Transport Management, 68*, 28–34.

Fan, D., Breslin, D., Callahan, J. L., & Iszatt-White, M. (2022). Advancing literature review methodology through rigour, generativity, scope and transparency. *International Journal of Management Reviews, 24*(2), 171–180.

Fisch, C., & Block, J. (2018). Six tips for your (systematic) literature review in business and management research. *Management Review Quarterly, 68*(2), 103–106.

Hair, J. F., Black, W. C., Babin, B. J., & Anderson, R. E. (2015). *Multivariate data analysis* (7th ed.). Pearson Education Limited.

Kaiser, H. F. (1974). An index of factorial simplicity. *Psychometrika, 39*(1), 31–36. https://doi.org/10.1007/BF02291575

Kamaruzzaman, S. N., Lou, E. C. W., Wong, P. F., Wood, R., & Che-Ani, A. I. (2018). Developing weighting system for refurbishment building assessment scheme in Malaysia through analytic hierarchy process (AHP) approach. *Energy Policy, 112*(October 2017), 280–290. https://doi.org/10.1016/j.enpol.2017.10.023

Ketchen, D. J., Jr., & Craighead, C. W. (2023). What constitutes an excellent literature review? Summarize, synthesize, conceptualize, and energize. *Journal of Business Logistics, 44*(2), 164–169.

Kunisch, S., zu Knyphausen-Aufsess, D., Bapuji, H., Aguinis, H., Bansal, T., Tsui, A. S., & Pinto, J. (2023). Using review articles to address societal grand challenges. *International Journal of Management Reviews, 25*(2), 240–250.

Lim, W. M., Kumar, S., & Ali, F. (2022). Advancing knowledge through literature reviews: 'What', 'why', and 'how to contribute'. *The Service Industries Journal, 42*(7–8), 481–513.

Mishra, V., & Singh, J. (2022). Health technology assessment of telemedicine interventions in diabetes management: Evidence from UAE. *FIIB Business Review*, 1–10. https://doi.org/10.1177/23197145221130651

Moher, D., Liberati, A., Tetzlaff, J., & Altman, D. G. (2009). Preferred reporting items for systematic reviews and meta-analyses: The PRISMA statement. *PLoS Medicine, 6*(7), e1000097.

Nunnally, J. C. (1978). *Psychometric theory.* McGraw-Hill. https://books.google.co.in/books?id=WE59AAAAMAAJ

Palmatier, R. W., Houston, M. B., & Hulland, J. (2018). Review articles: Purpose, process, and structure. *Journal of the Academy of Marketing Science, 46*(1), 1–5.

Patriotta, G. (2020). Writing impactful review articles. *Journal of Management Studies, 57*(6), 1272–1276.

Paul, J., & Barari, M. (2022). Meta-analysis and traditional systematic literature reviews—What, why, when, where, and how? *Psychology and Marketing, 39*(6), 1099–1115.

Paul, J., & Benito, G. R. G. (2018). A review of research on outward foreign direct investment from emerging countries, including China: What do we know, how do we know and where should we be heading? *Asia Pacific Business Review, 24*(1), 90–115.

Paul, J., & Criado, A. R. (2020). The art of writing literature review: What do we know and what do we need to know? *International Business Review, 29*(4), 101717.

Paul, J., Khatri, P., & Kaur Duggal, H. (2023). Frameworks for developing impactful systematic literature reviews and theory building: What, why and how? *Journal of Decision Systems, 1–14.*

Paul, J., Lim, W. M., O'Cass, A., Hao, A. W., & Bresciani, S. (2021). Scientific procedures and rationales for systematic literature reviews (SPAR-4-SLR). *International Journal of Consumer Studies, 45*(4), O1–O16.

Paul, J., Merchant, A., Dwivedi, Y. K., & Rose, G. (2021). Writing an impactful review article: What do we know and what do we need to know? *Journal of Business Research, 133*, 337–340.

Paul, J., & Rosado-Serrano, A. (2019). Gradual internationalization vs born-global/international new venture models. *International Marketing Review, 36*(6), 830–858.

Pituch, K., & Stevens, J. P. (2016). *Applied multivariate statistics for social sciences* (6th ed.). Routledge.

Post, C., Sarala, R., Gatrell, C., & Prescott, J. E. (2020). Advancing theory with review articles. *Journal of Management Studies, 57*(2), 351–376.

Rana, S., Sakshi, & Singh, J. (2022). Presenting the POWER framework of conducting literature review. In S. Rana, Sakshi, & J. Singh (Eds.), *Exploring the latest trends in management literature (Review of management literature)* (Vol. 1, pp. 1–13). Emerald Publishing Limited.

Saaty, T. L. (1988). What is the analytic hierarchy process? In G. Mitra, H. J. Greenberg, F. A. Lootsma, M. J. Rijkaert, & H. J. Zimmermann (Eds.), *Mathematical models for decision support*. Springer. https://doi.org/10.1007/978-3-642-83555-1_5

Saaty, T. L., & Ozdemir, M. S. (2003). Why the magic number seven plus or minus two. *Mathematical and Computer Modelling*, *38*(3–4), 233–244. https://doi.org/10.1016/S0895-7177(03)90083-5

Sauer, P. C., & Seuring, S. (2023). How to conduct systematic literature reviews in management research: A guide in 6 steps and 14 decisions. *Review of Managerial Science, 1–35*.

Shamseer, L., Moher, D., Clarke, M., Ghersi, D., Liberati, A., Petticrew, M., Shekelle, P., & Stewart, L. A. (2015). Preferred reporting items for systematic review and meta-analysis protocols (PRISMA-P) 2015: Elaboration and explanation. *BMJ*, *349*, g7647.

Singh, J., Sharma, S. K., & Srivastava, R. (2019). AHP-entropy based priority assessment of factors to reduce aviation fuel consumption. *International Journal of System Assurance Engineering and Management*, *10*(2), 212–227. https://doi.org/10.1007/s13198-019-00758-0

Snyder, H. (2019). Literature review as a research methodology: An overview and guidelines. *Journal of Business Research*, *104*, 333–339.

Tranfield, D., Denyer, D., & Smart, P. (2003). Towards a methodology for developing evidence-informed management knowledge by means of systematic review. *British Journal of Management*, *14*(3), 207–222.

Webster, J., & Watson, R. T. (2002). Analyzing the past to prepare for the future: Writing a literature review. *MIS Quarterly*, *26*(2), xiii–xxiii.

Whittemore, R., & Knafl, K. (2005). The integrative review: Updated methodology. *Journal of Advanced Nursing*, *52*, 546–553.

Xiao, Y., & Watson, M. (2019). Guidance on conducting a systematic literature review. *Journal of Planning Education and Research*, *39*(1), 93–112.

Yadav, V., & Sharma, M. K. (2016). Multi-criteria supplier selection model using the analytic hierarchy process approach. *Journal of Modelling in Management*, *11*(1), 326–354. http://doi.org/10.1108/JM2-06-2014-0052

APPENDIX A1. REVIEW PAPER TEMPLATE

Title:
Report specific review types in the system, such as systematic review, bibliometric review, meta-analysis, structured review, conceptual review, scoping review, etc.

Sections of literature review paper	Do's and Don'ts
Abstract: Purpose, methodology, finding, implications, original contribution	Should be clear and to the points. Make sure to answer why, how, what, and for whom in the abstract. Do not make a bulky abstract; either make a structured abstract or only one paragraph of abstract.
Keywords Six to eight keywords	Choose the keywords through which readers can search your paper. Avoid choosing complicated keywords.
1. Introduction What is being reviewed Why it is important to be reviewed Why it is important to be reviewed now Introduce the value and contribution briefly	Should be an impressive storyline. Make sure you use a sales pitch here to sell this idea to the readers.
2. Background and relevance Evolution, school of thoughts, overview of concepts, and definitions Critical assessment with the previous review studies available in the field Inconsistencies and questions raised in the literature. Objectives and research questions	Give brief but deep insight into the concepts that you are using (something that is not given in the previous literature; give it a space). Avoid repeating previous literature (something that is already given in some other paper/chapter; you don't need to repeat it). Highlight why this review is important and what is that previous studies have not done. Keep three to four objectives. Objectives and questions must not be limited to the documentation of previous literature. For example, exploring how many papers, influential journals, and influential authors have contributed to the field is not enough findings. Set review objectives. For example, how many research and which research clusters exist in the domain; what readers should read and what areas are not going to be in demand; what methods are more suitable for (1) conducting research on young generation, (2) a specific industry sector, (3) developed and emerging market contexts, and (4) setting future research agenda for next xx years.
3. Review methodology Planning the review Search strategy Search scope (database, libraries, and time frame) Search method (snowballing, forward looking, reference checking, etc.) Selection of keywords Literature extraction and handling duplicates Inclusion and exclusion criteria	Choose credible databases for search. Choose appropriate review methods and justify why you have chosen this review method. Make sure you define the quality of the documents you included to review. Do not perform review if you have below 40 papers to review. The keywords should be inclusive and fully related to the area of study. Make sure you don't leave any important keywords without searching them. Choose appropriate framework to review. One common mistake that review paper authors make is showing high number of papers in the search and choosing a few documents to review. Avoid it. Your search should be so strong that it includes only appropriate papers that you document for further screening. Clarify, on which bases you excluded papers from screening to full paper reading.

(Continued)

4. Review results Synthesis of included studies Clusters Mapping the concepts areas Exploring relationships Conceptual diagrams Learnings from prominent journals, authors, and influencing papers Methods suitable for the domain (suitable methods for different contexts) Theories incorporated (suitable theories concepts wise) Challenges suggested in the literature	Utilize the tables and figures carefully. The tables included should provide rich explanation. Do not provide a large number of tables; instead, think multiple times on how more information can be given in one table. Use figure/s to explain the results better. Use prepositions if you are introducing a conceptual diagram. Avoid suggesting only one or two mediator/moderator. If you have explored independent/dependent and moderators/mediators from the review, explain all the possible variables in each category. Do not forget to give the references/citations of the study suggesting these variables. Synthesize the main arguments from the literature.
5. Discussion Inconsistencies and new additions	Highlight the major challenges and opportunities in the area.
6. Implications Theoretical implications – addition and advancements Implications for practitioners and industry Implications for society	Implications should be derived from the literature. Do not forget to add your assessments and provide your suggestions based on your reading of the literature.
7. Future research agenda/directions and limitations	Give at least four to five major research areas in subheadings. For example, Area 1 Synthesize the related studies Area 2 Synthesize the related studies Guide future scholars on highlighting learnings from the related studies (cite these here so that one understands the important reading on this area).
8. Other Funding Registration Acknowledgment Author's bio	Write a proper bio in the cover letter to showcase your background. Use your updated ORCID ID. Write an impressive cover letter specifying what contribution this manuscript makes and why you are submitting it to the targeted journal.
9. References	Maintain consistency in the reference style.

SYSTEMATIC LITERATURE REVIEWS: STEPS AND PRACTICAL TIPS

Hussain G. Rammal

ABSTRACT

Literature reviews help summarize the field of a research area and identify gaps to be addressed as part of a future research agenda. Many types of literature reviews can be undertaken, including narrative literature reviews, scoping literature reviews, integrative literature reviews, and systematic literature reviews. While every researcher has undertaken some form of narrative literature review, the more advanced types of literature reviews require careful planning and following well-established protocols. This chapter discusses the various types of literature reviews, with an emphasis on the systematic literature review. It details the steps required in conducting a systematic literature review and provides some practical tips to enhance the quality of such studies and their contribution to the research field.

Keywords: Systematic review; review methods; writing review; quality review; reviewing literature; review process

1. INTRODUCTION

The business and management literature has witnessed a significant increase in research output. However, while these publications have added to the existing knowledge pool, it has also created a situation where research in some areas has become scattered. In addition, due to the large volume of publications, several studies remain unread.

Literature reviews provide the opportunity to capture all studies, summarize trends in the research field, and make theoretical contributions that can guide future research (Harris, 2019; Rana et al., 2022). Perhaps every researcher

Advancing Methodologies of Conducting Literature Review in Management Domain
Review of Management Literature, Volume 2, 27–35
Copyright © 2024 Hussain G. Rammal
Published under exclusive licence by Emerald Publishing Limited
ISSN: 2754-5865/doi:10.1108/S2754-586520230000002002

(student or professor) has undertaken a literature review (Snyder, 2019). The reasons for reviewing the literature may vary, but the primary intention is similar: to identify what the literature tells us about a research field (Aversano et al., 2012). However, literature reviews can go far beyond this basic focus and help extend a research field by providing unique perspectives on what has been studied and identifying new theoretical explanations for the phenomenon under study (Kraus et al., 2021). They can also help create new research fields and unique perspectives by bridging multiple research areas (Fink, 2019). Hence, the utility of literature review studies is far greater than what has previously been discussed (Williams et al., 2021).

Despite the critical value of these literature reviews, they remain undervalued. An obvious example of this attitude can be found in the thesis writing process for research degrees (Pickering et al., 2015). Individuals undertaking these degrees are expected to delve deep into the literature to seek unique research topics by identifying gaps in the literature (Ridley, 2012). Although every student undertakes an exhaustive literature review, only a few pursue the path of converting these reviews to stand-alone dedicated publications (Pickering & Byrne, 2014). In most instances where the literature review is used in publications, it is to briefly justify the motivation for the study.

But why is this the case? Why do we not see a greater conversion of these literature review chapters from research theses into journal articles or book chapters? The answer may lie in our understanding of the value of these reviews and, perhaps more crucially, our limited understanding of how such studies should be conducted (Dekkers et al., 2022). Not all literature reviews serve the same purpose, and researchers must select the type of literature review that is suitable for addressing the research motivation and questions.

This chapter provides an overview of the types of literature review that can be undertaken and articulates a detailed stepwise process for undertaking a systematic literature review.

2. TYPES OF LITERATURE REVIEWS

Many types of literature reviews can be undertaken. The selection of the relevant type needs to be linked to the research questions. This section provides an overview of some of the types of literature reviews most commonly used in business studies: narrative literature review, scoping literature review, integrative literature review, and systematic literature review.

Narrative literature reviews are the most common and traditional review used to identify gaps in the body of knowledge (Pautasso, 2019). The basic form of the narrative style of literature reviews is commonly found in journal publications (Meglio & Risberg, 2011). They do not typically follow a set pattern of searching in a specific database to retrieve studies or replicate any particular steps. Instead, the purpose of these reviews is usually to provide up-to-date knowledge about a specific topic. Most researchers are familiar with this technique as we read journal articles that follow this style and provide a mini-review. However, writing a full literature review paper using the narrative approach requires specific steps that need to be followed. Authors like Pautasso (2019) provide a user-friendly guide to undertaking narrative literature reviews.

Scoping literature reviews are useful when looking at complex topics or issues that have previously not been extensively examined (Pham et al., 2014). Scoping reviews share some similarities with systematic literature reviews as they both follow a rigorous and transparent path to selecting and analyzing relevant studies. The key difference between the two types is that while systematic literature reviews attempt to answer specific questions, scoping studies focus on mapping the literature in a specific field of research and provide a descriptive overview of the studies (Blake et al., 2019).

Integrative literature reviews are useful for bringing together a field of research where the studies are scattered. By integrating studies into themes, researchers can help generate new knowledge about a field (Torraco, 2005; Yorks, 2008), generating new frameworks (Burritt et al., 2020). Integrative literature reviews are also useful in looking at studies on a particular topic from across disciplines (Dang & Rammal, 2020). For example, research in the field of *knowledge* can be found in business management, information technology, medicine, etc. Bringing these studies together and generating new knowledge in the field can be achieved through integrative literature reviews (Elsbach & van Knippenberg, 2020).

The final type of literature review that we cover, and which is the main focus of this chapter, is the systematic literature review. *Systematic literature reviews* are considered to be the most rigorous review type that follows a well-defined approach (Fisch & Block, 2018; Lame, 2019). Compared to most other types of literature reviews, systematic literature reviews are comprehensive and focus on delving deep into particular research areas to seek answers to specific research questions (Linnenluecke et al., 2020; Xiao & Watson, 2019). Systematic literature reviews can be divided into two categories: meta-analysis and meta-synthesis. These categories depend on whether the analysis will be qualitative or quantitative.

Meta-analysis uses statistical procedures to analyze findings from several studies on a specific subject (Buckley et al., 2014). Meta-analysis is associated with a deductive research approach, where patterns and relationships are detected, and conclusions are drawn (Tang & Cheung, 2016). In contrast, meta-synthesis relies on nonstatistical techniques (Walsh & Downe, 2005). Meta-synthesis follows the inductive research approach, and the technique helps integrate, evaluate, and interpret the findings of multiple qualitative research studies (Walsh & Downe, 2005).

Both techniques have their particular focus and steps that they follow. In this chapter, we focus on the qualitative approach to undertaking a systematic literature review. Although the techniques differ, the motivations to conduct the study and some of the steps highlighted in the next section remain the same.

3. STEPS IN CONDUCTING A SYSTEMATIC LITERATURE REVIEW

A systematic literature review is used to answer specific research questions (Coombes & Nicholson, 2013). One of the key features of the systematic litera-ture review is that it should be undertaken in a way that is replicable (Tranfield et al., 2003). Hence, there are steps that need to be followed. While there may be differences in the number of steps followed, all authors tend to follow a standard process, even if some steps are consolidated and undertaken together.

The *first step* involves *defining the research question*. As discussed previously, systematic literature reviews are suitable when attempting to answer specific questions. Hence, the first task involves determining the need for the study, the research objectives, and the research questions (Booth et al., 2021).

The *second step* requires *identifying the inclusion and exclusion criteria that will be used to search within databases*. This is a critical step and determines the scope of the study (Hiebl, 2019). A limitation of several review studies is that the keywords and search strings for the search are selected ad-hoc. An effective way to address this issue is to select a sample of relevant publications and read through them to get a sense of the keywords and their relationships. If there is more than one author, then each member can undertake this activity and compare notes to arrive at the final list of keywords (Ferreira et al., 2021).

Once the keywords are determined, the scope of the search needs to be determined. For example, will the search include all publications or be limited to journal articles and books? Would publications in any language be included or a specific language (or languages)? Will the studies included in the search be restricted to a specific time range? The search for relevant publications can then be undertaken using the criteria. There are many databases available that can be used for the search, for example, Web of Science, Scopus, and Google Scholar. Depending on the search criteria being followed by the researcher, there may be some publications that are not captured by these databases. In that case, the search for publications would need to be broader. For specific databases, such as Web of Science and Scopus, the researcher can also restrict the search to a certain field(s) of study (for example, Business Economics). This step will result in the initial collection of articles for the review.

The *third step* involves the *cleaning and further refinement of the sample arti-cles*. There are many ways this step can be undertaken and is guided by the research field and the research objectives. If the field is developed and not new, then the second step would have resulted in a large number of publications. In that case, the researchers may wish to reduce this sample size. Some review studies achieve this by focusing on the ranking of the journals and only including those articles that are published in journals that are highly ranked in journal listings like the *Academic Journal Guide* published by the United Kingdom's Chartered Association of Business Schools or the Australian Business Deans' Council journal quality listing (Ott & Michailova, 2018).

The next part of this step is to clean the data by reading the remaining article to remove studies that may not be directly relevant to the research objectives.

For example, a study seeking relevant articles on the repatriation of employees by multinational enterprises (MNEs) after the completion of international assignments may end up finding articles that talk about the repatriation of profits from subsidiaries to headquarters by MNEs. Therefore, these studies would need to be removed from the sample. The process of cleaning the sample is time-consuming, and instead of reading the entire article at this stage, many researchers will restrict themselves to reading the abstracts. The use of text analysis software, such as NVivo, can be useful in undertaking this step.

Step four consists of the *analysis and synthesis of the evidence*. In this step, the researcher codes, synthesizes, and categorizes the data. This can be done to highlight themes in the literature that can reveal what issues and topics have been covered in the literature and what gaps remain. The initial analysis of the focal article may focus on listing the key features of each article, including the theoretical approach followed, whether the studies were conceptual or empirical, the methods used (where applicable), the keywords, and the research question or focus. Further analysis and categorization processes are driven by the research objectives and can be undertaken through manual and/or software coding.Manual coding can involve reading through the articles and coding the key terms. Some critics argue that manual coding can be subjective, questioning the reliability of the process. Elo et al. (2014) provide a checklist to improve the trustworthiness issue and break down the process into the preparation, organization, and reporting phases. Having described the preparation phase in Steps 1–3, the emphasis now is on the organization or categorization phase. Clear coding notes and patterns can demonstrate the reliability of how this process was conducted and can be replicated by others, enhancing its transparency. Another option, if working with other authors or a research assistant, would be for the researchers to conduct this step independently and then check to see whether there is agreement on the codes.Increasingly, there is a push for researchers to combine manual coding with software (van Dinter et al., 2021). For example, Leximancer is a text coding software that can generate codes automatically from PDFs of articles and show connections between different concepts (Dang et al., 2022). These codes can help validate the manual codes (Sinkovics, 2016). Other software, like NVivo, can be used to employ open coding to categorize studies (Sinkovics et al., 2008). Axial coding can be used to reduce the categories, draw connections between the codes, and organize the codes into subthemes under the main theme nodes. The NVivo "queries" search function allows for string search to be undertaken in the project database (Bandara et al., 2011). Using this function, one can search for combinations of sub-themes across the main nodes to understand how the literature discusses the issues. This function facilitates content analysis (Krippendorff, 2004) by counting the number of times certain phrases or subthemes appear in the text and highlighting the relevant sections within the paper (Rammal et al., 2022). The use of the query search helps highlight the relevant text in each article that links to the query terms and facilitates the qualitative analysis of the articles.The final step (*step five*) involves the *reporting or the presentation of the results* from the systematic literature review. This step is again guided by the research objectives and research questions. Some ways of presenting it include qualitative or quantitative meta-analyses or bibliographic mapping, including bibliometrics (Ferreira et al., 2022). The presentation can often be seen as merely reporting the findings. Regardless of the type of literature review being undertaken, the purpose of the final step is to present the analysis in a way that helps further the field. This may involve the introduction or extension of a theory, showing the most influential authors in the field, presenting the themes found in the literature, and so on. The important thing to remember is that the review's objective must involve adding something new to the field, which is what the final step should provide. Fig. 1 summarizes the five steps of the literature review.

4. SOME FINAL TIPS

Literature reviews are a useful resource that provides a state-of-the-play overview of a research field. As the number of research publications has increased, so has the number of literature reviews undertaken. While there are some journals that are dedicated to publishing review articles (for example, the *Academy of Management Review*, the *International Journal of Management Reviews*, and the *Human Resource Management Review*), many journals will only publish a few review articles or dedicate one issue annually to review articles. This means that there is a high level of competition to publish your literature review in quality journals. Here are some tips about issues to consider when preparing for a literature review:

(1) *Be clear about the purpose:* What is your motivation for undertaking the study? Have any other reviews been published that capture a similar topic? What are the objectives of your study, and what are the planned contribution? This is a primary reason why many manuscripts get rejected after being

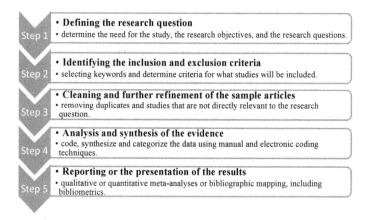

Fig. 1. Steps Involved in Conducting Systematic Literature Reviews.

reviewed. If editors and reviewers have to ask these questions and try to find the answers in the manuscript rather than it being explicitly stated, then the justification and need for the review are not strong. As authors, we need to grasp the attention of the reader and ensure that the need for and the contributions of the literature review are clearly articulated at the start of the manuscript.

(2) *Is the field developed sufficiently to undertake a literature review:* Another common limitation of literature review studies is that they are being undertaken for a research field that is relatively new, and there aren't enough studies to undertake an in-depth review of the literature. Of course, there are exceptions to this rule. If the study attempts to combine two or more areas of research across disciplines or fields of research, then the review can capture emerging trends and issues. Again, here the question can be asked whether the systematic literature review is the most appropriate form of review or whether another type is more relevant.

(3) *Are the steps followed replicable?* A key feature of literature review studies is that the process is transparent and replicable. Hence, not only do literature reviews advance the field of research, the detailed information about the steps followed in undertaking the review helps develop better processes to be applied in future studies. Therefore, it is not surprising that many reviewers highlight the lack of information about the steps followed as a major limitation of review studies. As researchers, we should ensure that every step is clearly explained and builds on previous studies. Furthermore, any new steps or processes should be justified and explained in the context of how it contributes to the field (think in terms of how the use of software for data analysis was introduced).

5. CONCLUSION

Literature reviews, like other types of research, require practice. The more a researcher systematically reviews literature, the better they will get at it and follow the process more efficiently. I hope this chapter provides the inspiration for more robust, transparent, and replicable literature reviews that will lead to substantial contributions in the business management and International Business fields.

REFERENCES

Aversano, L., Grasso, C., & Tortorella, M. (2012). A literature review of Business/IT Alignment Strategies. *Procedia Technology, 5,* 462–474. https://doi.org/10.1016/j.protcy.2012.09.051

Bandara, W., Miskon, S., & Fielt, E. (2011). A systematic, tool-supported method for conducting literature reviews in information systems. In *Proceedings of the 19th European Conference on Information Systems (ECIS 2011).* Helsinki, Finland.

Blake, M. R., Backholer, K., Lancsar, E., Boelsen-Robinson, T., Mah, C., Brimblecombe, J., Zorbas, C., Billich, N., & Peeters, A. (2019). Investigating business outcomes of healthy food retail strategies: A systematic scoping review. *Obesity Reviews, 20*(10), 1384–1399. https://doi.org/10.1111/obr.12912

Booth, A., Sutton, A., Clowes, M., & Martyn-St James, M. (2021). *Systematic approaches to a successful literature review* (3rd ed.). Sage.

Buckley, P. J., Devinney, T. M., & Tang, R. W. (2014). Meta-Analytic Research in International Business and International Management. In *The Multinational Enterprise and the Emergence of the Global Factory* (pp. 100–134). Palgrave Macmillan UK. https://doi.org/10.1057/9781137402387_5

Burritt, R. L., Christ, K. L., Rammal, H. G., & Schaltegger, S. (2020). Multinational enterprise strategies for addressing sustainability: The need for consolidation. *Journal of Business Ethics, 164*(2), 389–410. https://doi.org/10.1007/s10551-018-4066-0

Coombes, P. H., & Nicholson, J. D. (2013, July, 1). Business models and their relationship with marketing: A systematic literature review. *Industrial Marketing Management, 42*(5), 656–664. https://doi.org/10.1016/j.indmarman.2013.05.005

Dang, Q. T., & Rammal, H. G. (2020). Japanese expatriates' management in global assignments: A review and research agenda. *Thunderbird International Business Review, 62*(6), 689–705. https://doi.org/10.1002/tie.22140

Dang, Q. T., Rammal, H. G., & Michailova, S. (2022). Expatriates' families: A systematic literature review and research agenda. *Human Resource Management Review, 32*(4), 100877. https://doi.org/10.1016/j.hrmr.2021.100877

Dekkers, R., Carey, L., & Langhorne, P. (2022). *Making literature reviews work: A multidisciplinary guide to systematic approaches.* Springer.

van Dinter, R., Tekinerdogan, B., & Catal, C. (2021). Automation of systematic literature reviews: A systematic literature review. *Information and Software Technology, 136,* 2021. https://doi.org/10.1016/j.infsof.2021.106589

Elo, S., Kääriäinen, M., Kanste, O., Pölkki, T., Utriainen, K., & Kyngäs, H. (2014). Qualitative Content Analysis:A Focus on Trustworthiness. *Sage Open, 4*(1). https://doi.org/10.1177/2158244014522633

Elsbach, K. D., & van Knippenberg, D. (2020). Creating high-impact literature reviews: An argument for 'integrative reviews'. *Journal of Management Studies, 57*(6), 1277–1289. https://doi.org/10.1111/joms.12581

Ferreira, J. J., Fernandes, C. I., Guo, Y., & Rammal, H. G. (2022). Knowledge worker mobility and knowledge management in MNEs: A bibliometric analysis and research agenda. *Journal of Business Research, 142,* 464–475. https://doi.org/10.1016/j.jbusres.2021.12.056

Ferreira, J. J., Fernandes, C. I., Rammal, H. G., & Veiga, P. M. (2021). Wearable technology and consumer interaction: A systematic review and research agenda. *Computers in Human Behavior, 118.* https://doi.org/10.1016/j.chb.2021.106710

Fink, A. (2019). *Conducting research literature reviews: From the internet to paper.* Sage Publications.

Fisch, C., & Block, J. (2018, April 1). Six tips for your (systematic) literature review in business and management research. *Management Review Quarterly, 68*(2), 103–106. https://doi.org/10.1007/s11301-018-0142-x

Harris, D. (2019). *Literature review and research design: A guide to effective research practice.* Routledge.

Hiebl, M. R. W. (2019). Sample selection in systematic literature reviews of management research. *Organizational Research Methods.* https://doi.org/10.1177/1094428120986851

Kraus, S., Mahto, R. V., & Walsh, S. T. (2021). The importance of literature reviews in small business and entrepreneurship research. *Journal of Small Business Management,* 1–12. https://doi.org/10.1080/00472778.2021.1955128

Krippendorff, K. (2004). *Content analysis: An introduction to its methodology* (2nd ed.). SAGE.

Lame, G. (2019). Systematic literature reviews: An introduction. *Proceedings of the Design Society: International Conference on Engineering Design, 1*(1), 1633–1642. https://doi.org/10.1017/dsi.2019.169

Linnenluecke, M. K., Marrone, M., & Singh, A. K. (2020). Conducting systematic literature reviews and bibliometric analyses. *Australian Journal of Management, 45*(2), 175–194. https://doi.org/10.177/0312896219877678

Meglio, O., & Risberg, A. (2011). The (mis)measurement of M&A performance—A systematic narrative literature review. *Scandinavian Journal of Management, 27*(4), 418–433. https://doi. org/10.1016/j.scaman.2011.09.002

Ott, D. L., & Michailova, S. (2018). Cultural intelligence: A review and new research avenues. *International Journal of Management Reviews, 20*(1), 99–119. https://doi.org/10.1111/ijmr.12118

Pautasso, M. (2019). The structure and conduct of a narrative literature review. In *A Guide to the Scientific Career* (pp. 299–310). https://doi.org/10.1002/9781118907283.ch31

Pham, M. T., Rajić, A., Greig, J. D., Sargeant, J. M., Papadopoulos, A., & McEwen, S. A. (2014). A scoping review of scoping reviews: Advancing the approach and enhancing the consistency. *Research Synthesis Methods, 5*(4), 371–385. https://doi.org/10.1002/jrsm.1123

Pickering, C., & Byrne, J. (2014, May 4). The benefits of publishing systematic quantitative literature reviews for PhD candidates and other early-career researchers. *Higher Education Research and Development, 33*(3), 534–548. https://doi.org/10.1080/07294360.2013.841651

Pickering, C., Grignon, J., Steven, R., Guitart, D., & Byrne, J. (2015). Publishing not perishing: How research students transition from novice to knowledgeable using systematic quantitative literature reviews. *Studies in Higher Education, 40*(10), 1756–1769. https://doi.org/10.1080/03075079.2014.914907

Rammal, H. G., Rose, E. L., Ghauri, P. N., Ørberg Jensen, P. D., Kipping, M., Petersen, B., & Scerri, M. (2022). Economic nationalism and internationalization of services: Review and research agenda. *Journal of World Business, 57*(3). https://doi.org/10.1016/j.jwb.2022.101314

Rana, S., Sakshi, & Singh, J. (2022). Presenting the POWER framework of conducting literature review. In S. Rana, Sakshi, & J. Singh (Eds.), *Exploring the latest trends in management literature (review of management literature)* (Vol. 1, pp. 1–13). Emerald Publishing Limited. https://doi.org/10.1108/S2754-586520220000001001

Ridley, D. (2012). *The literature review: A step-by-step guide for students.* Sage.

Sinkovics, N. (2016). Enhancing the foundations for theorising through bibliometric mapping. *International Marketing Review, 33*(3), 327–350. https://doi.org/10.1108/IMR-10-2014-0341

Sinkovics, R. R., Penz, E., & Ghauri, P. N. (2008). Enhancing the trustworthiness of qualitative research in international business. *Management International Review, 48*(6), 689–714. https://doi.org/10.1007/s11575-008-0103-z

Snyder, H. (2019). Literature review as a research methodology: An overview and guidelines. *Journal of Business Research, 104*, 333–339. https://doi.org/10.1016/j.jbusres.2019.07.039

Tang, R. W., & Cheung, M. W. L. (2016). Testing IB theories with meta-analytic structural equation modeling. *Review of International Business and Strategy, 26*(4), 472–492. https://doi.org/10.1108/RIBS-04-2016-0022

Torraco, R. J. (2005). Writing integrative literature reviews: Guidelines and examples. *Human Resource Development Review, 4*(3), 356–367. https://doi.org/10.1177/1534484305278283

Tranfield, D., Denyer, D., & Smart, P. (2003). Towards a methodology for developing evidence-informed management knowledge by means of systematic review. *British Journal of Management, 14*(3), 207–222. https://doi.org/10.1111/1467-8551.00375

Walsh, D., & Downe, S. (2005). Meta-synthesis method for qualitative research: A literature review. *Journal of Advanced Nursing, 50*(2), 204–211. https://doi.org/10.1111/j.1365-2648.2005.03380.x

Williams, R. I., Clark, L. A., Clark, W. R., & Raffo, D. M. (2021, September 1). Re-examining systematic literature review in management research: Additional benefits and execution protocols. *European Management Journal, 39*(4), 521–533. https://doi.org/10.1016/j.emj.2020.09.007

Xiao, Y., & Watson, M. (2019). Guidance on conducting a systematic literature review. *Journal of Planning Education and Research, 39*(1), 93–112. https://doi.org/10.1177/0739456x17723971

Yorks, L. (2008). What we know, what we don't know, what we need to know—Integrative literature reviews are research. *Human Resource Development Review, 7*(2), 139–141. https://doi.org/10.1177/1534484308316395

HOW TO PLAN AND WRITE FOR SYSTEMATIC LITERATURE REVIEW PAPERS IN MANAGEMENT DOMAIN

Rahul Dhiman, Vimal Srivastava, Anubha Srivastava, Rajni and Aakanksha Uppal

ABSTRACT

Systematic literature review (SLR) papers have gained significant importance during the last years as many reputed journals have asked for literature review submissions from the authors. However, at the same time, authors are experiencing a high number of desk rejections because of a lack of quality and its contribution to the existing body of knowledge. Therefore, the purpose of this paper is to offer guidance to researchers who intend to communicate SLR papers in top-rated journals. We attempt to offer a guide to buddy researchers who plan to write SLR papers. This purpose is achieved by clearly stating how the traditional review method is different from SLR, when and how can each type of literature review method be used, writing effective motivation of a review paper and finally how to synthesize the available literature. We have also presented a few suggestions for writing an impactful SLR in the last. Overall, this chapter serves as a guide to various aspirants of SLR paper to understand the prerequisites of an SLR paper and offers deep insights to bring in more clarity before writing an SLR paper, thereby reducing the chances of desk rejection.

Keywords: Systematic literature review; traditional literature review; types of reviews; planning for SLR; writing for SLR; review methods

1. INTRODUCTION

Writing systematic literature review papers (SLR) has gained importance over time. This is because well-written SLR papers offer better decision-making for

Advancing Methodologies of Conducting Literature Review in Management Domain
Review of Management Literature, Volume 2, 37–55

ISSN: 2754-5865/doi:10.1108/S2754-586520230000002003

various stakeholders, viz., policymakers, entrepreneurs society, and researchers (Kraus et al., 2020). The word "systematic" means "to be structured" while writing a review (Tranfield et al., 2003) and SLR has emerged as a methodology for synthesizing the previously published literature to offer future research directions (Gusenbauer & Neal, 2020; Paul & Dhiman, 2021; Rana et al., 2022). The systematic literature review does not mean only a compilation of a few articles, but it requires an intelligent and insightful synthesis of existing literature. The SLR is a methodology that reviews, critiques, and synthesizes the published literature on a subject field in an integrated way, thereby coming up with new frameworks and perspectives (Nakano & Muniz, 2018). SLR does not mean merely synthesizing previous literature and presenting findings of the previous literature but SLR offers evidence-based guidelines for practitioners and researchers by presenting clear cut future research directions to all the stake-holders (Paul & Benito, 2018; Paul & Criado, 2020). This means that writing SLR is a skill which needs to be learnt; therefore, this paper is an attempt to offer guidance to aspirants of SLR. To achieve the purpose of this paper, we address the following research questions:

• How traditional review method is different to SLR?
• What are the roles of different types of reviews?
• When and how can each type of literature review method be used?
• What are the effective motivations for conducting a review paper?
• How to plan for writing the SLR?
• Over the past years, we have witnessed that many reputed journals in the year 2021 have come up with a call for SLR papers either in regular issues or special issues, specifically, asking for SLR papers (see Table 1). We have identified these journals by google search using keywords *special issue on SLR 2022, call for systematic reviews 2022*. In addition to this call for papers, many top journals such as *International Journal of Consumer Studies and European Management Journal* have already published SLR papers in their special issues in the year 2021 and 2022.

This means that SLR papers have captured the attention of both the Editors as well as the authors over time. Table 1 shows the list of journals (indexed in Scopus/ABDC) that have come up with the SLR papers. The purpose of creating this table is to reveal the fact that SLR papers have a huge scope of publication in top journals. Therefore, it is an interesting investigation to find out what SLR means and how an author should plan for writing SLR papers, which is the purpose of this paper.

The rest of the paper is structured is as follows:

The difference between "traditional literature review" and "systematic litera-ture review" is presented in the next section. In the next section, we focus on various types of reviews and also elaborate on when such types of reviews are to be conducted. The motivations for conducting an SLR are discussed in detail in the next section. The blueprint or plan for writing an impactful SLR is discussed

Table 1. Name of the Journals Asking for SLR Papers.

Name of the Journal	Publisher/ Indexing	Theme for SLR
International Journal of Consumer Studies	Wiley "A" in ABDC; Scopus; SSCI	Developing new research methods and advancing innovative techniques
International Marketing Review	Emerald "A" in ABDC; Scopus; SSCI	SLR in international marketing: From the past to the future
International Journal of Management Reviews	Wiley "A" in ABDC; Scopus	Advancing LR methodology through rigor, generativity, scope, and transparency
International Journal of Physical Distribution & Logistics Management	Emerald "A" in ABDC; Scopus	SLR to advance theories in logistic and supply chain management: A new paradigm
Technovation	Emerald "A" in ABDC; Scopus	SLR: New frontiers in innovation research
Organizational Research Method	Sage "A*" in ABDC; Scopus	How to conduct rigorous and impactful literature reviews?
Management Review Quarterly	Springer Scopus	SLR in entrepreneurship research – Setting the agenda
Journal of Business Research	Elsevier "A*" in ABDC; Scopus	Thematic literature reviews, bibliographic, and meta-analyses
International Journal of Consumer Studies	Wiley "A" in ABDC; Scopus; SSCI	SLR in Consumer Studies
European Management Journal	Elsevier "B" in ABDC; Scopus	SLR in management research: Exploring current challenges and setting future agendas

Source: Authors.

in the next section. We also offer general suggestions for writing SLR in the next section. In the last section, the conclusion is presented.

2. THE TRADITIONAL LITERATURE REVIEW VERSUS SYSTEMATIC LITERATURE REVIEW

A few years back, only the traditional literature review method was deployed by authors to come up with research gaps. Kraus et al. (2020) indicated the difference between SLR and traditional review. The major difference is that traditional review does not follow any specific methodology and is unstructured but SLR papers are systematic and offer a methodological approach and offer justification in terms of Why, What, Who, When, Where, and How also referred to as 5W1H principle (Lim, 2020). SLR papers justify the following:

- Why SLR is needed in the subject field?
- How many papers are downloaded to conduct the review?
- What was the inclusion criterion for the selection of papers and Why?
- How many papers were discarded from the review process and Why?
- What are the future research directions in terms of theory, contexts, constructs, and methodologies?

Some of the major difference between both these kinds of reviews is mentioned in Table 2.

Traditional reviews have to be part of each publication to present findings of previous literature; however, SLRs are only conducted if the need to conduct is well justified. Another difference is that in traditional reviews the author makes use of the literature that can support the hypotheses. However, in SLR, there is clear justification for the studies included and excluded. Also, SLR papers uncover various approaches of research methodologies in terms of selected parameters: method of data collection, sample size, sampled countries, and methodologies used. Apart from the methodologies, widely used theories, constructs, and contexts are also presented to offer guidance to researchers. It must also be noted that the traditional reviews are more opinion-based but SLR papers are evidence-based and each argument is justified. Since traditional reviews are unstructured and offer lesser transparency, therefore, are more likely to be biased by the subjectivity of the author (Briner & Denyer, 2012; Hodgkinson & Ford, 2014; Mulrow, 1994).

Nevertheless, the traditional review also offers a few advantages. The major advantage of writing a traditional review is that it can be written relatively easy since it is unstructured and opinion-based. However, as stated above, writing SLR is a skill and since it is structured it is time consuming but offers more clarity

Table 2. Systematic versus Traditional Review.

S. No.	Systematic Literature Reviews	Traditional Literature Reviews
1	SLR is need-based. Initially, the need to conduct SLR has to be well defined	Traditional reviews are done in almost every paper where we attempt to present the findings of previous studies in an unstructured manner
2	Developing a criterion or a methodology to conduct SLR is a must	No such criterion or methodology is required
3	SLRs are evidence-based review	Traditional reviews are author opinion-based review
4	Inclusion and exclusion criteria for the selection of papers are adopted to ensure the methodological nature of SLR	A review is taken that supports the hypothesis
5	The reason to conduct SLR is to create evidence to support the research questions	Traditional reviews establish a background of the study
6	SLRs are time-consuming	Relatively less time-consuming

Source: The Authors.

in terms of providing future research directions. But it also should be noted that due to the presence of robust databases these days it is easier to download the papers once the search criteria are well applied. It must be noted that the selection process of articles adopted should not create confusion and generates doubts about the reliability of the findings of the study. The strategy for synthesizing the findings of studies published must be clearly stated.

3. DIFFERENT TYPES OF REVIEWS

Various authors over the past have revealed that SLR papers are of various types such as structured review that focuses on widely used methods, theories, contexts, and constructs (Anlesinya et al., 2019; Mishra et al., 2021; Paul & Criado, 2020; Rebouças & Soares, 2021; Rosado-Serrano et al., 2018); framework-based (Lim et al., 2020; Paul & Benito, 2018); hybrid-narrative framework to set future research agenda (Kumar et al., 2020; Paul et al., 2017); theory-based review (Paul & Rosado-Serrano, 2019), meta-analysis based review (Rana & Paul, 2020), and bibliometric review (Randhawa et al., 2016), Review papers with a purpose to develop a model or framework (Paul & Mas, 2020; Paul, 2019) and systematic literature review articles which can be broadly classified as domain-based, theory-based, and method-based (Paul & Criado, 2020). Some other reviews include realist reviews (Best et al., 2012; Pawson et al., 2005), scoping reviews (Peters et al., 2015) and integrated reviews (Milne et al., 2016). The overview of all these reviews is mentioned in the following sub-sections. We also have attempted to guide when and how can each type of literature review method be used.

3.1 Structured Review

This type of review is structured with insightful information in the form of tables and figures (Canabal & White, 2008; Kahiya, 2018). Such tables and figures depict information in terms of broadly used theories, constructs and methodologies used in the previous studies. This method is used to enable buddy researchers to understand the most common methods and variables used in the existing literature (Paul & Feliciano Cestero, 2021). This method is useful to identify research gaps with reference to methodologies, constructs, contexts and theories based on the structured information. This type of review article can have 5–10 useful tables in a structured format (Paul & Criado, 2020).

3.2 Framework-Based Review

As it is clear from the name, this kind of review is used when an author wants to develop a framework to offer guidance in terms of future research directions. Framework-based review is also called a domain-based review. Various authors in the past made use of this kind of review and as an outcome came up with a new framework. For instance, 6W Framework was proposed by Callahan (2014). Similarly, Paul and Rosado-Serrano (2019) proposed the TCCM framework, where "T" means Theory; "C" is Construct; "C" is Characteristics; "M" is "Methodology" or the 7-P framework (Paul & Mas, 2020). This framework is useful when the researcher intends to present widely deployed theories, constructs, contexts, and methodologies in the existing literature. This kind of framework is useful for researchers in the initial stages of their research to identify theories, constructs, contexts, and methodologies and offers future research directions to carry forward the research. It should be noted that the authors who intend to make use of framework-based reviews must develop their framework to add value to the existing body of knowledge or must adopt an already existing framework as mentioned in this section.

3.3 Hybrid-Narrative Framework

This kind of framework offers both hybrid and narrative perspectives. Hybrid reviews can be developed when researchers put together a framework to offer future research directions in a more narrative-oriented form of review (Paul et al., 2017). A hybrid form of review takes into account both bibliometric and structured reviews. This type of review is useful when information is presented in a structured format and later such information can be presented by making use of tools/software. For instance, Bahoo et al. (2020) followed a similar approach by integrating the tenets of bibliometric review with that of a structured review.

3.4 Theory-Based Review

This kind of review is useful when a researcher intends to analyze the role of a definite theory in a subject field. This type of review article synthesizes and helps advancing a body of literature that uses and/or empirically applies a given underlying theory. For example, Kozlenkova et al. (2014) conducted a resource-based theory review in the marketing field. Also, Gilal et al. (2019) used "Role of self-determination theory in marketing science." Hence such kind of review can be helpful to explore the application of a single theory or various theories in a particular domain (Colquitt & Zapata-Phelan, 2007; Eisenhardt, 1989). A few examples of theory-based review can be systematically reviewing the role of agency theory in franchising, the theory of planned behavior in international marketing or entrepreneurship, and the theory of reasoned action to examine the behavioral intentions of customers. Some of the classic review-based articles are found in the work by Frank et al. (2010), Gardner et al. (2017), Lebek et al. (2014), and Schoor et al. (2015).

3.5 A Meta-Analysis Based Review

As suggested by the name itself, this kind of review is more analytical. One similarity between structured and meta-analysis based review is that both the reviews focus mainly on analyzing the volume of existing research. However, it should be noted that structured review attempts to synthesize the previous findings of published literature, but meta-analysis based review makes use of statistical analysis of available data and findings by examining correlations among variables from previous quantitative studies (Colquitt & Zapata-Phelan, 2007; Pati & Lorusso, 2018; Piper, 2013). In the present literature, this kind of review is a popular quantitative technique widely accepted as one of the best statistical assessments of previous literature. This kind of review is helpful to identify directions and effect sizes based on previous studies by using weighted average methods. Future research directions are also offered by studying the relationships of moderator variables also (Klier et al., 2017, p. 3). A few examples of meta-analysis based review in the existing literature are Knoll and Matthes (2017), Rauch et al. (2009), Tang and Buckley (2020), Schmid and Morschett (2020), and Field and Gillett (2010).

3.6 Bibliometric Reviews

This kind of review is used by authors to present data using the software. The widely deployed software currently used to write bibliometric reviews is VoS (Visualization of Similarities). The data can be presented to figure out trends and citations and/or co-citations of a particular theme, by year, country, author, journal, method, theory, and research problem (Bhaiswar et al., 2021; Pandey & Joshi, 2021; Rialp et al., 2019). The previous kind of review is more to do with theories, contexts, constructs, and methodologies; however, bibliometric reviews present systematic information in terms of authors, affiliations, countries, citations, and co-citations, etc. Some of the highly cited bibliometric articles are Ho and Kahn (2014), Linnenluecke et al. (2020), Zupic and Čater (2015).

3.7 Realist Reviews

Realist review is a relatively novel approach for synthesizing previous studies which has an explanatory rather than judgmental focus. Previous studies have stated that this kind of review is used for complex interventions (Best et al., 2012; Pawson et al., 2005). Realist review does not recommend both policymakers and managers regarding whether the investigated phenomenon will work or not, but this review offer practitioners and stakeholders with a comprehensive and pragmatic understanding of multifaceted social interventions. Such understanding offered in a realist review is of immense help while executing various social programs and local or national level.

3.8 Scoping Reviews

Scoping reviews are used to make clear operational definitions and conceptual boundaries of a particular subject field. Scoping reviews are for that reason predominantly helpful when a body of literature has not yet been reviewed in detail (Peters et al., 2015). Scoping reviews can also be used to find out the value and possible scope of a full systematic literature review. Further, this kind of review can also be undertaken to sum up and publish research findings, to discover research gaps, and to make a future research agenda.

3.9 Integrated Reviews

Another review method found in literature is integrated reviews. An exceptional integrative review is conducted with the similar rigidity as a systematic review; nevertheless, the main dissimilarity between both these reviews is the kind of studies included in the review and probably how the studies are compared and contrasted in the manuscript (McGrath, 2012). Integrative reviews are more oriented toward a discussion of findings within the framework of the needs of the clinical setting in question (Milne et al., 2016).

4. WHAT ARE THE EFFECTIVE MOTIVATIONS FOR CONDUCTING AN SLR?

As we are well aware of the fact that reviewers/editors of top-rated journals are more interested to know the motivation/rationale of the study. These days we could see many good papers getting rejected just because of weak underlying motivation. Therefore, it is vital to understand the motivation for conducting a review paper. It does not matter that motivation is only required in the case of empirical papers. In traditional reviews, motivation may not be of that importance as we only attempt to synthesize the findings of previous researchers to support our hypotheses. But writing motivation for conducting an SLR is vital. We present the following motivations for writing a review paper.

4.1 To Address the Research Questions

Conducting an SLR makes sense only when it is needed. So before we jump to writing SLR in any subject field it becomes important to understand why such kind of review is required? After a comprehensive examination if an author finds that SLR is required then a research question must be specified. The research question is a vital part of the SLR and is the underlying motivation (Fisch & Block, 2018). This is where SLR is different from the traditional literature reviews. The evidence the SLR aims to craft is very much related to the research question specified at the very beginning of the manuscript. In any review paper, we must clearly state the main research question is to synthesize what we know and what we do not know about a research question, hypotheses, applied methods or topics (Briner & Denyer, 2012; Paul & Criado, 2020). The research questions stated must be answered to present future research agenda in terms of theories, methodologies, and constructs. We cannot mention that unavailability of the sufficient literature is the purpose of conducting an SLR. But the availability of sufficient literature on the subject field should be the basis of writing an SLR (Hodgkinson & Ford, 2014). Therefore, as we mentioned at the beginning of the manuscript, writing SLR is an art and skill that should be learned. A review on a very narrow niche with a few cannot offer new insights or theories. Therefore, it should be noted that a broad range of literature is available supplemented by clear cut research questions that must be addressed.

Authors may find themselves in trouble if an SLR is already available on the subject field. In such cases, the focus should be made if different research questions can be asked that may be answered with new research. The author must take into consideration the following points:

- The originality of the idea for conducting SLR must be clearly defined
- Why SLR is required, specifically in the subject field and what is so unique that this phenomenon needs to be studied
- The introduction of the manuscript must further enhance the argumentation used regarding the motivation for conducting the review

4.2 To State the Future Research Agenda

Another motivation for writing an SLR should be to clearly state the future research agenda (Littell et al., 2008). Presenting research directions is a valuable addition to the existing body of knowledge, which should be the motivation for conducting an SLR. Paul and Criado (2020) clearly stated that at least 20–25% of the SLR should be dedicated to developing a comprehensive future research agenda with reference to theory, constructs, context and methodology. Hence, the motivation for an author to carry out SLR should be to come up with the theories, methods, contexts, and constructs that are rarely been used in prior studies.

5. HOW TO PLAN FOR WRITING THE SLR

An SLR can be conducted to be published as a standalone paper. Since writing an SLR includes a comprehensive synthesis of the existing literature and careful examination, therefore, conducting an SLR has to be effectively planned. Following are the steps that can offer researchers a guiding tool to move ahead while writing an SLR (see Table 3).

Table 3. Steps for Writing an Effective SLR.

Step 1	*Planning for SLR* *– Need identification* *– Develop a criterion for conducting a review*
Step 2	Identification and assessment of studies
Step 3	*Extracting and synthesizing data* *– Preparing for data extraction* *– Conducting data synthesis*
Step 4	Present the review findings

Source: The Authors.

5.1 Planning for SLR

It is necessary to plan or make a blueprint before an SLR is to be conducted. Planning involves identifying the need for conducting such a review and developing predefined criteria to move ahead in carrying out such a comprehensive review. Both such requirements of planning are mentioned in the following subsections.

5.1.1 Need Identification

The need for conducting an SLR must be identified by the author. The need can be identified by following certain steps.

- Initially, authors must check whether the SLR that is being planned is the very first of its kind or if there are already various kinds of reviews available in the subject field.
- To solve this issue, we suggest authors refer to various databases such as Google Scholar, Microsoft Academic, Scopus, ProQuest, EBSCO etc. depending on the availability as a majority of such software requires an institutional subscription.
- In case, the authors find that there is plentiful literature available, then it is an opportunity for a researcher to document a wonderful SLR, however, it has to be seen whether new research questions can be asked by conducting new research.

5.1.2 Develop a Criterion for Conducting a Review

Since the review is systematic, therefore, authors have to be methodological in their approach (Dhiman et al., 2018; Dhiman & Sharma, 2019). Being methodological means applying a well-established and justified criterion or protocol (Mittal et al., 2019; Tranfield et al., 2003). Criterion means applying methodology for various steps of an SLR (Pittaway et al., 2014) in terms of search strings, identifying a database (*Scopus/ABDC/WOS/SCI/SSCI* etc.), inclusion and exclusion criteria (such as PRISMA flow chart).

Various authors over the past indicated have asked authors to look for all kinds of available literature such as journal articles, magazine articles, authored/edited books, and conference proceedings (Briner & Denyer, 2012; Sharma & Dhiman, 2016). However, we suggest authors to limit and set a criterion for online databases and look for journal articles only, specifically in the business management research. This strategy seems more methodological and applies to the entire globe. We suggest not to include conference papers, working papers etc., also referred to as "gray literature" because journal articles published in indexed databases go through a stringent review process. However, gray literature does not go through that peer review process often (Podsakoff et al., 2005).

Based on the keywords applied by the researchers, the author searches the various databases. We also suggest applying justified criteria while selecting the time frame, because the author will come across too many papers which will be a cumbersome process to synthesize. However, justification has to be provided for the period selected. For instance, if an author intends to write an SLR on Indian international trade then the time period of 1991 onward can be selected as a criterion for downloading the papers because reforms in terms of liberalization, privatization, and globalization were formulated to expand the international trade.

Another significant question the author must be able to answer is where to search either "Only in Title" or "in Title or abstract" or even "in the text." This decision can be a challenge and depends upon the availability of papers in every search. If an author finds a lesser number of papers using one search then another search criterion can be applied to ensure more papers in the database.

5.2 Identification and Assessment of Studies

After developing a criterion, the authors will come across many relevant papers for conducting an SLR. Therefore, the identification and assessment of such papers becomes very important. While identifying the studies, the title alone can disclose whether a study fits the selected criteria or not. If a title is not sufficient to explain whether the paper should be taken as a part of SLR, then abstracts must be read to ensure that no relevant paper is missed from the database. Similarly, if abstracts are not able to identify the research questions then the author should start reading the text, however, we suggest that reading titles and abstracts should be sufficient to identify the relevant papers.

It has to be identified from the database which studies are to be kept and which one to be discarded. Tables specifying the "classification in terms of the number of papers published and the number of authors contributed" can support this step of planning for the review. Later, a table specifying the "distribution of papers in leading journals" can also be shown. This table will compile all the papers identified from each journal. Such a list can be displayed in order. For instance, any journal publishing the highest number of papers, say 40 articles in the subject field should come first and then followed by an order.

5.3 Extracting and Synthesizing Data

5.3.1 Preparing for Data Extraction

This is another important step to plan for the review and has to be systematic. At this stage, the authors should create a "data extraction bias" using the different judgments of the studies (Popay et al., 2006). To overcome the bias, avoid missing significant data and generate a higher level of objectivity. It is suggested that more than one author should conduct the data extraction (Rousseau et al., 2008). The table should be presented and must contain all the essential information for the synthesis and each paper reviewed should be outlined in that table. Also, a flow chart for inclusion and exclusion criteria of papers must be presented (see annexure for sample inclusion and exclusion criteria). The flow chart should depict the following points:

- Records identified through the database.
- Additional records identified through other sources.
- Records after duplicated removed.
- Title and abstracts screened.
- Records excluded.
- Articles after abstract and title screening.
- Records from backward and forward search strategies.
- Full-text articles accessed for eligibility.
- Full-text articles excluded.
- Studies included in our review.

5.3.2 Conducting Data Synthesis

Conducting data synthesis is one of the crucial steps while writing an SLR. Many of the papers face rejection because the synthesis of articles is not properly justified. Synthesis and summarizing are two different things. SLRs have to analyze and compare existing literature instead of just summarizing it (Jones & Gatrell, 2014). It is important to focus on underlying concepts that address the research questions and not on authors and their findings. This concept centric writing style needs to be constituted in the microstructure of the paper (Fisch & Block, 2018). Author-centric approach is not recommended for an SLR as this strategy will represent a summary only and not a synthesis (Webster & Watson, 2002). The authors must not only analyze the findings of the study but also the methodological gaps to identify problems and make cross country comparisons. Again, synthesis should be made in tables to bring in easier understanding. Tables can be presented in terms of "Determinants and Methodological Trends" of the subject field; "Theoretical Underpinnings" to synthesize the widely used theories used in the literature of the subject field; Tabular representation of previous contextual studies conducted, variables studied and their relationship. To have a look at the classical synthesis of reviews, we strongly recommend authors refer to these articles by Dabić et al. (2020), Denyer and Tranfield (2009), Jones and Gatrell (2014), Kumar et al. (2020), Paul et al. (2017), and Webster and Watson (2002).

5.4 Present the Review Findings

This part of the paper should form a roadmap for future researchers. This is probably the section where the author has to be very careful since this section is the backbone and is an outcome of an SLR. The review findings are to be presented in terms of the future research agenda. Here, an author should mention the theoretical gaps, methodological gaps and the constructs that can be further studied. In the theoretical gaps, authors must address what are the issues pertaining to theory extension and validation. Authors should come up with the rarely used theories in prior studies stating how these theories have the potential to explain more of the reasons for selected determinants across various industries and countries.

With respect to the investigated contexts, authors should present specific industries and countries where a majority of the studies are conducted. A comparison across developed and developing nations will also bring more clarity.

With respect to constructs, it needs to be clearly stated that authors in the past have attempted to establish linkages with various variables and their interrelationships, however, certain identified variables are still unexplored across diverse contextual settings.

Authors also can list out and anticipate the underexplored theories, major constructs and potentially novel methods that can be used in future research in this highly relevant section of an SLR.

6. GENERAL SUGGESTIONS FOR WRITING AN SLR

In this section, we attempt to offer a few suggestions to authors before they start writing an SLR. These points may be taken as a guide based on the publishing experience and a cursory glance at various highly cited SLR papers. We offer suggestions on various parameters such as the composition of a team for writing an SLR; the structure of a classic review article and the volume of articles.

6.1 Composition of a Team for Writing an SLR

Many times, we come across many single-authored empirical articles (for instance, Dhiman, 2018; Hakala, 2011; Hart, 1998; Oakley, 2002). But writing an SLR requires different skill sets which may not be possessed by a single author. Different skill requirements can be in terms of having an access to databases and proficiency while searching papers in the database, applying required keywords, inclusion and exclusion criteria, synthesis of papers, the art of writing an SLR etc. Therefore, we strongly urge authors to make an efficient team of authors (Akinci & Sadler-Smith, 2012; Jones & Gatrell, 2014). Those who do have not any prior publishing experience with SLR are suggested to identify at least one author who has published an SLR paper. Such an author can also serve as a critical peer reviewer apart from a coauthor.

6.2 Structure of a Classic Review Article

Unlike any other papers, SLR also starts with an introduction to build the background of the study; underlying motivation/need/rationale is also presented in this section (Webster & Watson, 2002). This is followed up by writing a methodology, synthesis of the literature, discussion, and conclusion (Denyer & Neely, 2004; Fisch & Block, 2018; Hakala, 2011). However, as stated above, more emphasis has to be laid on presenting future research agenda, which is the purpose of conducting an SLR. A clear structure and organization is also suggested by Rana et al. (2022) in one recently published paper in review of management literature.

6.3 Volume/Quantity of Articles

Many a times, researchers keep deliberating on the number of articles to be included for review. To be honest, we could not come across any thumb rule addressing this issue. We have seen SLR papers published in top-rated journals where less than 60 articles are also reviewed. For instance, please refer to Paul and Dhiman (2021), published in *International Marketing Review*; Tian et al. (2018), published in *Management Decision*. At the same time, we came across studies that reviewed only 20 articles. For instance, please see, Boelens et al. (2017). An SLR is also conducted by reviewing 670 articles, please see Cerniauskaite et al. (2011), published in *Disability and Rehabilitation*. This number may vary from subject to subject. In case there is ample number of articles available, then an attempt has to be made to ensure that different research questions are answered using a different type of review. On contrary, if the number of available articles is relatively less, then an attempt has to be made to ensure that a more comprehensive review can be conducted.

7. CONCLUSION

SLRs have turned out to be more popular in business management research. Many reputed journals have started to publish SLR papers now. The publishing experience of many authors reveals that the major reason for the rejection of SLR articles is attributed to the fact that the synthesis of these articles is not appropriate. Moreover, the majority of the articles just compile the information, which is not the purpose of conducting an SLR, hence becomes another chance of desk rejection at times. Over the period, we could see that writing traditional review articles are now replaced with SLR articles; this is because of the innovation in technology, availability of databases, and robust software. The major difference between a traditional and an SLR article is that an SLR article brings in more transparency due to its structured nature.

Earlier, literature review only means mere compiling of findings of previous authors. But with the passage of time and technological advancements, we could see software-oriented tables, graphs and charts, making an SLR more tables and picture-oriented, thereby making it reader-friendly, and better to understand.

Though the online databases and technology offer time-saving while writing an SLR paper, it is the art of synthesizing the available literature that must be learnt by the researchers. Planning for review is important before we start writing a review paper. A blueprint has to be developed in terms of need identification and developing a criterion for conducting a review. Later, identification and assessment of studies need a different skill altogether. It has to be ensured that no significant study is missed to be part of the review; therefore, selection of keywords, and screening through a title, abstract and the full text is vital. Since the review is systematic, therefore, inclusion and exclusion criteria also have to be well justified so that the final number of articles to be included for review are appropriate and make sense.

In the last, writing review findings in terms of stating future research agenda has to be well presented. We suggest that at least one-fourth of the article should be devoted to developing future research agenda, which is the major purpose of writing an SLR article.

8. IMPLICATIONS AND FUTURE SCOPE

This paper offers a few implications also. First, this paper will be of immense help to the researchers who plan to write SLR paper. This paper will serve as a guide for the buddy scholars and academicians who are in need of a paper that offers comprehensive guidance on planning and writing a SLR paper. Secondly, we could see many SLR papers on diverse subject fields but a sample guide offering planning and writing for SLR papers is still scarce in the existing body of the knowledge. Therefore, we believe this paper will of significant importance in the existing body of knowledge.

We also suggest researchers to also write a comprehensive guiding paper for planning various types of reviews such as hubris-narrative review, meta-analysis, and bibliometric review.

REFERENCES

Akinci, C., & Sadler-Smith, E. (2012). Intuition in management research: A historical review. *International Journal of Management Reviews, 14*(1), 104–122.

Anlesinya, A., Dartey-Baah, K., & Amponsah-Tawiah, K. (2019). A review of empirical research on global talent management. *FIIB Business Review, 8*(2), 147–160.

Bahoo, S., Alon, I., & Paltrinieri, A. (2020). Corruption in international business: A review and research agenda. *International Business Review, 29*(4), 101660.

Best, A., Greenhalgh, T., Lewis, S., Saul, J. E., Carroll, S., & Bitz, J. (2012). Large-system transformation in health care: A realist review. *The Milbank Quarterly, 90*(3), 421–456.

Bhaiswar, R., Meenakshi, N., & Chawla, D. (2021). Evolution of electronic word of mouth: A systematic literature review using bibliometric analysis of 20 Years (2000–2020). *FIIB Business Review, 10*(3), 215–231.

Boelens, R., De Wever, B., & Voet, M. (2017). Four key challenges to the design of blended learning: A systematic literature review. *Educational Research Review, 22*, 1–18.

Briner, R. B., & Denyer, D. (2012). Systematic review and evidence synthesis as a practice and scholarship tool. In *Handbook of evidence-based management: Companies, classrooms and research* (pp. 112–129).

Callahan, J. L. (2014). Writing literature reviews: A reprise and update. *Human Resource Development Review, 13*(3), 271–275. Oxford University Press.

Canabal, A., & White, G. O., III (2008). Entry mode research: Past and future. *International Business Review, 17*(3), 267–284.

Cerniauskaite, M., Quintas, R. U. I., Boldt, C., Raggi, A., Cieza, A., Bickenbach, J. E., & Leonardi, M. (2011). Systematic literature review on ICF from 2001 to 2009: Its use, implementation and operationalisation. *Disability & Rehabilitation, 33*(4), 281–309.

Colquitt, J. A., & Zapata-Phelan, C. P. (2007). Trends in theory building and theory testing: A five-decade study of the Academy of Management Journal. *Academy of Management Journal, 50*(6), 1281–1303.

Dabić, M., Vlačić, B., Paul, J., Dana, L. P., Sahasranamam, S., & Glinka, B. (2020). Immigrant entrepreneurship: A review and research agenda. *Journal of Business Research, 113*, 25–38.

Denyer, D., & Neely, A. (2004). Introduction to special issue: Innovation and productivity performance in the UK. *International Journal of Management Reviews, 5*(3–4), 131–135.

Denyer, D., & Tranfield, D. (2009). Producing a systematic review. In D. Buchanan & A. Bryman
(Eds.), *TheSage Handbook of Organizational Research Methods* (pp. 671–689). Sage.

Dhiman, R. (2018). Identifying the key indicators of financial stability and financial development: A
review of financial service sector. *Asian Journal of Management Science and Applications, 3*(4),
302–320.

Dhiman, R., Chand, P., & Gupta, S. (2018). Behavioural aspects influencing decision to purchase
apparels amongst young Indian consumers. *FIIB Business Review, 7*(3), 188–200.

Dhiman, R., & Sharma, M. (2019). Relation between labour productivity and export competitiveness
of Indian textile industry: Cointegration and causality approach. *Vision: The Journal of
Business Perspective, 23*(1), 22–30.

Eisenhardt, K. M. (1989). Agency theory: An assessment and review. *Academy of Management Review,
14*(1), 57–74.

Field, A. P., & Gillett, R. (2010). How to do a meta-analysis. *British Journal of Mathematical and
Statistical Psychology, 63*(3), 665–694.

Fisch, C., & Block, J. (2018). Six tips for your (systematic) literature review in business and management research. *Management Review Quarterly, 68*(2), 103–106.

Frank, H., Lueger, M., Nosé, L., & Suchy, D. (2010). The concept of "Familiness": Literature review
and systems theory-based reflections. *Journal of Family Business Strategy, 1*(3), 119–130.

Gardner, R. G., Harris, T. B., Li, N., Kirkman, B. L., & Mathieu, J. E. (2017). Understanding "it
depends" in organizational research: A theory-based taxonomy, review, and future research
agenda concerning interactive and quadratic relationships. *Organizational Research Methods,
20*(4), 610–638.

Gilal, F. G., Zhang, J., Paul, J., & Gilal, N. G. (2019). The role of self-determination theory in
marketing science: An integrative review and agenda for research. *European Management
Journal, 37*(1), 29–44.

Gusenbauer, M., & Neal, R. H. (2020). Which academic search systems are suitable for systematic
reviews or meta-analyses? Evaluating retrieval qualities of Google Scholar, PubMed, and 26
other resources. *Research Synthesis Methods, 11*(2), 181–217.

Hakala, H. (2011). Strategic orientations in management literature: Three approaches to understanding the interaction between market, technology, entrepreneurial and learning orientations.
International Journal of Management Reviews, 13(2), 199–217.

Hart, C. (1998). *Doing a literature review*. Sage Publications.

Hodgkinson, G. P., & Ford, J. K. (2014). Narrative, meta-analytic, and systematic reviews: What are
the differences and why do they matter? *Journal of Organizational Behavior, 35*(S1), S1–S5.

Ho, Y. S., & Kahn, M. (2014). A bibliometric study of highly cited reviews in the Science Citation
Index expanded™. *Journal of the Association for Information Science and Technology, 65*(2),
372–385.

Jones, O., & Gatrell, C. (2014). The future of writing and reviewing for IJMR. *International Journal of
Management Reviews, 16*(3), 249–264.

Kahiya, E. T. (2018). Five decades of research on export barriers: Review and future directions.
International Business Review, 27(6), 1172–1188.

Klier, H., Schwens, C., Zapkau, F. B., & Dikova, D. (2017). Which resources matter how and where?
A meta-analysis on firms' foreign establishment mode choice. *Journal of Management Studies,
54*(3), 304–339.

Knoll, J., & Matthes, J. (2017). The effectiveness of celebrity endorsements: A metaanalysis. *Journal of
the Academy of Marketing Science, 45*(1), 55–75.

Kozlenkova, I. V., Samaha, S. A., & Palmatier, R. W. (2014). Resource-based theory in marketing.
Journal of the Academy of Marketing Science, 42(1), 1–21.

Kraus, S., Breier, M., & Dasí-Rodríguez, S. (2020). The art of crafting a systematic literature review in
entrepreneurship research. *The International Entrepreneurship and Management Journal, 16*(3),
1023–1042.

Kumar, A., Paul, J., & Unnithan, A. B. (2020). 'Masstige' marketing: A review, synthesis and research
agenda. *Journal of Business Research, 113*, 384–398.

Lebek, B., Uffen, J., Neumann, M., Hohler, B., & Breitner, M. H. (2014). Information security awareness and behavior: A theory-based literature review. *Management Research Review*, *37*(12), 1049–1092.

Lim, W. M. (2020). Challenger marketing. *Industrial Marketing Management*, *84*, 342–345. https://doi.org/10.1016/j.indmarman. 2019.08.009

Lim, W. M., Yap, S. F., & Makkar, M. (2020). Home sharing in marketing and tourism at a at a tipping point: What do we know, how do we know, and where should we be heading? *Journal of Business Research*, *122*, 534–566.

Linnenluecke, M. K., Marrone, M., & Singh, A. K. (2020). Conducting systematic literature reviews and bibliometric analyses. *Australian Journal of Management*, *45*(2), 175–194.

Littell, J. H., Corcoran, J., & Pillai, V. (2008). *Systematic reviews and meta-analysis*. Oxford University Press.

McGrath, J. M. (2012). Systematic and integrative reviews of the literature: How are they changing our thoughts about practice? *Journal of Perinatal and Neonatal Nursing*, *26*(3), 193–195.

Milne, T., Creedy, D. K., & West, R. (2016). Integrated systematic review on educational strategies that promote academic success and resilience in undergraduate indigenous students. *Nurse Education Today*, *36*, 387–394.

Mishra, R., Singh, R. K., & Koles, B. (2021). Consumer decision-making in Omnichannel retailing: Literature review and future research agenda. *International Journal of Consumer Studies*, *45*(2), 147–174.

Mittal, A., Dhiman, R., & Lamba, P. (2019). Skill mapping for blue-collar employees and organisational performance: A qualitative assessment. *Benchmarking: An International Journal*, *26*(4), 1255–1274.

Mulrow, C. D. (1994). Systematic reviews: Rationale for systematic reviews. *British Medical Journal*, *309*, 597–599.

Nakano, D., & Muniz, J., Jr. (2018). Writing the literature review for empirical papers. *Production*, *28*.

Oakley, A. (2002). Social science and evidence-based everything: The case of education. *Education Review*, *54*, 277–286.

Pandey, K., & Joshi, S. (2021). Trends in destination choice in tourism research: A 25-year bibliometric review. *FIIB Business Review*, *10*(4), 371–392.

Pati, D., & Lorusso, L. N. (2018). How to write a systematic review of the literature. *HERD: Health Environments Research & Design Journal*, *11*(1), 15–30.

Paul, J. (2019). Marketing in emerging markets: A review, theoretical synthesis and extension. *International Journal of Emerging Markets*, *15*(3), 446–468.

Paul, J., & Benito, G. R. (2018). A review of research on outward foreign direct investment from emerging countries, including China: What do we know, how do we know and where should we be heading? *Asia Pacific Business Review*, *24*(1), 90–115.

Paul, J., & Criado, A. R. (2020). The art of writing literature review: What do we know and what do we need to know? *International Business Review*, *29*(4), 101717.

Paul, J., & Dhiman, R. (2021). Three decades of export competitiveness literature: Systematic review, synthesis and future research agenda. *International Marketing Review*, *38*(5), 1082–1111.

Paul, J., & Feliciano-Cestero, M. M. (2021). Five decades of research on foreign direct investment by MNEs: An overview and research agenda. *Journal of Business Research*, *124*, 800–812.

Paul, J., & Mas, E. (2020). Toward a 7-P framework for international marketing. *Journal of Strategic Marketing*, *28*(8), 681–701.

Paul, J., Parthasarathy, S., & Gupta, P. (2017). Exporting challenges of SMEs: A review and future research agenda. *Journal of World Business*, *52*(3), 327–342.

Paul, J., & Rosado-Serrano, A. (2019). Gradual internationalization versus born global/international new venture models. *International Marketing Review*, *36*(6), 830–858.

Pawson, R., Greenhalgh, T., Harvey, G., & Walshe, K. (2005). Realist review-a new method of systematic review designed for complex policy interventions. *Journal of Health Services Research & Policy*, *10*(1_Suppl), 21–34.

Peters, M. D., Godfrey, C. M., Khalil, H., McInerney, P., Parker, D., & Soares, C. B. (2015). Guidance for conducting systematic scoping reviews. *JBI Evidence Implementation*, *13*(3), 141–146.

Piper, R. J. (2013). How to write a systematic literature review: A guide for medical students. *National AMR, Fostering Medical Research, 1*, 1–8.

Pittaway, L., Holt, R., & Broad, J. (2014). Synthesising knowledge in entrepreneurship research-the role of systematic literature reviews. In *Handbook of research on small business and entrepreneurship*. Edward Elgar Publishing.

Podsakoff, P. M., MacKenzie, S. B., Bachrach, D. G., & Podsakoff, N. P. (2005). The influence of management journals in the 1980s and 1990s. *Strategic Management Journal, 26*(5), 473–488.

Popay, J., Roberts, H., Sowden, A., Petticrew, M., Arai, L., Rodgers, M., ... & Duffy, S. (2006). Guidance on the conduct of narrative synthesis in systematic reviews. *A product from the ESRC methods programme Version, 1*(1), b92.

Rana, J., & Paul, J. (2020). Health motive and the purchase of organic food: A meta-analytic review. *International Journal of Consumer Studies, 44*(2), 162–171.

Rana, S., Sakshi, & Singh, J. (2022). Presenting the POWER framework of conducting literature review. In S. Rana, Sakshi, & J. Singh (Eds.), *Exploring the latest trends in management literature (review of management literature* (Vol. 1, pp. 1–13). Emerald Publishing Limited. https://doi.org/10.1108/S2754-586520220000001001

Randhawa, K., Wilden, R., & Hohberger, J. (2016). A bibliometric review of open innovation: Setting a research agenda. *Journal of Product Innovation Management, 33*(6), 750–772.

Rauch, A., Wiklund, J., Lumpkin, G. T., & Frese, M. (2009). Entrepreneurial orientation and business performance: An assessment of past research and suggestions for the future. *Entrepreneurship Theory and Practice, 33*(3), 761–787.

Rebouças, R., & Soares, A. M. (2021). Voluntary simplicity: A literature review and research agenda. *International Journal of Consumer Studies, 45*(3), 303–319.

Rialp, A., Merigó, J. M., Cancino, C. A., & Urbano, D. (2019). Twenty-five years (1992–2016) of the international business review: A bibliometric overview. *International Business Review, 28*(6), 101587.

Rosado-Serrano, A., Paul, J., & Dikova, D. (2018). International franchising: A literature review and research agenda. *Journal of Business Research, 85*(September 2017), 238–257.

Rousseau, D. M., Manning, J., & Denyer, D. (2008). 11 Evidence in management and organizational science: Assembling the field's full weight of scientific knowledge through syntheses. *The Academy of Management Annals, 2*(1), 475–515.

Schmid, D., & Morschett, D. (2020). Decades of research on foreign subsidiary divestment: What do we really know about its antecedents? *International Business Review, 29*(4), 101653.

Schoor, C., Narciss, S., & Körndle, H. (2015). Regulation during cooperative and collaborative learning: A theory-based review of terms and concepts. *Educational Psychologist, 50*(2), 97–119.

Sharma, M., & Dhiman, R. (2016). Determinants affecting Indian textile exports: A review. *Biz and Bytes, 6*(2), 193–200.

Tang, R. W., & Buckley, P. J. (2020). Host country risk and foreign ownership strategy: Meta-analysis and theory on the moderating role of home country institutions. *International Business Review, 29*(4), 101666.

Tian, M., Deng, P., Zhang, Y., & Salmador, M. P. (2018). How does culture influence innovation? A systematic literature review. *Management Decision, 56*(5), 1088–1107.

Tranfield, D., Denyer, D., & Smart, P. (2003). Towards a methodology for developing evidence-informed management knowledge by means of systematic review. *British Journal of Management, 14*, 207–222.

Webster, J., & Watson, R. T. (2002). Analyzing the past to prepare for the future: Writing a literature review. *MIS Quarterly, 26*(2), 13–23.

Zupic, I., & Čater, T. (2015). Bibliometric methods in management and organization. *Organizational Research Methods, 18*(3), 429–472.

ANNEXURE

SAMPLE INCLUSION AND EXCLUSION CRITERIA

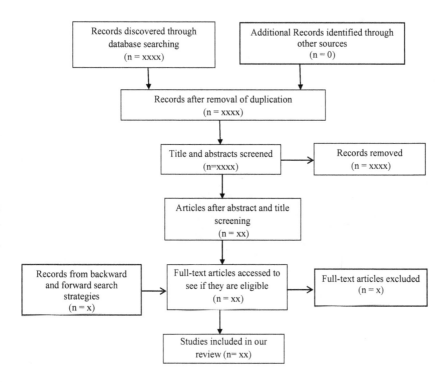

TECHNOLOGY AND THE CONDUCT OF BIBLIOMETRIC LITERATURE REVIEWS IN MANAGEMENT: THE SOFTWARE TOOLS, BENEFITS, AND CHALLENGES

Alex Anlesinya and Samuel Ato Dadzie

ABSTRACT

The use of structured literature review methods like bibliometric analysis is growing in the management fields, but there is limited knowledge on how they can be facilitated by technology. Hence, we conducted a broad overview of software tools, their roles, and limitations in structured (bibliometric) literature reviewing activities. Subsequently, we show that several software tools are freely available to aid in searching the literature, identifying/ extracting relevant publications, screening/assessing quality of the extracted data, and performing analyses to generate insights from the literature. However, their applications may be confronted with several challenges such as limited analytical and functional capabilities, inadequate technological skills of researchers, and the fact that the researcher's insights are still needed to generate compelling conclusions from the results produced by software tools. Consequently, we contribute toward advancing the methodologies for performing structured reviews by providing a comprehensive and updated overview of the knowledge base of key technological software tools and the conduct of structured or bibliometric literature reviews.

Keywords: Software tools; bibliometric analysis; structured literature reviews; review methodology; technology; writing quality literature review

Advancing Methodologies of Conducting Literature Review in Management Domain
Review of Management Literature, Volume 2, 57–78
Copyright © 2024 Alex Anlesinya and Samuel Ato Dadzie
Published under exclusive licence by Emerald Publishing Limited
ISSN: 2754-5865/doi:10.1108/S2754-586520230000002004

1. INTRODUCTION

Literature review constituents a critical part of academic research endeavors. A good literature review is necessary to understand the current state of knowledge in a particular academic field (Kunisch et al., 2018; Linnenluecke et al., 2020; Rana et al., 2022) and to provide a strong foundation to advance knowledge (Paul & Criado, 2020; Rana & Sharma, 2015; Xiao & Watson, 2019). Generally, there are two broad methods of literature review: traditional literature and structured (or systematic) reviews. The traditional method of reviewing the literature involves aggregating multiple findings and perspectives based on the exact relationships a researcher wishes to investigate (Raghuram et al., 2010; Zupic & Čater, 2015). These reviews are carried out mainly to provide conceptual and theoretical backgrounds and justifications for a new (empirical) study (Levy & Ellis, 2006; Raghuram et al., 2010; Templier & Paré, 2015). However, the arbitrariness, inexhaustiveness, subjectivity, and biases of traditional reviews (Denyer & Tranfield, 2009; Gough et al., 2012; Tranfield et al., 2003) affect the quality of such reviews, and can be addressed through the use of the structured or systematic method of literature review.

A systematic literature review is a standard methodology that identifies and locates all the studies relevant to an agreed research question, evaluates them, and then synthesizes their data, reporting on what is found "in such a way that allows reasonably clear conclusions to be reached about what is and is not known" (Denyer & Tranfield, 2009, p. 671). It follows a more transparent and repro-ducible method of producing scientific knowledge (Denyer & Tranfield, 2009; Tranfield et al., 2003). There are various forms of structured reviews such as meta-analysis, narrative evidence synthesis, science mapping, and bibliometric review/analysis – the focus of this chapter.

Bibliometric analysis is the use of quantitative techniques to summarize large amount of bibliometric data (e.g., units of citations, authors, keywords, journals, etc.) to highlight the state of the intellectual structure or knowledge anatomy of, as well as uncover emerging trends on a given research topic or field (Blanco-Mesa et al., 2017; Donthu et al., 2021). It provides an objective and a less time consuming evaluation of the impact of research outputs, researchers, and institutions (Havemann & Larsen, 2015). It is also useful in highlighting the nature and quality of collaborations among researchers. Bibliometric analysis further aids researchers to produce high research impact (Donthu et al., 2021). Thus, good bibliometric studies can assist in the development of strong foun-dations to advance a "field in novel and meaningful ways – it enables and empowers scholars to (1) gain a one-stop overview, (2) identify knowledge gaps, (3) derive novel ideas for investigation, and (4) position their intended contri-butions to the field" (Donthu et al., 2021, p. 285).

That said, conducting structured reviews like bibliometric studies is quite daunting, labor-intensive (Madden et al., 2018) and time-consuming, given that academic publications and knowledge are growing exponentially (Linnenluecke et al., 2020). Hence, to facilitate the process of conducting structured (e.g., bib-liometric analyses), several software tools have been developed to aid researchers (see Garfield, 2009; Persson et al., 2009; van Eck & Waltman, 2014; Xiao & Watson, 2019; Zupic & Čater, 2015) to perform a more systematic and transparent search of the extant academic literature (King et al., 2011; van Eck & Waltman, 2014). Consequently, a few studies have been conducted on the application of software tools in literature reviews (e.g., Cobo et al., 2011; Harrison et al., 2020; Moral-Muñoz et al., 2020; Pan et al., 2018; Sinkovics, 2016).

While the above studies have made some useful contributions to knowledge on the topic, there is still limited understanding of how and which software tools support systematic and transparent literature search. Besides, most of them focused more on the available software tools rather than how they collectively or individually facilitate a range of structured review activities. Besides, prior studies offered limited discussions on the challenges of using technology or software tools to perform structured literature reviews like bibliometric analyses.

In the views of Kitchenham and Charters (2007), the entire process of conducting a structured review consists of three major stages: planning the review, conducting the review (in this case, searching, organizing, and performing the bibliometric analysis), and reporting the review or findings. This chapter focuses on how software tools can facilitate key activities at the second stage of bibliometric literature review – conducting the review. Consequently, the objectives of this chapter are: First, to review key selected software tools that can be used to support the conduct of structured literature reviews – bibliometric studies; second, to examine how software tools facilitate bibliometric literature review activities, and thirdly, to ascertain the main challenges/limitations of using software tools to perform structured (bibliometric) reviews.

The contribution of our research is in threefold: First, we provided a comprehensive and updated overview of key software tools available to facilitate the conduct of structured literature reviews, and how these tools enable key structured review activities. Second, we extended the existing literature by providing insights on the limitations or challenges of applying technology to review the literature systematically and transparently. Third and finally, this chapter has provided a meaningful single-source reference material for researchers and research students in the management and other academic fields who want to learn about how they can leverage software tools to facilitate systematic and transparent review of the extant literature on topics of their choice.

The remainder of the chapter is organized into four sections. The first section examines the benefits of technology in structured and bibliometric literature reviewing processes. The second section discusses software tools to support the conduct of systematic literature reviews. The third section discusses the limitations/challenges of using software to conduct systematic reviews. The final section presents the implications and conclusion.

2. BENEFITS OF TECHNOLOGY – HOW SOFTWARE TOOLS FACILITATE BIBLIOMETRIC REVIEWS

Literature review is an important process of advancing knowledge by establishing where the knowledge frontier is (Xiao & Watson, 2019) through an assessment of relevant prior literature and the identification of potential gaps, weaknesses, and contradictions (Tranfield et al., 2003). This can better be achieved through the conduct of systematic or structured literature reviews. Structured literature reviews are normally performed via an iterative cycle of determining the problem or topic area, defining appropriate search keywords, searching the literature, and conducting analysis and interpretations (Madden et al., 2018; Tranfield et al., 2003).

In the views of Kitchenham and Charters (2007), the entire process of conducting a structured review can be seen as consisting of three major stages. The first stage is planning the review. Planning the literature involves identifying gaps to establish the need for the review, formulating appropriate research questions, and developing a protocol that will be used to conduct the review search. The second stage is conducting the review, which usually involves identifying and selecting publications using the established protocol, extracting, screening and performing quality assessment of the identified and selected publications, as well as analyzing and interpreting the data. The third stage, which is reporting the review, includes writing the report to facilitate the dissemination of the results or findings from the literature review.

As noted earlier, this chapter focuses on how software tools can support or facilitate key activities at the second stage of structured literature review (or bibliometric analysis in this case) – that is, conducting the review.

2.1 Literature Search and Identification

Searching for and identifying relevant publications on a topic of interest is a challenging and time-consuming venture. This task becomes even more challenging when the aim is to conduct an exhaustive structured search of the literature on a particular knowledge domain (Linnenluecke et al., 2020; van Eck & Waltman, 2014). To accomplish this, researchers usually deploy several manual ways of identifying additional studies from a large body of publications to ensure that no significant or relevant research is overlooked. For example, researchers may go through the reference section of included research publications or conduct a focused search in key journals with the aim of identifying relevant articles (see Anlesinya et al., 2019). They will also perform cited research search by examining publications that have cited the identified or included papers and papers citing them. While bibliographic databases like Web of Science (WoS) and Scopus can be deployed to carry out these search activities to ensure all relevant articles or publications are identified, they offer only limited functionalities to support systematic or structured literature searches (van Eck & Waltman, 2014).

Hence, the task of searching the extant literature in a structured manner to identify relevant publications on a particular research area or topic can be significantly facilitated by technology to save time and conduct exhaustive and reproducible search of the extant literature. In particular, structured literature review researchers can leverage software tools (e.g., CitNetExplorer, HistCite, etc.) to conduct cited reference search or reverse literature search based on citation relations to identify and select all relevant publications using forward and backward searches.

They can also help in properly defining and demarcating research areas and in doing so make it possible to easily search extant literature on one's topic to identify more publications for inclusion and exclusion. Besides, software tools (e.g., Cit-NetExplorer) are useful in a literature search that is targeted at identifying influential articles within a particular body of knowledge (see van Eck & Waltman, 2014).

2.2 Data Extraction

Another area of stage two of structured review (i.e., conducting the review) that software tools can be of immense help is data extraction as they offer researchers the potential to manage the large amount of reference data generated from the literature search (Hammick et al., 2010; King et al., 2011). Researchers usually create appropriate tables to extract relevant information from the research results to be used for analyses on their chosen topic. Again, this is a daunting task that can be greatly assisted with relevant technological applications. With the aid of software tools (e.g., BibExcel, VantagePoint, R-Bibliometrix; SciMAT, etc.) with bibliometric and exporting capabilities, researchers can extract relevant publications information or data from key databases (e.g., Scopus, WoS, etc.), import and store them, and retrieve them for further screening and analyses.

2.3 Data Screening and Quality Assessment

Every structured review of research is expected to be carried out in a manner that meets the highest standard. It must follow rigorous methods and, as much as possible, eliminate errors and biases (Cobo et al., 2011; Denyer & Tranfield, 2009; Tranfield et al., 2003). As a result, structured or bibliometric review researchers are required to carefully screen the extant articles identified to ensure that only those that meet the inclusion criteria are retained for analyses (Harrison et al., 2020). Technological software tools can be leveraged to screen and assure quality in the conduct of systematic reviews.

For instance, some software tools (e.g., Bibexcel, HistCite) are useful in detecting misspelled elements such names of the authors, and incomplete or wrong addresses of the authors. They also support quality assessment by detecting and removing duplicates and irrelevant publications. Furthermore, some software tools (e.g., Bibexcel, HistCite, Sci^2 Tool; SciMAT; VantagePoint, etc.) have preprocessing functional capabilities which allow researchers to facilitate the quality assessment of the extracted data by performing preprocessing activities and data cleaning of results of literature research to ensure they are devoid of mistakes or omissions that can undermine the findings.

This is consistent with Linnenluecke et al.'s (2020) assertion that software tools (e.g., HistCite) can be used to conduct triangulation of search results from multiple databases with the aim of ensuring that no relevant publication is missing or overlooked, duplicates are removed as well as automatically conducting cited reference check to achieve exhaustiveness in the searching process. This is because omissions of key publications in given literature can bias the results. Similarly, it is in line with Cobo et al.'s (2011) findings that Bibexcel allows "different preprocessing over the textual data to be performed, for example, an English word stemmer can be applied and duplicate documents can be deleted. Moreover, Bibexcel enables the deletion of low frequency items and keeps only the strongest links" (p. 1387).

2.4 Data Analysis and Interpretations

Data analysis and interpretation is one of the important tasks in conducting structured reviews (Denyer & Tranfield, 2009; Kitchenham & Charters, 2007; Tranfield et al., 2003). Data analysis or synthesis in a structured review is a process of putting the findings from individual studies together "into a new or different arrangement and developing knowledge that is not apparent from reading the individual studies in isolation" (Denyer & Tranfield, 2009, p. 685). Researchers can use software tools to perform a range of analyses such as descriptive, bibliometric, and science mapping calculations/analysis (e.g., co-citation analysis, co-author analysis, collaboration analysis, or co-occurrence analysis), thematic analysis, cartography, cluster analysis, and visualizing the extant literature to detect major trends and overarching themes.

For instance, VantagePoint which is a powerful text-mining software tool can be deployed to discover knowledge, patterns, and relationships from the results of a literature search (Cobo et al., 2011). Similarly, some software tools (e.g., VOSviewer, HistCite) can present a visualization map of a large set of publications on a specific topic to highlight impactful or most-cited articles studies, identify growth patterns, detect major trends and overarching themes to inform future research agenda (see Linnenluecke & Griffiths, 2013; Sinkovics, 2016; Van Eck & Waltman, 2010; Zupic & Čater, 2015). Since software tools are useful in highlighting growth patterns and discovering knowledge from search results, they make it easy for researchers to generate insights to facilitate the development and advancement of a knowledge domain beyond the current knowledge frontier.

The foregoing discussions regarding how software tools can facilitate the conduct of structured or bibliometric literature review are summarized and presented in Table 1.

3. SOFTWARE TOOLS TO SUPPORT THE CONDUCT OF BIBLIOMETRIC ANALYSIS

This section of the chapter reviews several software tools that can aid organization and management researchers to effectively perform bibliometric analysis and other related structured reviews. The details are as follows.

3.1 VOSviewer

VOSviewer was developed by the Leiden University of The Netherlands (Cobo et al., 2011; Li et al., 2021; Van Eck & Waltman, 2010), and is one of the most commonly used software tools for conducting different forms of literature review research (Li et al., 2021; Pan et al., 2018; Shah et al., 2020). It is freely accessible

Table 1. How Software Tools Facilitate Systematic Review Activities.

Conducting the Review's Activities	Potential Support of Software Tools	Possible Software Tools
Literature search and identification	Conducting cited reference search; defining and demarcating research areas; identifying and selecting all relevant publications using forward and backward searches based on citation relations	HistCite CitNetExplorer, etc.
Data extraction	Importing, storing, and retrieving publication or bibliographic data from key databases (e.g., Scopus, WoS)	R SciMAT, etc.
Screening and quality assessment	Preprocessing and data cleaning of results of literature researches (e.g., detecting and deleting duplicate documents; misspelled elements such names of the authors, incomplete or wrong addresses of the authors, etc., as well as performing cited reference check to identify missing articles)	Bibexcel, R HistCite SciMAT; VantagePoint
Analysis and interpretations	Highlighting the most-cited articles; detecting citation burst and identifying growth patterns; visualizing extant literature to detect major trends and overarching themes; detecting and analyzing emerging trends in a knowledge domain and how a particular scientific literature has evolved; conducting thematic analysis, cartography, and cluster analysis; discovering knowledge from search results – theory development	VOSviewer HistCite Sci² Tool VantagePoint CiteSpace II

Source: Constructed from the extant literature.

(Cobo et al., 2011; Li et al., 2021; Van Eck & Waltman, 2010), relatively easy to learn and apply software (Li et al., 2021), with the capacity to access or work with data from multiple databases such as Web of Science (WoS), Scopus, Dimensions, and PubMed (Moral-Muñoz et al., 2020).

It also offers researchers the ability to analyze a broad range of bibliometric networks composing of publications, authors, journals, authors, organizations, or countries (Van Eck & Waltman, 2010), conduct thematic analysis, cartography, and cluster analysis (Llanos-Herrera & Merigo, 2019).

Besides, VOSviewer has high quality visualization capability, permitting detailed examination of bibliometric maps and other visual representations through its zooming, scrolling, special labeling algorithms, and density metaphors functionalities. As a result, it offers users useful avenues to display and explore large bibliometric maps in ways that are easy to interpret and understand (Van Eck & Waltman, 2010).

However, VOSviewer does not offer users the opportunity to extract and build any co-occurrence matrix from bibliometric data (van Eck et al., 2010). Co-occurrence analysis is focused on "analyzing counts of co-occurring entities within a collection of unit. Typical data in co-occurrence analysis is the co-occurrence matrix, where the items form row and column headings and the intersection of the row and column represent the co-occurrence" (Zhou et al., 2022, p. 1). It is employed to examine whether there is any kind of relationship between two bibliographic items that are found or appeared in the same research article or publication (Zhou et al., 2022). This means that it is not possible to directly establish the existence of any correlation between bibliometric items in a given research publication using the VOSviewer software.

However, users who want to carry out co-occurrence analysis can leverage external processes with the aid of its VOS mapping technique (van Eck et al., 2010) which is used for building a map of similarity between bibliometric items (van Eck & Waltman, 2009). Furthermore, VOSviewer has no preprocessing capability (van Eck et al., 2010). The lack of preprocessing capability means that it does not allow researchers to perform proper data cleaning, such as checking for duplicates and misspelled elements like author names, journal titles, among others.

3.2 HistCite

HistCite is another software tool that is extensively used by researchers (Fetscherin & Heinrich, 2015; Shah et al., 2020). This software tool was developed by Eugene Garfield in 2001. It was however officially launched in 2007 (Herther, 2007). It was not freely accessible in the past because users were required to pay in order to access and use it but it is now free (Pan et al., 2018). HistCite is "a software system which generates chronological maps of bibliographic collections resulting from subject, author, institutional or source journal searches of the ISI Web of Science" (Garfield, 2009, p. 173). It is considered a robust software tool that allows users to analyze systematic literature reviews (Zupic & Čater, 2015).

Besides, it allows researchers to conduct cited reference or literature search by identifying all references that cited a particular research publication. The cited references are usually relevant to a given research topic but are missed by the researcher during the data collection (Linnenluecke et al., 2020). In addition, the HistCite software tool allows users to assess the development of thought on a particular topic (Börner et al., 2003; Janssen et al., 2006), and offers functionality that can be deployed to clean the data by way of removing duplicates (Linnenluecke et al., 2020).

However, HistCite can only source and import articles from WoS database (Linnenluecke et al., 2020; Shah et al., 2020). This suggests that articles not indexed or available in the WoS database cannot be accessed and included in systematic literature review on a topic even though they may be relevant.

3.3 BibExcel

The BibExcel is one of the software tools frequently used by management and organization researchers in performing bibliometric analysis (Zupic & Čater, 2015). This software was developed by Olle Persson (Persson et al., 2009). Subscription or payment is not required for a researcher to access and use this software. It has a high degree of flexibility in use due to its ability to work with data available in or imported from different databases such as the WoS and Scopus (Cobo et al., 2011; Persson et al., 2009).

BibExcel is easy to learn and apply to review the literature. It aids in performing a range of bibliometric analyses including co-word analysis (Cobo et al., 2011; Zupic & Čater, 2015), building maps, which can be read by other software tools like Microsoft Excel and SPSS (Borgatti et al., 2002), and its "exporting options include co-occurrence matrices for later use in statistical software and network formats that can be used in network analysis packages" (Zupic & Čater, 2015, p. 16). It can provide detailed data that may be analyzed using a range of network analysis tools like Gephi, VOSviewer, and Pajek (Persson et al., 2009). Different co-occurrence analyses can also be performed (Cobo et al., 2011).

Bibexcel has preprocessing functionality, meaning that it can aid researchers in cleaning data extracted (e.g., deletion of duplicates, low frequency items) prior to the main data analysis. For instance, duplicate documents can be deleted through the use of its English word stemmer (Cobo et al., 2011). However, it lacks advanced preprocessing capabilities for proper data cleaning. Besides, its user interface is not very friendly (Zupic & Čater, 2015) and has weak visualization capability or tool for representing outputs (Cobo et al., 2011). That being said, it "presents different export options that make data visualization possible using external software like Pajek, UCINET or SPSS. The bibliometric networks can also be exported" (Cobo et al., 2011, p. 1387).

3.4 Sitkis

Sitkis is a useful software tool that is employed to conduct bibliometric analysis. This software was developed by Henri A. Schildt at the Helsinki University of Technology to support reviews and bibliometric analyses (Schildt, 2005). It is easy to apply and can be utilized to carry out basic data preprocessing activities and its data can be exported to other software tools like Excel and UCINET network analysis software (Schildt & Mattsson, 2006). It can import data from WoS and Scopus (Gomez-Jauregui et al., 2014). Sitkis is capable of implementing a dense network subgrouping algorithm, which is a clustering procedure often used in bibliometric analysis. However, it is no longer being updated and it relies on legacy technology (Access) for database storage. Hence, only users with prior experience may be in position to apply it appropriately (Schildt & Mattsson, 2006).

3.5 SciMAT

SciMAT software tool was developed by researchers at the University of Granada to facilitate the conduct of research, principally, science mapping and bibliometric analyses (Cobo et al., 2012). This software has a user-friendly interface, advanced or superior preprocessing data capabilities (Zupic & Čater, 2015). It can be applied to perform bibliometric analyses, including visualizing and interpreting outputs as well as basic descriptive analyses like maximum, minimum, and average citations (Moral-Muñoz et al., 2020). Besides, no subscription or payment is required to access and use this software. Again, it can work with data from multiple databases and formats such as the WoS, Scopus, GS, Bitext, and data exported from EndNote. SciMAT also has the capacity to process or analyze data or information extracted from social media platforms such as Facebook, and other academic data in CSV format (Moral-Muñoz et al., 2020).

The main limitation or weakness of this software tool is that its interface does not allow data matrices to be exported for analyses in other statistical software. Users who want to carry out additional or further analyses with the aid of other statistical software tools can only do so by exporting the data using (undocumented) scripts. Alternatively, they may decide to limit their analyses to those permissible in SciMAT (Zupic & Čater, 2015).

3.6 CiteSpace

CiteSpace stands for Citation Space. It was developed by Chaomei Chen from the Drexel University in the United States of America (Moral-Muñoz et al., 2020) in 2003 and released in 2004 (Chen, 2006, 2019). It can be deployed to facilitate the visualization and identification of emerging trends and growth patterns on a particular research topic or knowledge domain. A range of bibliometric analyses (e.g., co-citation, co-author analysis, international collaboration, spectral clustering, citation burst detection, etc.) can be conducted using this software (Chen, 2006, 2019; Cobo et al., 2011; Moral-Muñoz et al., 2020) because it has comprehensive bibliometric capabilities (Chen, 2006; Cobo et al., 2011).

CiteSpace software works with data from multiple databases including the WoS, Scopus, PubMed, and others (Cobo et al., 2011; Moral-Muñoz et al., 2020). It can be used to trace how a particular field or topic has evolved because it offers options to build networks, or graphs for different time periods to detect and highlights its development over a given period. It has extensive visualization capabilities with options for visualization, namely, cluster view, time line, and time zone (Chen, 2006). The main challenge with the use of CiteSpace is that it has a steep learning curve. In other words, it is difficult to learn and apply (Cobo et al., 2011).

3.7 VantagePoint

VantagePoint which was developed by Search Technology Inc. in the United States (Cobo et al., 2011) is considered a powerful text-mining software tool that can be deployed to discover knowledge from the results of searches in patent and literature databases. It is useful in analyzing extant structured text to discover patterns and relationships. It can also be applied to perform a range of bibliometric calculations (Cobo et al., 2011). With 180 import filters, this software is able to facilitate the importation of data from a range of databases and can work with other software applications like Microsoft Excel, CSV, and Access by way of importing data from them (Cobo et al., 2011). As a result, it allows users to use different software tools to analyze the data to achieve their intended purpose.

Furthermore, its Thesaurus Editor (both predefined and user defined thesauruses) and Cleanup functionalities make it one of the powerful software tools for undertaking data preprocessing and cleaning activities during the conduct of literature reviews. However, this software tool is not freely accessible because it is commercial in nature. Users will have to pay to access and use it (Cobo et al., 2011).

3.8 Science of Science (Sci²) Tool

The Sci² Tool was developed by Cyberinfrastructure for Network Science Center and the Department of Information and Library Science in the School of Informatics and Computing of the Indiana University at Indiana University (USA). It is intended to aid in the study of science and so has the capacity to facilitate the conduct of several science mapping and bibliometric analyses ranging from network analysis, geospatial to visualization at different levels of analysis (Sci² Team, 2009). It is utilized to carry out temporal analysis by slicing the data into different time periods via citation burst detection. It is freely accessible, has a better capability for performing preliminary analysis, including data cleaning and with the ability to read or access data of research results in multiple databases such as WoS, Scopus, Bibtex, among others (Light et al., 2014).

While this software has a de-duplicating functionality (which means that it has the capacity to compare records in different electronic databases), it requires the support of external software tools (Cobo et al., 2011). It is easy to read and interpret because it has well-defined reference systems and legends (Light et al., 2014). Several tutorials are also available on the website of this software for users to learn and apply it to conduct literature reviews.

3.9 CitNetExplorer

The CitNetExplorer is one of the new software tools developed to aid the conduct of literature reviews. It "can for instance be used to study the development of a research field, to delineate the literature on a research topic, and to support literature reviewing" (van Eck & Waltman, 2014, p. 1). Besides, this software tool allows users to identify publications based on citation relations as well as to easily select all publications that cite, or are cited by a given set of publications (van Eck & Waltman, 2014). It has the capacity to analyze extant publications and citations, and can also be employed to carry out a range of bibliometric calculations, including citation networks of patents (van Eck & Waltman, 2014). It makes it possible for users to navigate through a large citation network and drill down to a small sub-network. CitNetExplorer "borrows various ideas from our VOSviewer tool. This applies in particular to certain features related to visualization (e.g., smart labeling) and user interaction (e.g., zooming and panning)" (van Eck & Waltman, 2014, p. 2).

3.10 R Software

R is a highly capable statistical software tool that provides users with a flexible and extensible free environment to perform research and analysis. It was developed by Robert Gentleman and Ross Ihaka of the Statistics Department of the

University of Auckland, and is currently being supported by the R Core Team and the R Foundation for Statistical Computing (R Core Team, 2019). It is freely accessible, and other scholars can extend its functionality through the development of new codes and packages. It has extensive statistical and visualization capabilities (Linnenluecke et al., 2020). R's packages such as the Bibliometrix (Aria & Cuccurullo, 2017), Revtools (Westgate, 2018), Litsearchr (Grames et al., 2019), Adjutant (Crisan et al., 2019), and Metagear (Lajeunesse, 2016) provide various avenues for researchers to leverage this software tool to support systematic reviewing of the literature on a given topic. However, Bibliometrix has been used in most studies relative to the other packages (Addor & Melsen, 2019; Lajeunesse, 2016).

The R software tool supports a range of descriptive and bibliometric calculations/analysis (e.g., co-citation analysis, co-author analysis, collaboration analysis, or co-occurrence analysis). The Bibliometrix package of R makes it possible to import search results from Scopus and WoS (Linnenluecke et al., 2020). However, R software has a steep learning curve; that is to say, it is difficult to learn and may require basic programming capabilities of users.

The above reviewed software tools which can support the conduct of bibliometric and other related structured literature reviews are summarized in Table 2.

4. CHALLENGES/LIMITATIONS OF USING SOFTWARE TOOLS TO PERFORM BIBLIOMETRIC REVIEWS

Despite the potential contributions of software tools to the conduct of structured literature reviews (e.g., bibliometric reviews), they are not without limitations. These challenges are discussed next.

4.1 Limitations on Access to Publication Databases

One of the challenges of using some software tools is that they have limited access to publication databases as they can only work with certain databases. As discussed earlier and shown in Table 2, although very powerful, HistCite only works with publications in WoS because it was not designed nor has functionalities that allow users to access and work with publications that are in other databases other than WoS. While a range of software tools can accommodate publications in WoS and Scopus, there are usually quality or relevant studies in other databases (e.g., Google Scholar, etc.) which may be overlooked in systematic reviews, thereby biasing the results of a review. This is similar to Shah et al.'s (2020) views that a bias might exist for high-quality publications because it is possible for non-WoS journal articles that can impact the findings of a review to be excluded from their analyses which were based on only WoS journal publications.

4.2 Limited Analytical and Functional Capabilities

Some of the software tools have limited analytical and functional capabilities and so may not provide the full support researchers may need in conducting

Table 2. Software Tools That can Support the Conduct of Bibliometric Literature Reviews.

Software Tools	Developers/Contributors	Data Source	User Interface	Website	Strengths/Benefits	Limitations/Weaknesses
VOSviewer	Van Eck and Waltman (2010) Leiden University, The Netherlands	WoS Scopus	Desktop	https://www.vosviewer.com/	Subscription or payment is not required to access and use it Useful in thematic analysis and cluster analysis Can access articles in multiple databases Displays large bibliometric maps in a manner that is easy to to-interpret or understand	No preprocessing capability – cannot help in data cleaning such as checking for duplicates and misspelled elements like Not possible to directly establish relationship between bibliometric items in the same research (e.g., co-occurrence analysis from bibliometric data)
HistCite	Garfield (2001); Herther (2007)	WoS		http://www.histcite.com/	Identifying influential articles Freely accessible For conducting reverse/cited literature search	Can only source articles from WoS database Useful for only quantitative analyses
BibExcel	Persson et al. (2009) University of Umeå (Sweden)	WoS Scopus	Desktop	https://homepage.univie.ac.at/juan.gorraiz/bibexcel/	Very easy to learn and apply to perform literature reviews Can access articles in multiple databases - can be applied to retrieve articles from both WoS and Scopus Subscription/payment is not required to use it Useful for producing quick and basic bibliometric calculations/analysis Has significant exporting functionality and also collaborates with different statistical software (e.g., SPSS, Excel) Modest preprocessing capability	Limited capability for advanced analysis in literature Not very effective in cleaning data for analysis Relatively weak data visualization capacity

Table 2. (*Continued*)

Software Tools	Developers/ Contributors	Data Source	User Interface	Website	Strengths/Benefits	Limitations/Weaknesses
Sitkis	Schildt (2005) Helsinki University of Technology	WoS, Scopus	Desktop	https://sites.google.com/site/sitkisbibliometricanalysis/home	Easy to use Collaborates with other software tools (e.g., Excel) Subscription is not required Can be used to carry out basic preliminary data analyses, basic bibliometric calculations/analysis (e.g., co-citation and co-author analysis)	It relies on only legacy technology (Access) Basic data preprocessing capability Requires prior Sitkis experience
SciMAT	University of Granada	WoS, Scopus	Desktop	https://sci2s.ugr.es/scimat/	Has friendly user interface Subscription or payment is not required to access and use it Can access articles in multiple databases including data/information from social media platforms like Facebook Has better capability for performing preliminary analysis including data cleaning (e.g., preprocessing)	Difficult to export data matrices for analyses in other statistical software
CiteSpace II	Chen (2006) Drexel University (USA)	WoS, Scopus	Desktop	http://cluster.cis.drexel.edu/~cchen/citespace/	Can access articles in multiple databases Comprehensive bibliometric capabilities Identifying emerging trends in a particular knowledge domain	Difficulty to learn and apply
VantagePoint	Search Technology, Inc.	WoS, Scopus	Desktop	https://www.thevantagepoint.com/	Powerful text-mining software tool with capacity to discover knowledge from search results Significant data importation of search results	Commercial software – payment is required to access and apply

Tool	Developer	Database	Platform	URL	Capabilities	Limitations
Science of Science (Sci²) Tool	Indiana University (USA)	WoS Scopus	Desktop	https://sci2.cns.iu.edu/user/index.php	Can access articles in multiple databases and collaborate with other software (e.g., Excel, CSV) Has data preprocessing and cleaning capabilities Has better capability for performing preprocessing analysis and data cleaning Can be used to carry out basic preliminary data analyses, basic bibliometric analysis (e.g., co-citation, co-author analysis, etc.) Subscription is not required	
CitNetExplorer	van Eck and Waltman (2014); Leiden University, The Netherlands	WoS Scopus	Desktop	http://www.citnetexplorer.nl/	Subscription is not required Can access articles in multiple databases Supports literature reviewing by delineating research areas Identifying publications based on citation relations User friendly	
R	Robert Gentleman and Ross Ihaka Statistics Department of the University of Auckland	WoS Scopus	Desktop	https://www.r-project.org/contributors.html	Subscription is not required Can be used to carry a range of descriptive and bibliometric calculations/analysis (e.g., co-citation and co-author analysis) High statistical and visualization capabilities	Steep learning curve; difficulty to learn Basic programming skills or experience of users may be needed

Source: constructed from the extant literature.

systematic reviews. Some have no preprocessing and data cleaning capabilities, while others have limited visualization and importation functionalities, among others. This means that a user may have to complement different software tools or require the support of external applications or software tools to be able to realize the full potential of technological software use in literature reviews.

For instance, and as presented earlier, the SciMAT software tool does not allow data matrices to be exported for analyses in other statistical software. It is not possible to directly establish the existence of any correlation between bibliometric items in a given research publication using the VOSviewer software because it lacks the capacity to generate co-occurrence matrix from bibliometric data. Besides, VOSviewer software has no preprocessing capability while Bibexcel lacks advanced preprocessing capabilities for proper data cleaning, and the Sci^2 Tool requires the support of external software tools. This is consistent with Cobo et al.'s (2011) assertion that not all software tools have the functionalities to extract all bibliometric data and may require external processes or software tools.

4.3 Lack of Required Technological Skills of Researchers

Most software tools for conducting bibliometric literature reviews require basic information technological skills, and programming knowledge. So individual researchers without the required technological skills may find it difficult to learn these software tools and leverage them to conduct high quality structured reviews properly. Unfortunately, Zupic and Čater (2015) argued that while some doctoral programs are training doctoral students to use software tools to carry out literature reviews, the level of diffusion is still very low.

Besides, some of the software tools (e.g., CiteSpace and R) have a steep learning curve. This implies that they are not easy to learn and apply. This can impact their adoption and proper use to carry out quality literature reviews. Moreover, Zupic and Čater (2015) noted that Sitkis is not being actively updated, and it relies on legacy technology (Access) for database storage and so their utilization in the conduct of systematic reviews requires prior Sitkis experience.

4.4 Researcher's Insights Are Still Needed

While software tools play vital roles in supporting the various activities involved in performing systematic and transparent review of the extant literature, researchers still have to interpret and generate conclusions that are grounded in the results of the review. This is seen as an important but challenging aspect of literature reviews (Cobo et al., 2011; Zupic & Čater, 2015). Researchers with "in-depth knowledge of the field have a distinct advantage here. However, they need to be careful not to try to fit the analysis to their existing preconceptions, but the opposite: to use their knowledge to enhance the findings" (Zupic & Čater, 2015, p. 21). Thus, researchers must still read wide and use their experience and subject knowledge to generate compelling insights from the analyses of the literature, which may be aided to a great extent by software tools.

5. IMPLICATIONS AND CONCLUSION

Literature review, whether based on the traditional literature review method or structured review method (e.g., bibliometric analysis), are crucial in understanding the current state of knowledge in a particular academic field and to provide a strong foundation to advance knowledge. However, the arbitrariness, inexhaustiveness, subjectivity, and biases of the traditional review method affect the quality of such reviews, and can be addressed through the structured method of literature reviews, but structured literature reviews are quite daunting and time-consuming given that academic publications and knowledge are growing at an exponential rate. Hence, to facilitate the processes of conducting structured reviews like bibliometric studies, several software tools have been developed to aid researchers to perform a more systematic and transparent search of the extant academic literature within a specific knowledge domain.

Though a few studies have been conducted on the use of software tools in literature reviews (see Cobo et al., 2011; Harrison et al., 2020; Moral-Muñoz et al., 2020; Pan et al., 2018), and have made some useful contributions to knowledge on the topic, there is still the need for further exposition on the topic. Accordingly, we reviewed key selected software tools to support the conduct of structured literature reviews in the management and organization fields, noting their specific benefits and challenges or limitations.

We show that several software tools (e.g., HistCite, VOSviewer, CitNetExplorer, BibExcel, R, Sitkis, SciMAT, CiteSpace, Sci^2 Tool etc.) are freely available in addition to a few commercial ones (e.g., VantagePoint) that management and organization researchers can leverage to facilitate the conduct of structured literature reviews like bibliometric analysis. In particular, these software tools can aid structured review researchers in searching the literature and identify relevant articles or publications on a topic; extracting relevant publications information or data from key databases; carefully screening the extant articles and facilitating the quality assessment of the extracted data by performing preprocessing activities and data cleaning of results of literature research to ensure they are devoid of mistakes or omissions that can potentially bias the results; as well as performing a range of bibliometric and science mapping analyses (e.g., co-citation analysis, co-author analysis, collaboration analysis or co-occurrence analysis, etc.), thematic analysis, cartography, cluster analysis and visualizing the extant literature to detect major trends and overarching themes, among others.

However, the choice and application of some of these software tools in performing transparent and systematic literature search may be limited by challenges such as their limited access to publication databases, inadequate analytical and functional capabilities, lack of required technological skills of researchers concerned, and the fact that the researcher's insights are still needed to generate compelling conclusions from the results of the analyses produced by the software tools.

5.1 Practical Implications

Our chapter offers some useful implications for research practice. First, scholars should explore the development of new software tools or design of packages for existing software tools that will allow researchers to not only access relevant publications on a topic of interest from the well-established databases (e.g., WoS and Scopus) but also from databases and quality journal outlets outside these major bibliometric sources. This will ensure that biases in the literature review findings due to the overlooking of publications and journals outside the major databases (WoS and Scopus) are minimized to a great extent.

Second, training of researchers, particularly research students, in the use of software tools to conduct literature reviews is not encouraging, especially in most developing countries, and should be stepped up. Consequently, we reechoed Zupic and Čater's (2015) call for higher educational institutions to offer opportunities for research students, particularly doctoral students to be trained in the use of software tools to successfully carry out quality systematic literature reviews. This is because one's specific skill set plays an important role in the choice of software tools for conducting systematic reviews (Harrison et al., 2020) and the efficiency and confidence with which they are used to facilitate quality reviews.

Third, there is the need for researchers to carefully analyze and interpret results generated by software tools in order to generate insights that will advance the frontier of the existing knowledge on a given topic or academic literature. Fourth and finally, we urge researchers to deploy multiple collaborative and complementary software tools to conduct quality structured (or bibliometric) reviews if the intention is to apply technological software to support the review activities. This is similar to Cobo et al.'s (2011) assertion that researchers should leverage synergies that exist between cooperative software tools to perform a complete science mapping analysis.

5.2 Limitations and Future Research Implications

The following are potential limitations of this research with implications for further studies. First, the articles and publications used to develop our research were not identified through a systematic review method and so can limit the findings. Hence, future studies may use a systematic review method to examine technology's role in conducting structured reviews. Second, our discussions on software tools supportive of the conduct of literature reviews is not exhaustive because others (e.g., CoPalRed, NVivo, Network Workbench (NWB) Tool IN-SPIRE, Leydesdorff's Software, ResGap, etc.) were not covered in this review and could be considered in future studies. That being said, the 10 software tools discussed in this chapter are most commonly used techniques within the management and organization fields. Besides, researchers should explore the role of qualitative software tools like NVivo and ATLAS.ti because Xiao and Watson (2019) argued that they could play useful roles in coding qualitative and quantitative studies through nodes or by topical area and subsequently extracting relevant quotes from the included papers for analysis and synthesis.

Third and finally, our chapter has not covered the dos and don'ts of technology use in the conduct of structured reviews or bibliometric analyses. Given that this aspect has been less discussed in the literature, future studies are strongly recommended to explore dos and don'ts during the process using technology tools to perform structured literature reviews.

5.3 Conclusion

In conclusion, our chapter shows that structured review of the literature is a difficult task which can be made easier if researchers are adequately trained to leverage several freely available software tools to carry out the core activities at the conducting the review stage of a typical structured review (e.g., bibliometric analysis) process. Since the use of structured literature review methods like bibliometric analysis is growing across various academic fields, but there is limited knowledge on how each of the structured review activities can be facilitated by technology, our chapter contributes toward advancing the methodologies for performing structured reviews by providing a comprehensive and an updated overview of key software tools and how they can aid the conduct of structured literature reviews such as bibliometric studies. Second, it provides a meaningful single-source reference material for researchers and research students in the management fields and other academic disciplines who want to learn about how they can leverage software tools to facilitate the conduct of state-of-the-art systematic and transparent review of the extant literature on their topic of choice. Finally, we extend the existing literature by providing insights on the limitations or challenges of applying technology to systematically and transparently review the literature.

REFERENCES

Addor, N., & Melsen, L. A. (2019). Legacy, rather than adequacy, drives the selection of hydrological models. *Water Resources Research*, *55*(1), 378–390. https://doi.org/10.1029/2018WR022958

Anlesinya, A., Dartey-Baah, K., & Amponsah-Tawiah, K. (2019). Strategic talent management scholarship: A review of current foci and future directions. *Industrial and Commercial Training*, *51*(5), 299–314. https://doi.org/10.1108/ICT-11-2018-0095

Aria, M., & Cuccurullo, C. (2017). Bibliometrix: An R-tool for comprehensive science mapping analysis. *Journal of Informetrics*, *11*(4), 959–975. https://doi.org/10.1016/j.joi.2017.08.007

Blanco-Mesa, F., Merigó, J. M., & Gil-Lafuente, A. M. (2017). Fuzzy decision making: A bibliometric-based review. *Journal of Intelligent & Fuzzy Systems*, *32*(3), 2033–2050. https://doi.org/10.3233/JIFS-161640

Borgatti, S. P., Everett, M. G., & Freeman, L. C. (2002). *UCINET for windows: Software for social network analysis*. Analytic Technologies.

Börner, K., Chen, C., & Boyack, K. W. (2003). Visualizing knowledge domains. *Annual Review of Information Science and Technology*, *37*(1), 179–255. https://doi.org/10.1002/aris.1440370106

Chen, C. (2006). CiteSpace II: Detecting and visualizing emerging trends and transient patterns in scientific literature. *Journal of the American Society for Information Science and Technology*, *57*, 359–377. https://doi.org/10.1002/asi.20317

Chen, C. (2019). *How to use CiteSpace*. Leanpub.

Cobo, M. J., López-Herrera, A. G., Herrera-Viedma, E., & Herrera, F. (2011). Science mapping software tools: Review, analysis, and cooperative study among tools. *Journal of the American Society for Information Science and Technology*, *62*(7), 1382–1402. https://doi.org/10.1002/asi.21525

Cobo, M. J., López-Herrera, A. G., Herrera-Viedma, E., & Herrera, F. (2012). SciMAT: A new science mapping analysis software tool. *Journal of the American Society for Information Science and Technology, 63*(8), 1609–1630.

Crisan, A., Munzner, T., & Gardy, J. L. (2019). Adjutant: An R-based tool to support topic discovery for systematic and literature reviews. *Bioinformatics, 35*(6), 1070–1072. https://doi.org/10.1093/bioinformatics/bty722

Denyer, D., & Tranfield, D. (2009). Producing a systematic review. In D. A. Buchanan & A. Bryman (Eds.), *The Sage handbook of organizational research methods* (pp. 671–689). Sage Publications Ltd.

Donthu, N., Kumar, S., Mukherjee, D., Pandey, N., & Lim, W. M. (2021). How to conduct a bibliometric analysis: An overview and guidelines. *Journal of Business Research, 133,* 285–296. https://doi.org/10.1016/j.jbusres.2021.04.070

Fetscherin, M., & Heinrich, D. (2015). Consumer brand relationships research: A bibliometric citation meta-analysis. *Journal of Business Research, 68*(2), 380–390. https://doi.org/10.1016/j.jbusres.2014.06.010

Garfield, E. (2001). From computational linguistics to algorithmic historiography. Paper presented at *The Symposium in Honor of Casimir Borkowski at the University of Pittsburgh School of Information Sciences*, Pittsburgh, PA 15260.

Garfield, E. (2009). From the science of science to Scientometrics visualizing the history of science with HistCite software. *Journal of Informetrics, 3*(3), 173–179. https://doi.org/10.1016/j.joi.2009.03.009

Gomez-Jauregui, V., Gomez-Jauregui, C., Manchado, C., & Otero, C. (2014). Information management and improvement of citation indices. *International Journal of Information Management, 34*(2), 257–271. https://doi.org/10.1016/j.ijinfomgt.2014.01.002

Gough, D., Thomas, J., & Oliver, S. (2012). Clarifying differences between review designs and methods. *Systematic Reviews, 1*(1), 1–9. http://www.systematicreviewsjournal.com/content/1/1/28

Grames, E. M., Stillman, A. N., Tingley, M. W., & Elphick, C. S. (2019). An automated approach to identifying search terms for systematic reviews using keyword co-occurrence networks. *Methods in Ecology and Evolution, 10*(10), 1645–1654. https://doi.org/10.1111/2041-210X.13268

Hammick, M., Dornan, T., & Steinert, Y. (2010). Conducting a best evidence systematic review. Part 1: From idea to data coding. BEME Guide No. 13. *Medical Teacher, 32*(1), 3–15. https://doi.org/10.3109/01421590903414245

Harrison, H., Griffin, S. J., Kuhn, I., & Usher-Smith, J. A. (2020). Software tools to support title and abstract screening for systematic reviews in healthcare: An evaluation. *BMC Medical Research Methodology, 20*(1), 1–12. https://doi.org/10.1186/s12874-020-0897-3

Havemann, F., & Larsen, B. (2015). Bibliometric indicators of young authors in astrophysics: Can later stars be predicted? *Scientometrics, 102*(2), 1413–1434. https://doi.org/10.1007/s11192-014-1476-3

Herther, N. K. (2007). Thomson scientific and the citation indexes. *Searcher: Magazine for Database Professionals, 15*(10), 8–17.

Janssen, M. A., Schoon, M. L., Ke, W., & Börner, K. (2006). Scholarly networks on resilience, vulnerability and adaptation within the human dimensions of global environmental change. *Global Environmental Change, 16*(3), 240–252. https://doi.org/10.1016/j.gloenvcha.2006.04.001

King, R., Hooper, B., & Wood, W. (2011). Using bibliographic software to appraise and code data in educational systematic review research. *Medical Teacher, 33*(9), 719–723. https://doi.org/10.3109/0142159X.2011.558138

Kitchenham, B., & Charters, S. (2007). *Guidelines for performing systematic literature reviews in software engineering.* Technical Report EBSE-2007-01, School of Computer Science and Mathematics. Keele University, Keele.

Kunisch, S., Menz, M., Bartunek, J. M., Cardinal, L. B., & Denyer, D. (2018). Feature topic at organizational research methods: How to conduct rigorous and impactful literature reviews? *Organizational Research Methods, 21*(3), 519–523. https://doi.org/10.1177/1094428118770750

Lajeunesse, M. J. (2016). Facilitating systematic reviews, data extraction and meta-analysis with the metagear package for R. *Methods in Ecology and Evolution, 7*(3), 323–330. https://doi.org/10.1111/2041-210X.12472

Levy, Y., & Ellis, T. J. (2006). A systems approach to conduct an effective literature review in support of information systems research. *Informing Science*, *9*, 181–212. https://doi.org/10.28945/479

Light, R. P., Polley, D. E., & Börner, K. (2014). Open data and open code for big science of science studies. *Scientometrics*, *101*(2), 1535–1551. https://doi.org/10.1007/s11192-014-1238-2

Li, J., Goerlandt, F., & Reniers, G. (2021). An overview of scientometric mapping for the safety science community: Methods, tools, and framework. *Safety Science*, *134*, 105093. https://doi.org/10.1016/j.ssci.2020.105093

Linnenluecke, M. K., & Griffiths, A. (2013). Firms and sustainability: Mapping the intellectual origins and structure of the corporate sustainability field. *Global Environmental Change*, *23*(1), 382–391. https://doi.org/10.1016/j.gloenvcha.2012.07.007

Linnenluecke, M. K., Marrone, M., & Singh, A. K. (2020). Conducting systematic literature reviews and bibliometric analyses. *Australian Journal of Management*, *45*(2), 175–194. https://doi.org/10.1177/0312896219877678

Llanos-Herrera, G. R., & Merigo, J. M. (2019). Overview of brand personality research with bibliometric indicators. *Kybernetes*, *48*(3), 546–569. https://doi.org/10.1108/K-02-2018-0051

Madden, A., Bailey, C., Alfes, K., & Fletcher, L. (2018). Using narrative evidence synthesis in HRM research: An overview of the method, its application, and the lessons learned. *Human Resource Management*, *57*(2), 641–657. https://doi.org/10.1002/hrm.21858

Moral-Muñoz, J. A., Herrera-Viedma, E., Santisteban-Espejo, A., & Cobo, M. J. (2020). Software tools for conducting bibliometric analysis in science: An up-to-date review. *Profesional de la Información*, *29*(1), e290103. https://doi.org/10.3145/epi.2020.ene.03

Pan, X., Yan, E., Cui, M., & Hua, W. (2018). Examining the usage, citation, and diffusion patterns of bibliometric mapping software: A comparative study of three tools. *Journal of Informetrics*, *12*(2), 481–493. https://doi.org/10.1016/j.joi.2018.03.005

Paul, J., & Criado, A. R. (2020). The art of writing literature review: What do we know and what do we need to know? *International Business Review*, *29*(4), 101717. https://doi.org/10.1016/j.ibusrev.2020.101717

Persson, O., Danell, R., & Schneider, J. W. (2009). How to use Bibexcel for various types of bibliometric analysis. *Celebrating Scholarly Communication Studies: A Festschrift for Olle Persson at his 60th Birthday*, *5*, 9–24.

R Core Team. (2019). *R: A language and environment for statistical computing*. R Foundation for Statistical Computing.

Raghuram, S., Tuertscher, P., & Garud, R. (2010). Research note—Mapping the field of virtual work: A cocitation analysis. *Information Systems Research*, *21*(4), 983–999. https://doi.org/10.1287/isre.1080.0227

Rana, S., Sakshi, & Singh, J. (2022). Presenting the POWER framework of conducting literature review. In S. Rana, Sakshi, & J. Singh (Eds.), *Exploring the latest trends in management literature (Review of management literature, Vol. 1)* (pp. 1–13). Emerald Publishing Limited. https://doi.org/10.1108/S2754-586520220000001001

Rana, S., & Sharma, S. K. (2015). A literature review, classification, and simple, meta-analysis on the conceptual domain of international marketing: 1990–2012. *Entrepreneurship in International Marketing Advances in International Marketing*, *25*, 189–222. https://doi.org/10.1108/S1474-797920140000025009

Schildt, H. A. (2005). *Sitkis, a software tool for bibliometric analysis*. Helsinki University of Technology.

Schildt, H. A., & Mattsson, J. T. (2006). A dense network sub-grouping algorithm for co-citation analysis and its implementation in the software tool Sitkis. *Scientometrics*, *67*(1), 143–163. https://doi.org/10.1007/s11192-006-0054-8

Sci² Team. (2009). *Science of Science (Sci2) Tool*. Indiana University and SciTech Strategies. https://sci2.cns.iu.edu

Shah, S. H. H., Lei, S., Ali, M., Doronin, D., & Hussain, S. T. (2020). Prosumption: Bibliometric analysis using HistCite and VOSviewer. *Kybernetes*, *49*(3), 1020–1045. https://doi.org/10.1108/K-12-2018-0696

Sinkovics, N. (2016). Enhancing the foundations for theorising through bibliometric mapping. *International Marketing Review*, *33*(3), 327–350. https://doi.org/10.1108/IMR-10-2014-0341

Templier, M., & Paré, G. (2015). A framework for guiding and evaluating literature reviews. *Communications of the Association for Information Systems*, *37*(6), 112–137. https://doi.org/10. 17705/1CAIS.03706

Tranfield, D., Denyer, D., & Smart, P. (2003). Towards a methodology for developing evidence-informed management knowledge by means of systematic review. *British Journal of Management*, *14*(3), 207–222. https://doi.org/10.1111/1467-8551.00375

van Eck, N. J. V., & Waltman, L. (2009). How to normalize cooccurrence data? An analysis of some well-known similarity measures. *Journal of the American Society for Information Science and Technology*, *60*(8), 1635–1651. https://doi.org/10.1002/asi.21075

Van Eck, N., & Waltman, L. (2010). Software survey: VOSviewer, a computer program for bibliometric mapping. *Scientometrics*, *84*(2), 523–538. https://doi.org/10.1007/s11192-009-0146-3

van Eck, N. J., & Waltman, L. (2014). CitNetExplorer: A new software tool for analyzing and visualizing citation networks. *Journal of Informetrics*, *8*(4), 802–823. https://doi.org/10.1016/j.joi. 2014.07.006

van Eck, N. J., Waltman, L., Dekker, R., & Van Den Berg, J. (2010). A comparison of two techniques for bibliometric mapping: Multidimensional scaling and VOS. *Journal of the American Society for Information Science and Technology*, *61*(12), 2405–2416. https://doi.org/10.1002/asi.21421

Westgate, M. J. (2018). Revtools: Bibliographic data visualization for evidence synthesis in R. *bioRxiv*, *10*, 262881. http://doi.org/10.1101/262881

Xiao, Y., & Watson, M. (2019). Guidance on conducting a systematic literature review. *Journal of Planning Education and Research*, *39*(1), 93–112. https://doi.org/10.1177/0739456X17723971

Zhou, X., Zhou, M., Huang, D., & Cui, L. (2022). A probabilistic model for co-occurrence analysis in bibliometrics. *Journal of Biomedical Informatics*, *128*, 104047. https://doi.org/10.1016/j.jbi.2022. 104047

Zupic, I., & Čater, T. (2015). Bibliometric methods in management and organization. *Organizational Research Methods*, *18*(3), 429–472. https://doi.org/10.1177/1094428114562629

WHAT? WHY? WHEN? HOW? WHERE? OF TECHNOLOGY-BASED BIBLIOMETRIC REVIEW

Shalini Sahni and Rahul Pratap Singh Kaurav

ABSTRACT

The proliferation of bibliometric review articles is a true reflection of how bibliometrics is gaining popularity and has been widely adopted in various disciplines. The growing interest of scholars has encouraged us to dwell upon the what, why, when, how, *and* where *of bibliometric literature reviews. The study explained the bibliometric review with the standpoint that it can be considered a strong review method for analyzing a large volume of data and scholars can supplement their traditional reviews with bibliometric reviews to strengthen their knowledge. This will help researchers to justify the (a) need for a study on the particular topic; (b) type or method of review chosen; (c) number of articles selected; (d) inclusion and exclusion criterion; (e) method of analysis; and (f) presentation of the findings.*

Keywords: Bibliometric analysis; bibliometric methodology; technology-based review; bibliometric software; literature review; review methodology

1. INTRODUCTION

Bibliometrics is one of the most popular literature review techniques and is now established as a scientific method that provides quantitative analysis of the published literature (Beckendorff & Zehrer, 2013; Ellegaard & Wallin, 2015; Rana et al., 2022). With time, researchers have widely adopted bibliometric reviews in various disciplines such as economics, business management, accounting, social sciences, medicine, information technology, and agriculture. Social sciences and medicine scholars were the pioneers in using bibliometric

Advancing Methodologies of Conducting Literature Review in Management Domain
Review of Management Literature, Volume 2, 79–101
Copyright © 2024 Shalini Sahni and Rahul Pratap Singh Kaurav
Published under exclusive licence by Emerald Publishing Limited
ISSN: 2754-5865/doi:10.1108/S2754-586520230000002005

methods as shown by Scopus with 10,573 and 10,300 publications (July 2022) with the first article published in 1969. According to the Web of Science (WOS), the information and library science category used bibliometric methods in 1900. Much of the bibliometric method's growth and popularity can be attributed to its (a) ability to handle a large volume of published articles and (b) systematically visualizing large networks of various authors, journals, countries, and keywords (Fig. 1).

In 1985, when bibliometrics was first used in academics in business management and social sciences discipline, only three articles were published under the search bibliometrics in the WOS database. By 2010, the number rose to 52 and in 2022, the number had risen to 364, a 121-fold increase in WOS and Scopus. The number of published bibliometric studies was 300 in 2010 and it further rose to 1,390 in 2022.

The increase in the number of publications is a true reflection of how bibliometrics has been widely applied and accepted within the discipline of business management and social sciences. In a real sense, this is good interdisciplinary adoption of a methodology from the library and information science to any discipline one can recall. There are numerous evidences of how bibliometric research has grown over the years and has been widely accepted by leading journals, which include but are not limited to

(1) the call for recognition of bibliometric reviews and literature reviews by editors of premier journals. For example, call by the *International Journal of Consumer Studies* (2022) and Palmatier et al. (2018). The editorial in the *JAMS* (*Journal of the Academy of Marketing Science*) is evidence of the commitment of the journals to publishing review (i.e., bibliometric, systematic literature reviews [SLR], meta, integrative, framework-based) articles.
(2) the number of citations received by bibliometric reviews published in seminal journals. For example, the *International Journal of Management Reviews*, a well-known management journal established in 1999, received a very high impact factor (IF) based on citations received on review articles (i.e., 2-year

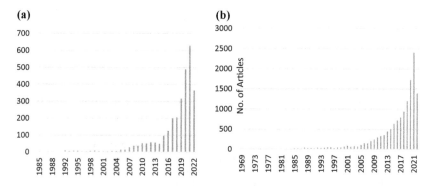

Fig. 1. Growth of Bibliometrics in Business Management and Social Sciences (a) Scopus and (b) Web of Science (WOS). *Source:* Scopus and Web of Science Database.

IF: 8.631; 5-year IF: 9.896) and rankings (i.e., business: 5/152; management: 5/266) in the 2019 *Journal Citation Reports* (Clarivate Analytics).

(3) the publication of bibliometric reviews in premier journals. For example, Weingarten and Goodman's (2021) review on experiential advantage in the *Journal of Consumer Research* and White et al.'s (2019) review on sustainable consumer behavior in the *Journal of Marketing*.

(4) the special issues and call for papers, particularly for publishing literature review articles in leading journals such as the *Journal of the Academy of Marketing Science* (Hulland & Houston, 2020) and the *International Business Review* (Paul & Criado, 2020).

(5) the number of citations received by the author for bibliometric reviews. For example, Van Eck and Waltman (2010) have been cited 4,481 times, Geissdoerfer et al. (2017) have cited 2,162 times, and Aria and Cuccurullo (2017) have been cited 1,610 times.

Given that the proliferation of bibliometric research encourages us to curate knowledge about bibliometric reviews. The study conducted by Donthu et al. (2021) explained the *how* part of the bibliometric review and offered guidelines on "how" bibliometric review should be conducted, leaving *what, why, when*, and *where* of bibliometric literature reviews. Therefore, the current study aims to bridge the gap by offering and explaining the missing links and also expanding *how* part of conducting bibliometric literature reviews. Therefore, to guide research scholars, an in-depth understanding of conducting bibliometric reviews is provided by introducing the steps that will enable them to justify the decisions taken for and during the review. For example, it will help them to justify the (a) need for a review on the particular topic; (b) the type or method of review chosen; (c) the number of articles selected; (d) inclusion and exclusion criterion; (e) method of analysis; and (f) presentation of the findings. In particular, the aim is to offer guidance to aspiring authors in deciding what topic to review and the type of review to write and outline a step-wise procedure that can be adopted for writing a bibliometric review paper. This paper specifically deals with the five research questions (RQs). These are as follows:

RQ1: What are the reasons for conducting bibliometric analysis?

RQ2: Why bibliometric analysis papers are needed?

RQ3: When the bibliometric analysis is conducted?

RQ4: How the bibliometric analysis is processed? What are the process and tools?

RQ5: Where bibliometric analysis papers can be published?

2. *WHAT* IS A BIBLIOMETRIC REVIEW: ASSESSMENT OF THE MATURITY OF THE FIELD

Systematic literature reviews were originally used in the field of medicine where a consistent method of reporting is followed (Cronin et al., 2007; Higgins & Green, 2011). In recent years, this approach is further developed and has been made more appropriate to be used in any discipline, including areas where publications are not as consistent (Tranfield et al., 2003), and assessment of the maturity of the field is required. This gave rise to another stronger method of reviewing literature using bibliometric methods that can be conducted in different research areas (Archambault & Larivière, 2010; Hicks, 1999; Hood & Wilson, 2001; Patra & Mishra, 2006; Schoepflin & Glänzel, 2001). In other words, bibliometric review stemmed from SLRs (Fan et al., 2022; Lim et al., 2022) and created a strong application potential (Van Raan, 2019) by evaluating the extant literature by applying various statistical techniques like factorial analysis, multidimensional scaling, descriptive analysis, etc., on bibliographic data (such as authors, sources, keywords, citations) (Donthu et al., 2021). It further assesses the development of the topic and suggests the maturity of a research field over time with a specific interest in the creation, growth, and dissemination of knowledge (Keathley-Herring et al., 2016). Pritchard (1969) defined bibliometrics as "the application of mathematics and statistical methods to books and other media of communication," and Broadus (1987) redefined it as a "quantitative study of physical published units, or of bibliographic units, or the surrogates for either."

One distinguishing feature that makes bibliometric reviews noteworthy is that it uses objective and statistical measures to evaluate the large volume of data (articles), and provides network visualizations that are not offered by other literature review types. Consequently, this widens the scope of bibliometric studies. For example, the bibliometric reviews can be conducted on (a) domains such as tourism and finance (Koseoglu et al., 2016; Kumar et al., 2021); (b) constructs such as trust (Mumu et al., 2022); (c) methods such as structural equation modeling (Blanco-Encomienda & Rosillo-Díaz, 2021); (d) highly cited review articles (Ivanović & Ho, 2019); (e) systematic reviews (Wieland et al., 2021); (f) journals (Donthu et al., 2021); and (g) theories such as the theory of planned behavior, unified theory of acceptance and use of technology (Si et al., 2019; Williams & Baláž, 2012). In this manner, a systematic bibliometric review synthesizes evidence of the maturity of the research field to inform knowledge and practice in a particular discipline (Tranfield et al., 2003). Furthermore, the bibliometric review has the potential to analyze the current state of the research area and how a particular discipline is developing (Romanelli et al., 2021), reveal the stricture of the research area (Nakagawa et al., 2019), and identify the current knowledge status and future trends (Baber et al., 2022; Cabeza-Ramírez et al., 2020; Kaurav & Gupta, 2022; Kaushal et al., 2021; Pilkington & Chai, 2008; Romanelli et al., 2021) which consequently suggests the maturity of a research area.

3. WHEN IS A BIBLIOMETRIC REVIEW "APPROPRIATE"?

Given the popularity of bibliometric methods, the use of bibliometric review often requires additional discussion to explain the rationale behind choosing it by comparing it with SLR and meta-analysis. For building the criteria of *when* to use bibliometric review, 30 bibliometric articles were collected from Scopus and WOS databases. Table 1 summarizes the few seminal papers that have adopted bibliometric review from the discipline of business and management and social sciences that helped authors to make informed decisions with respect to the selection of the bibliometric review method.

Based on the previous studies reviewed, the most prominent justifications for using bibliometric reviews are attributed to the following, which are briefly discussed as under:

• Scope of the research area and RQs.
• Sample size (amount of literature published and age of journals).

3.1 Scope of the Research Area and Type of Research Questions

The scope of the research area refers to the extent to which the research area in a particular domain or field will be explored. Bibliometric reviews are appropriate

Table 1. Bibliometric Review Studies From Business Management and Social Sciences Discipline.

Author	Title	Journal	# Of Studies	Period	Reasons for Considering Bibliometric Review
Geissdoerfer et al. (2017)	"The Circular Economy – A New Sustainability Paradigm?"	*Journal of Cleaner Production*	295	1950–2016	Type of research questions framed
Fahimnia et al. (2015)	"Green Supply Chain Management: A Review and Bibliometric Analysis"	*International Journal of Production Economics*	884	1992–2013	Sample size
Martínez-López et al. (2018)	"Fifty Years of the European Journal of Marketing: A Bibliometric Analysis"	*European Journal of Marketing*	50 years	1967–2016	Age of journal (50 years)
Ramos-Rodríguez and Ruíz-Navarro (2004)	"Changes in the Intellectual Structure of Strategic Management Research: A Bibliometric Study of the Strategic Management Journal, 1980–2000"	*Strategic Management Journal*	870	1980–2000	Amount of published work in the area over an extended period, evolution of discipline of strategic management (Scope)
Kraus et al. (2020)	"The Sharing Economy: A Bibliometric Analysis of the State-of-the-Art"	*International Journal of Entrepreneurial Behavior & Research*	326	2013–2020	A large number of publications

Source: Authors' Creation.

Note: All articles reviewed did not provide justifications for using bibliometric reviews.

when the scope of the research area is broad and the RQs are aimed to answer the following queries:

- Whether there has been an upward trend or decline in the particular discipline or sub-fields making it possible to examine how disciplines are developing (Romanelli et al., 2021)?
- What are the leading past and present trends of a particular journal (Schwert, 1993), for example, the bibliometric review of the *Journal of Business Research* (Merigó et al., 2015) for the years 1973 and 2014; bibliometric analysis of the *European Journal of Marketing* from 1967 to 2017?
- How was the performance of authors, institutes, and countries as compared to others (Bhattacharya & Sharma, 2022)?

3.2 Sample Size

Sample size in bibliometric studies refers to the number of articles considered by a researcher for a review. This is an important consideration as the choice of the type of review depends on the number of articles selected. Literature suggests that one should consider a bibliometric review if the number of articles is at least above 60. Bibliometric reviews are considered good if the articles lie between 200 and 500 and are considered excellent if the number is above 500. A bibliometric review is deemed appropriate when the amount of published research is high and the number of literature reviews available is less (Fig. 2).

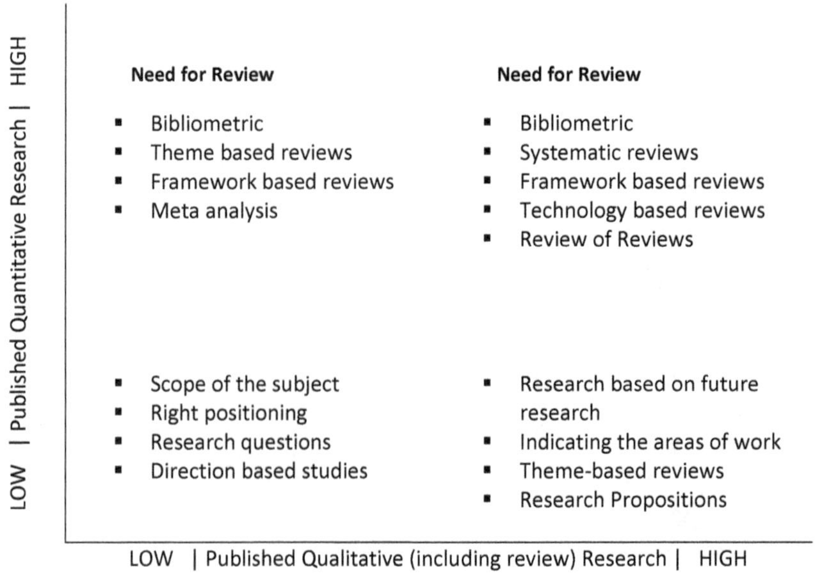

	Need for Review	**Need for Review**
HIGH	▪ Bibliometric ▪ Theme based reviews ▪ Framework based reviews ▪ Meta analysis	▪ Bibliometric ▪ Systematic reviews ▪ Framework based reviews ▪ Technology based reviews ▪ Review of Reviews
LOW	▪ Scope of the subject ▪ Right positioning ▪ Research questions ▪ Direction based studies	▪ Research based on future research ▪ Indicating the areas of work ▪ Theme-based reviews ▪ Research Propositions

Published Quantitative Research

LOW | Published Qualitative (including review) Research | HIGH

Fig. 2.   Need for Literature Review. *Source:* Modified by Authors adapted from Pautasso (2013).

4. *WHY* OF BIBLIOMETRIC REVIEW

Although the bibliometric methodology is not new (Kessler, 1963; Small, 1973), its proliferation started with the easy accessibility of databases in the universities and the free software available online. Bibliometric methods have been more rapidly adopted in a few fields (such as strategic management, entrepreneurship, education, innovation, and medicine), while other fields such as organizational behavior and psychology are relatively slow (Zupic & Čater, 2015).

In recent years, the amount of published literature is increasing exponentially, and tracking the relevant literature is becoming more difficult. Therefore, a researcher needs to understand the use of bibliometric methods which can handle a large volume of data and can keep track of the performance of the various elements (such as most prolific authors, journals in the particular discipline, highly cited countries, institutions, etc.) One must use bibliometric methods as it complements the traditional way of doing a literature review. Zupic and Čater (2015) suggest that bibliometric methods are useful in mapping the relevant literature from all disciplines and can show various patterns in the literature. The advanced bibliometric methods can help in examining the correlation matrix that can be further analyzed using quantitative statistical techniques that can be used to test the hypothesis.

However, topic selection is one of the most crucial steps of why one should write a bibliometric review. Scholars should not select a very recurring topic that already has some reviews on a similar topic.

5. *HOW* OF BIBLIOMETRIC REVIEW

5.1 Databases and Database Coverage

To perform a bibliometric analysis, the first step is to decide on the best data source that fits the requirement of a researcher and has the maximum scientific coverage of that particular area. There are many bibliographic databases available; however, most of them are subscription based, while free databases available provided limited information. Databases that can be used for performing bibliometric analysis are summarized in Table 2.

Researchers can use multiple databases to extract data and here one needs to answer "which database" should be considered. The answer lies in the fact that the identification of that provides the largest number of relevant articles for a limited number of searches (Livoreil et al., 2017). Further, retrieving articles from the database is another essential component of a bibliometric review. Once an area of study is decided, the investigator chooses a database based on the number of scholarly articles present in a particular chosen study. The three widely used databases for bibliometric research are WOS, Scopus, and Pubmed. If researchers have limited access to the databases, they may use - Medline, Embase, Publish or Perish and Dimensions. One should perform a search query on all databases to evaluate the search results. Pubmed, Medline, and Embase are preferred for medical studies. For business and management studies, both WOS and Scopus

Table 2. Databases for Bibliometrics.

Database/ Software	Subscription Required	Data Download	Records Limit for Downloading	File Extension Formats	Analysis
WOS (Database)	Yes	Yes	500 records at one time	.txt	Complete information available
Scopus (Database)	Yes	Yes	2,000 records	.csv and .ris	Complete information available
Dimensions (Database)	No/ subscription also available	Yes	50,000	.csv	Complete information available
Google Scholar (Database)	No	Yes (External support is required by POP)	NA	.csv	Limited information available in CSV
Microsoft Academic (Database)	No	Using API	NA	NA	NA
Mendeley (software)	No	Yes	NA	.ris	Limited information available thereby limited analysis is possible

Source: Authors' Creation.

Note: Web of Science (WOS), Comma delimited file (CSV), .txt (text file), research information systems (.ris), application programming interface (API), publish or perish (POP) retrieved from https://harzing.com/resources/publish-or-perish.

are the most preferred databases and dimensions are gaining popularity as a database but are not widely used. The journal coverage of both WOS and Scopus varies greatly. While evaluating the publication status of the keyword "panic buying" in WOS (225 articles) and Scopus (278 articles) would provide different results (Scopus covers approximately 43,685 journals vs. 21,429 journals). For example, pharmaceutical journals are better covered in WOS as compared to Scopus. Therefore, scholars must evaluate databases as a prime step for bibliometric research.

5.2 Searching Articles in Databases Using Keywords

Search options related to data fields are available in all databases. A researcher must define the search string in the paper as this stage lays the foundation of all subsequent steps in the review. Keywords used for searching the articles are based on the topic, context, and research questions or objectives framed in the study. One can start an article search for a bibliometric review by using the context of interest, which can be a discipline or a particular research topic. Selecting key terms require looking at author keywords, and abstracts, and reading published reviews (Romanelli et al., 2021). It is also recommended to use various synonyms, acronyms, or abbreviations as keywords in the search string, for example, authors usually use SEM for structural equation modeling. Researchers may also face the challenge at the time of combining search terms, which can be overcome by using Boolean operators and double quotes.

Furthermore, one must consider the following questions while searching articles in any database:

- Should reviews, case reports, editorials, and communication to the editor be considered?
- Are the keywords used in the search bar good enough to answer objectives and RQs?

The answers to these questions along with the database coverage must be combined to determine the next step of identifying and downloading the articles from the database.

5.3 Identifying Studies for Review

The scholar has to identify the relevant studies from the pool of articles and select the study based on the operational problems that belong to the pertinent population identified for the study (Baber et al., 2023; Guzzo et al., 1987). The inclusion of the study in the review is based on the kind of RQs raised in the research by the scholar. Hence, bibliometric studies are free from researcher biases because as a protocol, bibliometric methodology emphasizes that all studies (both qualitative and quantitative) conducted on a topic should be included. The important questions one might consider are as follows:

- Should unpublished articles be included?
- Should technical reports be included?
- Should conference proceedings, editorials, and communication with the editors be considered?
- Which discipline one should consider while selecting articles?
- Should article selection be based on the journal's performance?

One must answer all these questions while selecting the articles that develop a base for inclusion and exclusion criteria for writing a bibliometric review. Once the articles are selected, the researcher must consider the methodological comparison of different types of reviews (bibliometric analysis, meta-analysis, and SLRs) to make an informed decision about the selection of appropriate review technique and takes a decision on "which" bibliometric tool should be used.

5.4 Bibliometric Tools and Indicators

In the following section, the performance of bibliometrics is presented using various bibliographic tools and indicators that can be used to demonstrate bibliographic modeling and topic modeling. There are many bibliographic tools available and a few important ones which are widely used are summarized here. For this purpose, 20 articles were analyzed using the keywords "bibliometric"

OR "Bibliography*" from A and A* star journals and mapped how these articles have analyzed the bibliographic data and which type of metrics have been used most frequently. It was found that VOSviewer is the most widely used bibliographic tool followed by Gephi and Bibexcel. HistCite™ was used only in two documents and CiteNet explorer, and R programming language was used only in one document. Interestingly, MS Excel was also used for bibliometric calculations. All bibliometric software take raw bibliographic data (e.g. an export from WOS, Scopus, Dimensions, Pubmed), perform bibliometric calculations, and calculate the similarity matrices between various unit of analysis (documents, authors, journals, words, institutes, and countries). Based on the earlier-drawn facts, the study briefly describes only those bibliometric software's and indicators that are being used in the studies analyzed.

5.4.1 VOSviewer
The software is an open-source program and is freely available for download (see www.vosviewer.com). VOSviewer can be used to do scientific mapping of authors, journals, and keywords based on citation analysis or co-occurrences. It generates two types of maps, namely, (a) distance-based maps; and (b) graph-based maps. Distance-based maps present the distance between two items (authors or journals or countries or institutes) indicating the strength of the relationship. Graph-based maps indicate a relationship between items. Both distance-based and graph-based mapping form clusters in different colors for easy identification of elements falling under each cluster.

5.4.2 HistCite
Clarivate Analytics' HistCite™ is free software and is widely used in informetrics research (Bornmann & Marx, 2012; Garfield, 2004; Garfield & Pudovkin, 2004; Garfield et al., 2003a, b). It helps in generating a chronological map of citations for articles, journals, universities, and research institutions. The method highlights key articles and the relationships between them. It generates chronological historiography that highlights the most-cited works in the corpus of articles, thereby giving the user a snapshot of the key literature on any current topic (Garfield et al., 2003a; Van Eck & Waltman, 2011).

5.4.3 Gephi
Gephi is open-source software for network maps and rendering graphs in real time. It can deal with a large network (i.e. over 20,000 nodes) as it is built on a multitask model. Gephi can use files from different software as it specializes in dynamic analyses (Xu et al., 2018). Most of the bibliometric papers that were analyzed used VOSviewer and Gephi together as authors did the co-word analysis using VOSviewer, while the co-citation and dynamic co-citation analyses were performed using Gephi (Khanra et al., 2021). The advance prestige or performance analysis can also be performed using Gephi as it follows a sophisticated ranking algorithm (Xu et al., 2018).

5.4.4 Bibexcel

Bibexcel is a very versatile bibliometric tool as it allows easy interaction with other software, such as Pajek, Excel, SPSS, etc. Bibexcel provides various types of files, at every step. It generates a new file with a different extension. However, creating an OUT-file is always the first step for carrying out various bibliometric analyses. One of the important noteworthy features of Bibexcel is that enables a user to produce correlation matrices for export to statistical software such as SPSS, R, JAMOVI, etc.

5.4.5 CiteSpace

CiteSpace is free software that creates interactive visualizations of structural and temporal trends in a scientific field. It also provides a "remove duplicates" function for removing duplicates which is absent in all software except SCI2. CiteSpace software provides clusters in the network visualization map by identifying subject areas and citations received by an article. It interprets the chronological structure and connects with previous research patterns and offers clusters through geospatial collaboration patterns. The clusters are based on a time-slicing strategy and play a key role in predicting the evolution of the research field.

5.4.6 CiteNet Explorer

CiteNet Explorer is also free software and performs performance analysis and scientific mapping. It builds the network based on the most important publication and shows the citation relations between these publications to indicate how publications build on each other. Other citation networks of journals or authors cannot be analyzed using CitNet Explorer. Hence, each node in CitNet Explorer, in a citation network represents a publication.

5.4.7 Biblioshiny

The researchers who are not much comfortable with programming/coding, Biblioshiny offers a web interface for bibliometrix (R package). Biblioshiny is meant for the R language lovers. It aids scholars in making simple use of bibliometrix's key features like importing data, converting it to a data frame, and collecting it. Data acquisition is possible through Dimensions, PubMed, Scopus, and WOS. Biblioshiny analyses and plots the data using four different level metrics. These are authors, documents, sources, and coupling via clustering. Biblioshiny uses three popular knowledge structures, namely, intellectual structure, conceptual structure, and social structure.

The comparison of the earlier-mentioned software is described in Table 3.

5.5 Bibliometric Indicators

The "how" of bibliometric review encapsulates the use of quantitative techniques on bibliographic data extracted from various databases. The techniques range

Table 3. Comparison of the Software.

Name of Software	Present Version	Developers	Interface (CUI or GUI), Web or Desktop	Database Supported							Pre-processing		Analysis					
				WOS	Scopus	Dimensions	Google Scholar	Microsoft Academic	Citation Related Software	Duplicate	Time Slice	Filter	Author/Affiliation Network	Country Network	Thematic Analysis	Evolution	Visualization	Multivariate
VOS Viewer, 2022	1.6.18	Leiden University, The Netherlands	GUI, Desktop, Web	✓	✓	✓	✓	×	✓ (Using POP)	×	×	✓	✓	✓	✓	×	✓	✓
Biblioshiny (bibliometrix), 2022	4.0.0	University of Naples, Italy	GUI, Web	✓	✓	✓	×	×	×	×	✓	✓	✓	✓	✓	✓	✓	✓
Cite Space, 2022	6.1.R2	Drexel University, USA	GUI, Desktop	✓	✓	✓	×	✓	✓	×	✓	✓	✓	✓	✓	×	✓	✓
Sci², 2018*	1.3	Cyberinfrastructure for Network Science, Center, USA	GUI, Desktop	✓	✓	×	✓	×	×	✓	✓	✓	✓	✓	✓	×	✓	✓
Gephi	0.9	Mathieu Bastian, Eduardo Ramos Ibañez, Mathieu Jacomy, and Nine others	GUI, Desktop	✓	✓	×	×	×	×	×	×	✓	✓	✓	✓	✓	✓	✓
Bibexcel	2017	Olle Persson	GUI, Desktop	✓	✓	✓	×	✓	✓	✓	×	✓	✓	✓	✓	✓	✓	✓
HisCite ™	12.3.17	Eugene Garfield, the Founder of the ISI	GUI, Web-based Interface	✓	×	×	×	×	✓	×	×	✓	✓	✓	×	✓	✓	×
CiteNet Explorer	1.0.0	Leiden University, The Netherlands	GUI, Desktop, Web	✓	×	×	×	×	×	×	✓	×	✓	✓	✓	✓	✓	×

Source: Authors' Own Creation.

Note: *Was not used in the articles reviewed. Character user interface (CUI); graphical user interface (GUI).

from studying the simple performance of the various bibliographic data (journals, authors, countries, sources, institutes) to network visualizations and collaborations that fall into two broad categories: (a) performance analysis; (b) scientific mapping.

5.5.1 Performance Analysis

Performance analysis is performed on the bibliographic data and provides information on how authors, journals, countries, and institutions are performing in the particular field of inquiry, which is akin to scientific mapping. Scholars can compare and analyze the publication and citation performance of both author (number of citations and h index) and journal (impact factor and citations) based on year, institution performance (academic vs. non-academic), and country publication (developed vs. developing) as part of performance analysis. One of the most critically important points while doing the performance analysis is the normalization of bibliometric data, which is usually ignored in most studies. It is recommended that source-normalized impact per paper (SNIP) should be used for journals, particularly as compared to the impact factor (IF) score. The SNIP is a metric that intrinsically allows citations to be compared among various journals across research fields and eliminates the need of categorizing journals into various categories (Moed, 2010).

5.5.2 Scientific Mapping
Further based on the performance analysis, scientific mapping involves the application of quantitative and statistical techniques (e.g., descriptive statistics analysis, cluster analysis, and factorial analysis) on bibliographic data (e.g., sources and citations) (Broadus, 1987; Cobo et al., 2011; Donthu et al., 2021). The mapping provides visualization networks that pertain to the intellectual structure and development of scientific fields (Baker et al., 2020; Tunger & Eulerich, 2018). Table 4 summarizes various bibliometric indicators and metrics used for various types of bibliometric analysis in the articles selected for analysis.

It was found that innumerable measures exist for bibliometric analysis. The most prominent measure used in the articles reviewed is the performance (descriptive) analysis (Ford et al., 2021; Guo et al., 2019; Hollebeek et al., 2021; Subramony et al., 2021; Varma et al., 2022), followed by bibliographic coupling and co-citation analysis (Budler et al., 2021; Guo et al., 2019; Khanra et al., 2021; Mortazavi et al., 2021; Norder et al., 2022; Perez-Vega et al., 2022; Subramony et al., 2021). Besides these techniques, recently introduced social- and web-based metrics known as Altmetric scores were used in one article (Guo et al., 2019). The altimetric score was obtained from http://www.altmetric.com to measure how many times each paper has been mentioned in social media such as Twitter, Facebook, Mendeley, blogs, and Wikipedia influence. Akbari et al. (2022) used a degree of centrality and eigenvector centrality to find the keywords' relative importance. One of the interesting analyses used by Varma et al. (2022) sheds light on the performance analysis of articles, journals, and other research elements using negative binomial regression which is in line with the recommendations provided by Donthu et al. (2021) and recent demonstrations of bibliometric methodology in premier journals.

6. "WHERE" OF BIBLIOMETRIC REVIEW

Bibliometric tools allow us to evaluate a huge volume of data and offer quantitative assessments of the various bibliographic elements. However, a true evaluation of data is just not obtained by examining the citations and publications but should include the most sought future directions for the scholars. If bibliometric methods are used to their full extent, then it has the potential to

Table 4. Bibliometric Indicators Suitable for Performance Analysis.

S.No.	Category of Analysis	Type of Indicator	Unit of Analysis	Description	Can be Used for	Metrics Used	Research Questions
1	Performance analysis	Citation analysis	Document Author Journal	The descriptive method involves studying a discipline or a research field by identifying the major publications, authors, sources, institutions, and countries using citations	Impact or influence (Most cited article, author, and journal)	h index, g index, TLC, TGC, TC, Ratios (TGC/TC, TLC/TC)	Who are the most prolific authors in the research field? Which are the most impactful or influential journals in the particular discipline? Which are the seminal articles in a specific research area?
		Publication counts/journal impact	Author Journal	The simplest bibliometric indicator provides a number of published articles that a researcher or a journal has produced	Impact or influence	Counts: TP, h index, g index	Which author has published the most in the particular research field? Which journal has got the highest number of publications related to a particular field?
2	Scientific mapping	Co-citation analysis	Document Author Journal	Connects various documents, authors, or sources on the basis of common reference lists	Cluster analysis and thematic evolution, major developments, maturity assessment	Hierarchical clustering Correlation Binomial regression Factorial analysis Multidimensional scaling Eigen vector centrality (EVC) (For keyword relative importance) Degree of centrality (DC) (For key word relative importance) Weighted degree of centrality (WDOC)	What is the intellectual or knowledge structure of a particular construct or domain in the literature? Which are the most influential articles on a particular topic in the research field? How has the proliferation or diffusion of the concept taken place in the literature? What is the social structure of the scientific community in a particular field? How has the knowledge structure developed over time?

Method	Unit	Description	Structure	Research questions	Metrics
Co-author analysis	Author	Provides evidence of collaboration	Social structure/ collaboration structure	Which authors have co-authored together? Has co-authorship influenced the citations? What is the pattern or structure of co-authorship or collaboration among authors? What is the social structure of the research field? What is the intellectual association in scientific research?	Page rank (PR)/ Altmetrics
Bibliographic coupling	Articles	A network of publications is said to be bibliographically coupled if they have one or more common references	Intellectual structure and highlights contemporary themes	What is the intellectual structure of recent/emerging literature? What are the important themes in a particular research area that have developed over time?	
Co-word analysis	Key words	Provides important terms and their frequencies used in the research field	Thematic evolution and cluster analysis	What is the conceptual structure of a research field? What are the major themes that have been studied over time? How have the themes evolved over the year?	
Algorithmic historiography*		Provides the chronological development of the research field by visualizing the important publications and is performed on Citenet explorer	Cluster analysis and thematic evolution	Which are the important domains that contribute to the important theoretical underpinnings?	

Source: Authors.

Note: Total publications (TP); Total citations (TC); Total local citations (TLC); Total global citations (TGC); DOC: measures an article's contribution to the overall literature; WDOC: article relative popularity within the network; EVC: article relative influence; PR: measures article prestige on the webpages when a keyword search is used; Altmetrics: this is comparatively a recent matrix which is social- and web-based metrics. It measures the impact of papers promptly after publication by tracking the online attention they receive. *performed on CiteNet Explorer.

publish in journals of high repute. All the journals are open for publishing review papers, particularly bibliometric review-based papers. To the best of our knowledge, no journals have made the guidelines that they will not publish papers based on the bibliometric analysis. However, the manuscript needs to be aligned with the scope and objectives of the journal. In a recent survey on Scopus a list of journals has been found, where bibliometric analysis papers were published at high frequency (Table 5).

7. DISCUSSION

The integrative approach of presenting *what, why, when, how,* and *where* of bibliometric review as presented in Table 6 will help scholars to understand the strengths of bibliometric review and they can have a global perspective of their performance a few years later. Like other types of literature reviews, SLR, Meta-analysis, Narrative Reviews, Integrative Reviews, and bibliometric reviews are equally published and acknowledged as they contribute to the advancement of knowledge and can suggest new directions for future research. However, despite the growing importance of bibliometric studies, they do not reveal theoretical insights (Mukherjee et al., 2022; Post et al., 2020). In other words, one must extend bibliometric studies beyond the descriptive and quantitative findings and should make a theoretical contribution. Another critically important point, while analyzing the data for bibliometrics is the normalization of the data, that is, to account for the differences between various fields, subfields, and nations in their publication and patenting patterns (Narin et al., 1994).

Considering the need and desire of the research community to be more scientific, it is not surprising that scholars quickly adopt new literature review methods that are more objective and precise in nature. The rapid increase in the

Table 5. List of Journals With Highest Publications of Papers With Bibliometric Analysis.

Sr. No.	Source Title	# of Articles
1	Scientometrics	512
2	Library Philosophy and Practice	366
3	Sustainability Switzerland	359
4	Journal of Cleaner Production	111
5	Journal of Business Research	62
6	Technological Forecasting and Social Change	50
7	Science and Technology Libraries	46
8	Journal of Informetrics	32
9	Journal of Scientometric Research	28
10	Benchmarking	27
11	Management Review Quarterly	27

Source: Authors.

Table 6. Understanding the Overall Ecosystem of Bibliometric-Based Papers.

Question	Response
What?	Establish the importance and impact of research
	Identify the strength and weaknesses of a particular research field
	Identifying the top researchers in the subject area
	To identify past, present, and forecast future publishing trends
	To study the productivity of the institutions/individual and the disciplines
	To get publications in top-tier journals
When?	Type of RQs framed
	Sample size
	Age of journal (10, 30, 50 years)
	Amount of published work in the area over an extended period, Evolution of discipline of strategic management (scope)
	A large number of publications
Why?	To identify the research gaps
	Understanding over-explored and under-exposed areas (emerging themes)
	Decipher evolutionary nuances of a selected field
How?	Use any or combination of these software: VOSviewer, HistCite, Gephi, Bibexcel, CiteSpace, CiteNet Explorer, and Biblioshiny. There are many other software as well
Where?	Popularly for WOS and Scopus indexed journals

Source: Authors' Creation.

use of bibliometric studies in recent years is an indication that it may become an obligatory method of doing a literature review. It is, therefore, important for both scholars and consumers of bibliometric research to know the important challenges one might come across while planning a bibliometric review. These are as follows:

(1) Sometimes different disciplines have different citation patterns. For example, it is easy to attract citations in life sciences, material sciences, and core sciences. Whereas in social sciences like business management, marketing, and sociology it is difficult to attract citations due to a large number of theories and prevailing criticism. In other words, it is therefore quite misleading to compare the citations of an article of discipline A with B. Moreover, self-citation to a researcher's articles, and to the work of colleagues from his institution, which probably will take more time to diffuse through the scientific network also needs some kind of manual intervention while writing inferences.

(2) For bibliometric analysis, only good sources (like indexing, Scopus, WOS, and others) can be used. Therefore, a large number of papers have been left unused. They might be published in popular conference proceedings, not indexed journals, and book chapters (Block & Fisch, 2020).

(3) It is possible that the paper may be cited in a negative sense, i.e. for criticism, yet the citation would still be counted. Which portrays a misleading academic reputation of researcher and science as well.

(4) Bibliometric researchers should carefully choose the search string. Following the principles of systematic reviews and maps (Haddaway et al., 2015), the search process should be as comprehensive as possible and yield reliable results.
(5) The biggest challenge with bibliometric analysis-based papers is that it includes only academic documents. Informal publications and communications, i.e. magazine articles, newspaper reports, industry white and yellow papers, blogs, Wikipedia entries, academic presentations and discussions, documentaries, monologues, etc., are not a part of the bibliographic data. Thus, predicting the scientific development/evolutions cannot be appraised properly as they do not represent the complete academic activity.

Thus, to conduct a more robust and reliable bibliometric review, a scholar is recommended to check the answers to the under-mentioned questions and then follow the step-by-step procedure of conducting bibliometric analysis as shown in Fig. 3:

- When was the last review done on the topic chosen?
- What were the objectives of the past reviews?
- What techniques were used to analyze the data?
- Which database was used to extract the articles?
- How was the quality of the articles?
- How can my review be different from the previous ones?

7.1 Implications

Literature reviews are conducted for several reasons but bibliometric reviews are conducted for three main reasons. These are as follows: (a) analyzing the maturity of the field; (b) analyzing the performance of various bibliographic elements; and (c) analyzing the intellectual social structure. In recent bibliometric reviews, hybrid methods combining the existing bibliometric approaches and content analysis, using more than two bibliometric software for various kinds of outputs have been adopted (Ford et al., 2021; Guo et al., 2019; Hollebeek et al., 2021; Subramony et al., 2021; Varma et al., 2022). Such methods can improve the accuracy of clustering and overcome the problems of synonyms being used in different forms and spelling differences due to American and British English.

This chapter will inform scholars about how to structure literature reviews using various bibliometric methods that can increase the rigor and structure of literature reviews. Scientific mapping builds an understanding of the social processes (coauthorship and co-citation analysis) and helps a scholar in understanding relationship networks that may help him in establishing future network connections. It suggests future scholarly opportunities that can contribute to the development of the field. The knowledge clusters and thematic evolution helps a scholar in understanding research gaps and recognize the important areas that have been ignored, which serves as a key building block of theory development

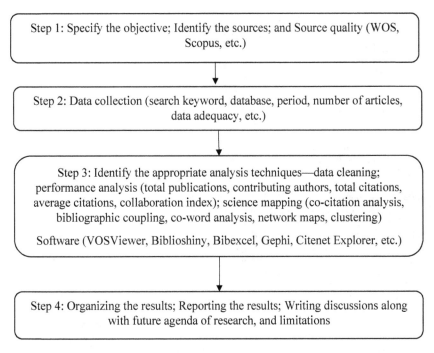

Fig. 3. Overall Process of Conducting Bibliometric Analysis Paper.
Source: Authors.

(Jaakkola, 2020; Rana et al., 2020). The bibliometric studies can contribute to practice and be utilized by the universities that evaluate the relative performance of the authors and help them in justifiable decision-making. Additionally, this review will help the reviewers to understand the important components of bibliometric papers and in evaluating the bibliometric review articles appropriately.

8. CONCLUSION

The study explained the bibliometric review with the standpoint that it can be considered a strong review method for analyzing a large volume of data and scholars can supplement their traditional reviews with bibliometric reviews to strengthen their knowledge base. In doing so, the *what, when, why, how,* and *where* of the bibliometric review were explained. The study highlighted two main categories of bibliometric analysis, namely, citation-based performance analysis and scientific mapping. Different types of analysis were explained through bibliometric indicators along with various research questions that will help scholars in understanding the output and draw meaningful inferences. In addition, the ideas presented to conduct the bibliometric reviews have been suggested based on the articles published in the A and A* categories of journals. Therefore, scholars can use this approach for clarifying construct definition and advancing theory and practice by exposing emerging perspectives (Post et al., 2020) through bibliometric findings.

REFERENCES

Akbari, M., Foroudi, P., Fashami, R. Z., Mahavarpour, N., & Khodayari, M. (2022). Let us talk about something: The evolution of e-WOM from the past to the future. *Journal of Business Research*, *149*, 663–689.

Archambault, É., & Larivière, V. (2010). The limits of bibliometrics for the analysis of the social sciences and humanities literature. *World Social Science Report 2009/2010*, 251–254.

Aria, M., & Cuccurullo, C. (2017). Bibliometrix: An R-tool for comprehensive science mapping analysis. *Journal of Informetrics*, *11*(4), 959–975.

Baber, R., Upadhyay, Y., Baber, P., & Kaurav, R. P. S. (2022). Three decades of consumer ethnocentrism research: A bibliometric analysis. *Business Perspectives and Research*. https://doi.org/ 10.1177/22785337221098472

Baber, R., Upadhyay, Y., Baber, P., & Kaurav, R. P. S. (2023). Three decades of consumer ethnocentrism research: A bibliometric analysis. *Business Perspectives and Research*, *11*(1), 137–158.

Baker, H. K., Pandey, N., Kumar, S., & Haldar, A. (2020). A bibliometric analysis of board diversity: Current status, development, and future research directions. *Journal of Business Research*, *108*, 232–246.

Beckendorff, P., & Zehrer, A. (2013). A network analysis of tourism research. *Annals of Tourism Research*, *43*, 121–149.

Bhattacharya, S., & Sharma, R. P. (2022). Advanced services accelerating servitization: A review synthesis and future research agenda. In S. Rana, Sakshi, & J. Singh (Eds.), *Exploring the latest trends in management literature (Review of management literature, Vol. 1)* (pp. 169–183). Emerald Publishing Limited. https://doi.org/10.1108/S2754-586520220000001009

Blanco-Encomienda, F. J., & Rosillo-Díaz, E. (2021). Quantitative evaluation of the production and trends in research applying the structural equation modelling method. *Scientometrics*, *126*(2), 1599–1617.

Block, J. H., & Fisch, C. (2020). Eight tips and questions for your bibliographic study in business and management research. *Management Review Quarterly*, *70*, 307–312. https://doi.org/10.1007/ s11301-020-00188-4

Bornmann, L., & Marx, W. (2012). HistCite analysis of papers constituting the h index research front. *Journal of Informetrics*, *6*(2), 285–288.

Broadus, R. N. (1987). Toward a definition of "bibliometrics". *Scientometrics*, *12*(5), 373–379.

Budler, M., Župič, I., & Trkman, P. (2021). The development of business model research: A bibliometric review. *Journal of Business Research*, *135*, 480–495.

Cabeza-Ramírez, L. J., Cañizares, S. M. S., & Fuentes-García, F. J. (2020). From bibliometrics to entrepreneurship: A study of studies. *Revista Española de Documentación Científica*, *43*, 37.

Cobo, M. J., López-Herrera, A. G., Herrera-Viedma, E., & Herrera, F. (2011). Science mapping software tools: Review, analysis, and cooperative study among tools. *Journal of the American Society for Information Science and Technology*, *62*(7), 1382–1402.

Cronin, S., Hardiman, O., & Traynor, B. J. (2007). Ethnic variation in the incidence of ALS: A systematic review. *Neurology*, *68*(13), 1002–1007.

Donthu, N., Kumar, S., Mukherjee, D., Pandey, N., & Lim, W. M. (2021). How to conduct a bibliometric analysis: An overview and guidelines. *Journal of Business Research*, *133*, 285–296.

Ellegaard, O., & Wallin, J. A. (2015). The bibliometric analysis of scholarly production: How great is the impact? *Scientometrics*, *105*(3), 1809–1831.

Fahimnia, B., Sarkis, J., & Davarzani, H. (2015). Green supply chain management: A review and bibliometric analysis. *International Journal of Production Economics*, *162*, 101–114.

Fan, D., Breslin, D., Callahan, J. L., & Iszatt-White, M. (2022). Advancing literature review methodology through rigour, generativity, scope and transparency. *International Journal of Management Reviews*, *24*(2), 171–180.

Ford, J. B., Bezbaruah, S., Mukherji, P., Jain, V., & Merchant, A. (2021). A decade (2008–2019) of advertising research productivity: A bibliometric review. *Journal of Business Research*, *136*, 137–163.

Garfield, E. (2004). Historiographic mapping of knowledge domains literature. *Journal of Information Science, 30*(2), 119–145.

Garfield, E., & Pudovkin, A. I. (2004, November). The HistCite system for mapping and bibliometric analysis of the output of searches using the ISI Web of Knowledge. In *Proceedings of the 67th annual meeting of the American society for information science and technology* (Vol. 83). Information Today Inc.

Garfield, E., Pudovkin, A. I., & Istomin, V. S. (2003a). Why do we need algorithmic historiography? *Journal of the American Society for Information Science and Technology, 54*(5), 400–412.

Garfield, E., Pudovkin, A. I., & Istomin, V. S. (2003b). Mapping the output of topical searches in the Web of Knowledge and the case of Watson-Crick. *Information Technology and Libraries, 22*(4), 183–187.

Geissdoerfer, M., Savaget, P., Bocken, N. M., & Hultink, E. J. (2017). The circular economy – A new sustainability paradigm? *Journal of Cleaner Production, 143*, 757–768.

Guo, F., Ye, G., Hudders, L., Lv, W., Li, M., & Duffy, V. G. (2019). Product placement in mass media: A review and bibliometric analysis. *Journal of Advertising, 48*(2), 215–231.

Guzzo, R. A., Jackson, S. E., & Katzell, R. A. (1987). Meta-analysis analysis. *Research in Organizational Behavior, 9*(1), 407–442.

Haddaway, N. R., Woodcock, P., Macura, B., & Collins, A. (2015). Making literature reviews more reliable through application of lessons from systematic reviews. *Conservation Biology, 29*(6), 1596–1605.

Hicks, D. (1999). The difficulty of achieving full coverage of international social science literature and the bibliometric consequences. *Scientometrics, 44*(2), 193–215.

Higgins, J. P. T., & Green, S. (2011). *Cochrane Handbook for Systematic Reviews of Interventions Version 5.1.0* [updated March 2011]. The Cochrane Collaboration. www.cochrane-handbook. org

Hollebeek, L. D., Sharma, T. G., Pandey, R., Sanyal, P., & Clark, M. K. (2021). Fifteen years of customer engagement research: A bibliometric and network analysis. *Journal of Product & Brand Management, 31*(2), 293–309.

Hood, W., & Wilson, C. (2001). The literature of bibliometrics, scientometrics, and informetrics. *Scientometrics, 52*(2), 291–314.

Hulland, J., & Houston, M. B. (2020). Why systematic review papers and meta-analyses matter: An introduction to the special issue on generalizations in marketing. *Journal of the Academy of Marketing Science, 48*(3), 351–359.

Ivanović, L., & Ho, Y. S. (2019). Highly cited articles in the education and educational research category in the social science citation index: A bibliometric analysis. *Educational Review, 71*(3), 277–286.

Jaakkola, E. (2020). Designing conceptual articles: Four approaches. *AMS Review, 10*(1), 18–26.

Kaurav, R. P. S., & Gupta, P. (2022). Trends in multidiscipline management research: Past, present and future of FIIB Business Review. *FIIB Business Review.* https://doi.org/10.1177/23197145221136966

Kaushal, N., Kaurav, R. P. S., Sivathanu, B., & Kaushik, N. (2021). Artificial intelligence and HRM: Identifying future research agenda using systematic literature review and bibliometric analysis. *Management Review Quarterly*, 1–39. https://doi.org/10.1007/s11301-021-00249-2

Keathley-Herring, H., Van Aken, E., Gonzalez-Aleu, F., Deschamps, F., Letens, G., & Orlandini, P. C. (2016). Assessing the maturity of a research area: Bibliometric review and proposed framework. *Scientometrics, 109*(2), 927–951.

Kessler, M. M. (1963). Bibliographic coupling between scientific papers. *American Documentation, 14*(1), 10–25.

Khanra, S., Dhir, A., Parida, V., & Kohtamäki, M. (2021). Servitization research: A review and bibliometric analysis of past achievements and future promises. *Journal of Business Research, 131*, 151–166.

Koseoglu, M. A., Rahimi, R., Okumus, F., & Liu, J. (2016). Bibliometric studies in tourism. *Annals of Tourism Research, 61*, 180–198.

Kraus, S., Li, H., Kang, Q., Westhead, P., & Tiberius, V. (2020). The sharing economy: A bibliometric analysis of the state-of-the-art. *International Journal of Entrepreneurial Behavior & Research*, 26(8), 1769–1786.

Kumar, A., Sharma, S., & Mahdavi, M. (2021). Machine learning (ML) technologies for digital credit scoring in rural finance: A literature review. *Risks*, 9(11), 192.

Lim, W. M., Kumar, S., & Ali, F. (2022). Advancing knowledge through literature reviews: "What", "why", and "how to contribute". *The Service Industries Journal*, 42(7–8), 481–513.

Livoreil, B., Glanville, J., Haddaway, N. R., Bayliss, H., Bethel, A., de Lachapelle, F. F, ... & Frampton, G. (2017). Systematic searching for environmental evidence using multiple tools and sources. *Environmental Evidence*, 6(1), 1–14.

Martínez-López, F. J., Merigó, J. M., Valenzuela-Fernández, L., & Nicolás, C. (2018). Fifty years of the European Journal of Marketing: A bibliometric analysis. *European Journal of Marketing*, 52(1/2), 439–468.

Merigó, J. M., Mas-Tur, A., Roig-Tierno, N., & Ribeiro-Soriano, D. (2015). A bibliometric overview of the Journal of Business Research between 1973 and 2014. *Journal of Business Research*, 68(12), 2645–2653.

Moed, H. F. (2010). Measuring contextual citation impact of scientific journals. *Journal of Informetrics*, 4(3), 265–277.

Mortazavi, S., Eslami, M. H., Hajikhani, A., & Väätänen, J. (2021). Mapping inclusive innovation: A bibliometric study and literature review. *Journal of Business Research*, 122, 736–750.

Mukherjee, D., Lim, W. M., Kumar, S., & Donthu, N. (2022). Guidelines for advancing theory and practice through bibliometric research. *Journal of Business Research*, 148, 101–115.

Mumu, J. R., Saona, P., Mamun, M. A. A., & Azad, M. A. K. (2022). Is trust gender biased? A bibliometric review of trust in E-commerce. *Journal of Internet Commerce*, 21(2), 217–245.

Nakagawa, S., Samarasinghe, G., Haddaway, N. R., Westgate, M. J., O'Dea, R. E., Noble, D. W., & Lagisz, M. (2019). Research weaving: Visualizing the future of research synthesis. *Trends in Ecology & Evolution*, 34(3), 224–238.

Narin, F., Olivastro, D., & Stevens, K. A. (1994). Bibliometrics/theory, practice and problems. *Evaluation Review*, 18(1), 65–76.

Norder, K., Emich, K., Kanar, A., Sawhney, A., & Behrend, T. S. (2022). A house divided: A multilevel bibliometric review of the job search literature 1973–2020. *Journal of Business Research*, 151, 100–117.

Palmatier, R. W., Houston, M. B., & Hulland, J. (2018). Review articles: Purpose, process, and structure. *Journal of the Academy of Marketing Science*, 46(1), 1–5.

Patra, S. K., & Mishra, S. (2006). Bibliometric study of bioinformatics literature. *Scientometrics*, 67(3), 477–489.

Paul, J., & Criado, A. R. (2020). The art of writing literature review: What do we know and what do we need to know? *International Business Review*, 29(4), 101717.

Pautasso, M. (2013). Ten simple rules for writing a literature review. *PLoS Computational Biology*, 9(7), e1003149.

Perez-Vega, R., Hopkinson, P., Singhal, A., & Mariani, M. M. (2022). From CRM to social CRM: A bibliometric review and research agenda for consumer research. *Journal of Business Research*, 151, 1–16.

Pilkington, A., & Chai, K. H. (2008). Research themes, concepts and relationships: A study of International Journal of Service Industry Management (1990–2005). *International Journal of Service Industry Management*, 19(1), 83–110.

Post, C., Sarala, R., Gatrell, C., & Prescott, J. E. (2020). Advancing theory with review articles. *Journal of Management Studies*, 57(2), 351–376.

Pritchard, A. (1969). Statistical bibliography or bibliometrics. *Journal of Documentation*, 25(4), 348.

Ramos-Rodríguez, A. R., & Ruíz-Navarro, J. (2004). Changes in the intellectual structure of strategic management research: A bibliometric study of the Strategic Management Journal, 1980–2000. *Strategic Management Journal*, 25(10), 981–1004.

Rana, S., Raut, S. K., Prashar, S., & Hamid, A. B. A. (2020). Promoting through consumer nostalgia: A conceptual framework and future research agenda. *Journal of Promotion Management*, 27(2), 211–249.

Rana, S., Sakshi, & Singh, J. (2022). Presenting the POWER Framework of Conducting Literature Review. In S. Rana, Sakshi, & J. Singh (Eds.), *Exploring the latest trends in management literature (Review of management literature, Vol. 1)* (pp. 1–13). Emerald Publishing Limited. https://doi.org/10.1108/S2754-586520220000001001

Romanelli, J. P., Gonçalves, M. C. P., de Abreu Pestana, L. F., Soares, J. A. H., Boschi, R. S., & Andrade, D. F. (2021). Four challenges when conducting bibliometric reviews and how to deal with them. *Environmental Science and Pollution Research, 28*(43), 60448–60458.

Schoepflin, U., & Glänzel, W. (2001). Two decades of "Scientometrics". An interdisciplinary field represented by its leading journal. *Scientometrics, 50*(2), 301–312.

Schwert, G. W. (1993, June). The Journal of Financial Economics: A retrospective evaluation (1974–1991). *Journal of Financial Economics,* 369–424.

Si, H., Shi, J. G., Tang, D., Wen, S., Miao, W., & Duan, K. (2019). Application of the theory of planned behavior in environmental science: A comprehensive bibliometric analysis. *International Journal of Environmental Research and Public Health, 16*(15), 2788.

Small, H. (1973). Co-citation in the scientific literature: A new measure of the relationship between two documents. *Journal of the American Society for Information Science, 24*(4), 265–269.

Subramony, M., Groth, M., Hu, X. J., & Wu, Y. (2021). Four decades of frontline service employee research: An integrative bibliometric review. *Journal of Service Research, 24*(2), 230–248.

Tranfield, D., Denyer, D., & Smart, P. (2003). Towards a methodology for developing evidence-informed management knowledge by means of a systematic review. *British Journal of Management, 14*(3), 207–222.

Tunger, D., & Eulerich, M. (2018). Bibliometric analysis of corporate governance research in German-speaking countries: Applying bibliometrics to business research using a custom-made database. *Scientometrics, 117*(3), 2041–2059.

Van Eck, N., & Waltman, L. (2010). Software survey: VOSviewer, a computer program for biblio-metric mapping. *Scientometrics, 84*(2), 523–538.

Van Eck, N. J., & Waltman, L. (2011). Text mining and visualization using VOSviewer. *ISSI News-letter, 7*(3), 50–54.

Van Raan, A. (2019). Measuring science: Basic principles and application of advanced bibliometrics. In *Springer Handbook of Science and Technology Indicators* (pp. 237–280). Springer.

Varma, A., Kumar, S., Lim, W. M. M., & Pandey, N. (2022). Personnel review at age 50: A retro-spective using bibliometric analysis. *Personnel Review.* https://doi.org/10.1108/PR-05-2021-0313

Weingarten, E., & Goodman, J. K. (2021). Re-examining the experiential advantage in consumption: A meta-analysis and review. *Journal of Consumer Research, 47*(6), 855–877.

White, K., Habib, R., & Hardisty, D. J. (2019). How to SHIFT consumer behaviors to be more sustainable: A literature review and guiding framework. *Journal of Marketing, 83*(3), 22–49. https://doi.org/10.1177/0022242919825649

Wieland, L. S., Cramer, H., Lauche, R., Verstappen, A., Parker, E. A., & Pilkington, K. (2021). Evidence on yoga for health: A bibliometric analysis of systematic reviews. *Complementary Therapies in Medicine, 60,* 102746.

Williams, A. M., & Baláž, V. (2012). Migration, risk, and uncertainty: Theoretical perspectives. *Population, Space and Place, 18*(2), 167–180.

Xu, X., Chen, X., Jia, F., Brown, S., Gong, Y., & Xu, Y. (2018). Supply chain finance: A systematic literature review and bibliometric analysis. *International Journal of Production Economics, 204,* 160–173.

Zupic, I., & Čater, T. (2015). Bibliometric methods in management and organization. *Organizational Research Methods, 18*(3), 429–472.

A CRITICAL REVIEW OF LITERATURE REVIEW METHODOLOGIES

Amna Farrukh and Aymen Sajjad

ABSTRACT

A literature review or review article is an integral part of a scientific body of research which synthesizes prior knowledge and provides a holistic overview of a subject domain. While several studies emphasize the significance of literature reviews and include the guidelines for conducting a review, limited studies demonstrated different types of literature review methodologies in a comprehensive way. Accordingly, this chapter presents various types of review methodologies which includes narrative, descriptive, systematic, meta-analysis, hybrid, umbrella, scoping, theoretical, and critical reviews. In addition, the authors' skills including logical reasoning, content analysis, literature mapping, critical writing, and ethical consideration are presented. Further, quality aspects of the literature review are discussed such as the rigor and relevance of the selected studies. Overall, this chapter provides implications for researchers in understanding types of literature review methodologies along with their objectives, strengths, and weaknesses which can assist them in selecting a suitable methodology while conducting a review.

Keywords: Literature review; review methodologies; authors' skills; critical reasoning; quality of literature review; management literature

1. INTRODUCTION

High-quality literature reviews are imperative for accumulating knowledge, synthesizing empirical findings, developing novel theories, understanding the depth and breadth of a research phenomenon, and identifying unexplored areas for future research, which require further investigation. By accumulating

Advancing Methodologies of Conducting Literature Review in Management Domain
Review of Management Literature, Volume 2, 103–123
Copyright © 2024 Amna Farrukh and Aymen Sajjad
Published under exclusive licence by Emerald Publishing Limited
ISSN: 2754-5865/doi:10.1108/S2754-586520230000002006

scattered findings and integrating diverse knowledge streams on a particular area of inquiry, literature reviews play an important role in developing academic scholarship (Paré et al., 2015; Rana et al., 2022). Further, an effective and well-structured review helps in building a strong foundation for advancing knowledge and theory development of a phenomenon under consideration (Paré et al., 2015). By critically analyzing and synthesizing findings of diverse conceptual and/or empirical studies in a systematic way, a review of literature can help in offering potential pathways for research that are to be explored in future research endeavors (Snyder, 2019).

Fink (2019, p. 6) defined a literature review as "a systematic, explicit, and reproducible method for identifying, evaluating, and interpreting the existing body of original work." Similarly, a review of literature can be broadly described as a "more or less systematic way of collecting and synthesizing previous research" (Snyder, 2019). It must include the following two elements: (i) a review of selected studies, different theories, problems, emerging areas, and main themes in a research domain and (ii) an illustration of studies and framing them into a theoretical context (Alajami, 2021). Hence, the literature review process not merely serves the purpose of surveying the literature but also critically and systematically analyzing the studies relevant to a research topic (Cooper, 1985). According to Hart (1998), a literature review aims to (i) present the existing body of knowledge by revealing the work which has been done and the research gaps, (ii) identify key variables pertinent to a research area, (iii) accumulate prior research studies and their results, (iv) reveal significant methodologies and techniques used in a research domain, and (v) justify the significance of a research problem.

While literature reviews are generally found in journals, books, conference proceedings, and other modes of research writing to summarize the significant findings in a subject domain, there is a lack of information about how studies are selected, analyzed, integrated, and the findings are presented in a robust manner (Jaidka et al., 2013). In addition, there is a lack of well-structured theory and method-based reviews published in recognized journals (Paul & Criado, 2020). Further, there are not many articles presenting the literature review types in a comprehensive way (Grant & Booth, 2009). To bridge the above gaps, the primary objective of this chapter is to highlight the significance of the literature review, illustrate different types of literature review, and demonstrate the quality aspects of conducting a quality review. The remainder of the chapter is organized as follows. Section 2 presents the importance and value of the literature review in developing academic scholarship. Section 3 explains various types of literature review methodologies and Section 4 highlights the author's (review author) skills while conducting a review. Section 5 discusses the quality concerns in the literature review, which is followed by the summary and conclusion section.

2. SIGNIFICANCE OF LITERATURE REVIEWS

In the academic context, the term "review" is used interchangeably with similar terminologies and concepts such as "literature review" and "theoretical background" (Paré et al., 2015). The literature review section of an article includes the theoretical background, an overview of a topic, and gaps related to a specific field leading to a research question (Okoli & Schabram, 2010). It is recognized as an "essential first step and foundation when undertaking a research project" (Baker, 2000). Thus, a literature review section enables a researcher to provide careful synthesis and analysis of the theoretical background of the selected issue, phenomenon or topic of research inquiry, articulate a research problem, present adequate research methodologies, and justify the purpose of a study by highlighting the gaps in the existing body of knowledge, which finally lead to a research question (Paré et al., 2015).

The literature review methodology is centered around the nature of the research question to be addressed in the study. Following the research question, the discussion on the topic should narrow down to the specific issue from a broad topic (Denney & Tewksbury, 2013). As a result, the reader can understand the existing knowledge, research gaps, scope of the study, and justification of the study. A well-presented literature review not only presents an overview of the research area but also provides the reader with an in-depth understanding of a research issue/problem along with its justification (Alajami, 2021). Hence, a literature review revolves around the knowledge about a research topic including the conceptual understanding and recent findings in an area under scrutiny. Additionally, a literature review is recognized as a "multidimensional concept" linked with certain aspects of research which require profound research abilities (Alajami, 2021). Accordingly, the significance of the literature review stems from the fact that by conducting the review, a researcher develops a better understanding of the research topic that is obtained through in-depth knowledge of a research topic and by critically reviewing the theoretical and practical dimensions of the selected studies (Hart, 2018).

Pautasso (2013) has recommended the following key points which need to be considered in reviewing the literature: (i) a clear presentation of the research topic/problem for the audience including supervisors, the public, examiners, policymakers, researchers, and practitioners who can benefit from the review, (ii) continuous search of the appropriate review material, (iii) data collection and storage of the reviewed material, (iv) selection of the adequate review methodology, (v) logical structure of the review, and (vi) quality assurance of the review based on the relevance and validity (Mohammed & Ahmed, 2019).

The concept of "literature review" is defined as an overview of academic research in a particular subject domain and can be conducted as part of a conceptual/ empirical study and an independent (standalone) study (Lim et al., 2022). From a conceptual or empirical study perspective, the literature review fosters developing the theoretical background of a study and familiarizing readers with the main areas and key concepts in the existing body of knowledge. Accordingly, a literature review provides the basis of knowledge which supports developing a particular study (Lim et al., 2022). Being an independent study, a review article is centered around the literature review regarding a specific research issue. In this way, the literature review primarily presents an in-depth reflection and provides readers with "a bird's eye view of the state of the body of knowledge" of a particular research domain along with the major contributions and future research directions (Lim et al., 2022). While a literature review can be used as part of an empirical or conceptual study and as a standalone review, it does not create new knowledge, instead, it integrates the existing knowledge in a coherent fashion, which in turn provides a foundation for further development of new knowledge in a particular area of research inquiry (Lim et al., 2022).

In addition, the value of a literature review can be determined by analyzing its necessity. Literature reviews are necessary for empirical or conceptual research as they provide a theoretical background to justify the need for the study and logical reasoning behind developing hypotheses and propositions as well as key research questions (Lim et al., 2022). In an independent study, the literature reviews are essential to identify the key themes from the accumulated knowledge which can facilitate evaluating the main streams and emerging streams of research along with the contributions and research gaps (Lim et al., 2022).

3. TYPES OF LITERATURE REVIEW METHODOLOGIES

The following section provides details on different types of literature review methodologies including narrative, descriptive, systematic, meta-analysis, hybrid, umbrella, theoretical, and critical reviews.

3.1 Narrative Review

A narrative review is one of the most frequently used methodologies to conduct a literature review in which the author reads available literature in a specific domain, determines its significance, synthesizes the current body of knowledge, and then presents the analysis of the reviewed literature (Green, 2009; Pickering et al., 2014). Narrative reviews are commonly used in a variety of literature disciplines such as pharmacy (Toma & Crişan, 2018), dentistry (Piedra-Cascon et al., 2021), and manufacturing (Sony et al., 2020). Additionally, narrative reviews offer valuable insights into issues such as the state of existing research, research domains/areas, and locations which can be utilized by other researchers to plan and conduct further research (Collins & Fauser, 2005). For example, a study followed a narrative review on reporting biases, particularly on selective outcome reporting and publication bias to analyze the intensity of the problem in the medical field (McGauran et al., 2010). This type of review is often invited by journals in which subject area experts are contacted to conduct an in-depth review of a specific topic (Pickering et al., 2014). Narrative reviews depend primarily on the author/reviewer's knowledge and interpretation of the subject domain and generally focus on what is known, rather than what is not known (Pickering et al., 2014). Therefore, narrative reviews are often undertaken by researchers who are experts in their subject areas (Green, 2009).

Narrative reviews aim to identify the information regarding a topic or subject; however, the generalization aspects of knowledge accumulation in a specific research domain are not considered in this type of review (Davies, 2000; Green et al., 2006). In particular, narrative reviews distinguish from other review types in several aspects as these reviews search only those studies which are readily accessible and do not follow a comprehensive and systematic search methodology for identifying the research articles (Davies, 2000). Further, the limitation of these reviews is a lack of explanation regarding the process and procedures of conducting the literature review, thereby considered to be more subjective in nature owing to transparent and well-documented procedures for selecting review papers. This limitation of narrative review further results in a lack of reproducibility and replicability of the review results in case someone follows this method even if there is no biasedness (Paré et al., 2015). In addition to the limitation regarding the relevant literature identification, the narrative review follows informal methods of data analysis to synthesize prior literature such as interpretation or commentary (Dixon-Woods et al., 2005; Paré et al., 2015).

Despite presenting useful information and its application in a variety of fields, this type of review inherits biases such as these are largely dependent on the expertise, judgments, and competencies of the author (Borenstein et al., 2021; Pickering et al., 2014) compared to systematic literature reviews (Borenstein et al., 2021). Though research students also conduct narrative reviews, their chances of acceptance and publication are low due to the biases and limitations of this review type (Kamler, 2008; Pickering & Byrne, 2014). The methodology used to generate knowledge and information is selective and based on the author's personal criteria, thus, lacking rigor, standardization, and transparency (Pickering et al., 2014). Additionally, the structure of this review is more descriptive and narrative and not aligned with the format of research papers which follows the traditional pattern of abstract, introduction, methodology, findings, discussion, and conclusion (Pickering et al., 2014).

3.2 Descriptive Reviews

Descriptive reviews enable the emergence of logical patterns and trends from the empirical studies while considering prior theories, findings, methodologies, and propositions in a specific research domain (King & He, 2005). Accordingly, this type of review captures, categorizes and analyses numerical data related to authors, methods, and frequency of research topics in the existing body of literature, thus addressing the generalization aspects (King & He, 2005; Rumrill et al., 2010). Descriptive reviews follow a structured method of identifying research studies and evaluating data. For example, descriptive reviews include frequency analysis to generate quantitative results using the information extracted from each study such as the year of publication and research methodology, as well as a demonstration of significant and non-significant findings. In particular, each study in the descriptive review is considered as a unit of analysis and the whole database comprise existing literature in a particular domain. By conducting descriptive reviews, the author aims to determine the logical patterns to provide an overall picture of the existing theories, methodologies, concepts, and findings of studies (Paré et al., 2015). For example, a study performed a descriptive review to examine the ethical considerations regarding digital technologies for mental health which primarily focused on patients suffering from schizophrenia (Chivilgina et al., 2021). Similarly, a recent study investigated the impact of the COVID-19 pandemic on global supply chain sustainability addressing the issues of social sustainability and resilience in global supply chains. The study also presented potential pathways for future research such as protecting employees, building resilience, embracing advanced digital technologies, promoting a delicate balance between diversification, regionalization, and localization, and most importantly focusing on collaboration aspects among a range of stakeholder groups (Sajjad, 2021).

3.3 Scoping Reviews

Scoping reviews facilitate researchers in identifying key research activities, research gaps, and the significance of the comprehensive systematic literature review (Arksey & O'Malley, 2005; Rumrill et al., 2010). It focuses on the breadth of literature on a specific topic similar to the narrative and descriptive review methodologies. However, the scoping review aims to cover a research topic holistically as compared to the narrative and descriptive literature review (Paré et al., 2015). In doing so, the researcher needs to consider different constraints including time, financial resources, and accessibility while addressing the feasibility and comprehensiveness (Pieper et al., 2012).

Scoping reviews initially establish the inclusion and exclusion criteria which aid researchers in eliminating the out-of-scope research studies or studies that do not address the research question. As a requirement of the scoping reviews, at least two independent researchers first need to review and codify the studies' abstracts after applying the search strategy and then analyze full articles to be included in the final sample (Daudt et al., 2013). Scoping reviews synthesize salient findings of the selected studies through content analysis and thematic analysis and present these in a tabular form (Paré et al., 2015). In addition, scoping reviews focus on exploring the scope and nature of a broad research area, thereby examining the research trends in a particular topic which leads to answering a "generic" research question (Paré et al., 2015). For example, La Rosa et al. (2020) conducted a scoping review to summarize the evidence-based knowledge on the occurrence and persistence of coronavirus in water environments including wastewater, drinking water, seawater, freshwater, and surface water.

Scoping reviews aim to examine the type and scope of the research phenomenon, generally ongoing research. Moreover, the scoping reviews share several commonalities with the systematic literature reviews including transparency, replicability, and systematicity. By doing so, these reviews facilitate researchers in deciding whether a comprehensive systematic literature review is needed (Grant & Booth, 2009). Although, scoping review is a comprehensive method, quality assessment of the selected studies is a challenge due to the risks of including grey literature in the final selection of the articles (Levac et al., 2010; Paré et al., 2015). Another limitation of the scoping reviews is the lack of rigor and quality assessment in the study selection. Consequently, the findings of the scoping reviews lack practical and policy implications (Grant & Booth, 2009).

3.4 Systematic Reviews

Systematic reviews emerged as a result of the "evidence-based medicine movement" (Paré et al., 2015) during the late 1970s and early 1980s to assist researchers in collecting and synthesizing the available knowledge and information regarding the health case interferences to be reliably used in effective decision-making (Grant & Booth, 2009). The typology of the systematic reviews and methods of conducting the systematic review has evolved over time in different research fields and among different groups of researchers and authors (Grant & Booth, 2009; Schagrin et al., 2011).

Systematic literature reviews are different from narrative reviews as these are transparent and follow a standardized and explicit methodology to identify the relevant literature, hence falling into a positivist paradigm. Following this, the research findings are reproducible (Petticrew & Roberts, 2006; Pickering & Byrne, 2013). In addition, systematic reviews are more comprehensive in creating knowledge and information in a research area (Petticrew & Roberts, 2006). Nevertheless, the systematic literature reviews include narrow and pre-defined research questions, hence covering a limited area in a subject domain (Borenstein et al., 2021; Pickering et al., 2014). This type of review is further categorized into quantitative, weighted, and meta-analysis based on the requirements and extent of the quantitative and statistical analysis of the data extracted from the papers (Pickering et al., 2014).

3.5 Meta-Analysis

Meta-analysis includes the implementation of statistical techniques to retrieve and aggregate data and information and present it in the form of correlation coefficients, mean, and risk ratios from two or more similar types of research studies (King & He, 2005; Paré et al., 2015). This review methodology has four main objectives which are: (i) to assess the consistency and/or variability between the research studies, (ii) to examine and rationalize the causes of heterogeneity (if any) between the studies, (iii) to provide the confidence interval along with cumulative effect size, and (iv) analyze the robustness of the overall effect size applying sensitivity analyses and evaluating the potential causes of biasedness and variability emanating from the primary studies which could affect the cumulative effect size. Following this, meta-analyses combine "statistically significant and non-significant findings" resulting from the selected studies (Paré et al., 2015). In this way, meta-analyses can provide precise estimates of the effects of a research phenomenon compared to the individual studies investigated through discrete sources of information (Paré et al., 2015; Rosenthal & DiMatteo, 2001). Thus, meta-analysis is recognized as one of the strong review methodologies facilitating researchers to extract useful information and meaningful inferences from the studies in the review. Compared with the qualitative systematic reviews that narratively present the knowledge, this methodology is more precise due to the use of statistical techniques for data evaluation and can observe the patterns, moderators, and mediators emerging from the data and examine the relationship between the study findings (Paré et al., 2015; Rosenthal & DiMatteo, 2001). For instance, a study evaluated the carbon footprint of three systems of dairy milk production namely pasture-based production system, mixed production system, and confinement production system (zero grazing during lactation) using a meta-analysis methodology (Lorenz et al., 2019).

Meta-analysis statistically aggregates the findings of quantitative studies to "provide a more precise effect of the results" (Grant & Booth, 2009). An effective meta-analysis primarily includes similar studies and characteristics such as the population being studied, and comparisons and interferences examined in the studies. Above all, the meta-analysis emphasizes the same study characteristics to be measured in the same way against the same time intervals. However, a risk associated with the meta-analysis methodology is to include the combination of "apples and oranges" (Grant & Booth, 2009) i.e., synthesis of the studies which are not similar and may mislead the concluding results (Grant & Booth, 2009).

3.6 Qualitative Systematic Reviews

Qualitative systematic reviews aim to investigate, explore, and summarize the data from quantitative research studies to determine the direction, size, consistency, and strength of the effect of studies selected in a review. Qualitative systematic reviews focus on integrating and comparing the findings leading to developing a new theory by evaluating the emergent themes and constructs from within and across the individual qualitative studies (Grant & Booth, 2009). This methodology follows the traditional process of systematic literature review; however, it is different from the meta-analysis as it synthesizes and presents the findings using narrative and subjective techniques as compared to the statistical ones (Higgins et al., 2019; Paré et al., 2015). While statistical and numerical analysis of the data including correction analysis, confidence interval, ratios, and p-values can be employed simultaneously, the key characteristic of this methodology is to present the findings in a textual format/approach after analyzing the data extracted from the review of the empirical studies (Paré et al., 2015). Following this, the review author(s) generally employ the content analysis technique as part of the data analysis methodology comprising frameworks, clusters, categorization, and tabular presentation of various characteristics (such as limitations, objectives, and purpose) of the studies. Using this technique, aggregating, and summarizing the key findings of the studies; the authors present the conclusion, recommendations, research gaps, and future research direction (Paré et al., 2015). For example, Farrukh et al. (2022a) conducted a qualitative systematic review to analyze the environmental burden of flexible packaging such as greenhouse gas emissions, soil pollution, health hazards, energy footprint, food waste, and marine pollution associated with its manufacturing and post-consumer use. Similarly, another study in the area of sustainable supply chain management performed a content analysis technique including the descriptive analysis (such as research methodology adopted in the selected studies, journal publications according to time period, articles distribution in different journals, and sustainability dimensions addressed in articles) along with a conceptual framework development (Seuring & Müller, 2008). The framework comprised three parts: (i) triggers for sustainable supply chain management, (ii) risk and performance management related to suppliers, and (iii) supply chain management for sustainable products.

In addition to the narrative explanation, qualitative systematic reviews may also use a quasi-quantitative technique known as vote counting to investigate the direction and consistency of the effect or relationship between studies selected for the review. Vote counting is also recognized as box scoring which uses statistical interpretation such as *p*-values and probabilities determined in the individual studies to compare the significant and non-significant results of several studies accepting or rejecting a hypothesis (Hedges & Olkin, 1980; King & He, 2005). For example, vote counting can be used to determine the number of studies about a specific environmental management system (e.g., ISO 14001) to be positively correlated with organizational characteristics such as discrete or process industry and large or small and medium-sized companies.

Qualitative systematic review methods are still evolving and there is considerable disagreement regarding the use of different approaches to conducting this methodology such as either comprehensive search strategies are needed to identify relevant qualitative studies or a selective approach is required to determine the sample research studies representing a holistic picture of a research phenomenon (Grant & Booth, 2009). Although it is an easy and straightforward technique, it can mislead the overall synthesis/results and significant statistical interpretation of the analysis in case if relatively a small sample size of studies is selected in a review (Hedges & Olkin, 1980; Paré et al., 2015).

3.7 Umbrella Reviews

Umbrella reviews are recognized as "overview of reviews" (Paré et al., 2015) and are considered as a tertiary technique that combines relevant knowledge and information from multiple types of reviews (such as qualitative and quantitative reviews) into a single document addressing a narrow research question (Paré et al., 2015; Smith et al., 2011). It is an emerging methodology in the health sciences domain to synthesize the evidence due to an increasing number of systematic reviews published in journals (Hartling et al., 2012). According to Bastian et al. (2010), nearly 11 new systematic reviews and 75 trials are published and listed in MEDLINE (medical literature analysis and retrieval system online). In addition, the growing number of systematic reviews attempt to answer similar types of research questions with a constant increase in contradictory findings and misleading interpretations (Paré et al., 2015). Such conflicting results can mislead and pose significant challenges for the potential audience including researchers, policymakers, stakeholders, decision-makers, and practitioners in effective decision-making who largely rely on the evidence and knowledge generated from these reviews (Jadad et al., 1997). Accordingly, umbrella reviews are considered as a strong review methodology to present an overview of reviews which can address the above shortcomings. A study conducted an umbrella review in the field of sport and exercise psychology to examine reviews published on mental health and exercise/physical activities (Faulkner et al., 2021). However, there is no standard technical term for this methodology and it is known as "overview of systematic reviews," "systematic review of systematic reviews," "umbrella reviews," and "meta-reviews" (Paré et al., 2015).

While this methodology is evolving, it enhances the methodological rigor of the findings of the systematic reviews by employing explicit techniques such as AMSTAR (assessment of multiple systematic reviews) (Shea et al., 2009) and GRADE (grading of recommendations assessment, development, and evaluation) (Atkins et al., 2004). Umbrella reviews compare and reconcile the findings considering biases (if any) in each systematic review and then finally compile these results into a single table (Paré et al., 2015). Overall, this type of review follows the same standards and data analysis techniques which are employed in qualitative or quantitative systematic reviews (Pieper et al., 2012). Since it is relatively a new methodology, the guidelines and procedures for conducting the review are still in the developing phase to ensure the reliability and validity of the generated results (Smith et al., 2011).

3.8 Theoretical Reviews

Theoretical reviews focus on explanation building using conceptual and empirical studies in the current literature that aim to identify, explain, and transform the extracted knowledge into concepts, constructs, relationships, and theoretical structures and frameworks. The main purpose of the theoretical reviews is to develop conceptual frameworks or models using hypotheses and research propositions (Paré et al., 2015). They can be useful in addressing the emerging issues in a research domain by building on new theoretical underpinnings and/or the existing body of knowledge on a mature topic on which there is a lack of theories or the existing theories are inadequate to address the current research gaps (Paré et al., 2015). In general, theoretical reviews synthesize the diverse streams of research in a subject domain through categorization systems, morphologies, and framework development. By doing so, theoretical reviews effectively organize prior research, investigate the interrelationships, and determine the similarities and emerging patterns from the selected studies in a review that aid in developing new theories (Paré et al., 2015). For instance, an article in the field of education examined the studies focusing on the professional development of teachers after completing their basic teacher training (Postholm, 2012).

This type of review has significant importance as it can bring novel concepts, develop new theories, and extend the existing theories (such as natural resource-based view and practice-based view theories originating from the resource-based view theory (Hart et al., 2010; Tiwari et al., 2020)) based on the knowledge and research gaps (Paré et al., 2015). Theoretical reviews initially focus on a broad research question and refined it after analyzing the accumulative evidence and knowledge (Paré et al., 2015). In addition, both the interpretive and positivist methods including grounded theory, meta-synthesis, meta-triangulation, meta-narratives, content analysis, and qualitative comparative analysis can be used for data analysis in theoretical reviews (Eakin & Mykhalovskiy, 2003; Oates et al., 2012).

3.9 Critical Reviews

This methodology in the literature review taxonomies critically examines the extant literature in a broad research area to identify inconsistencies, paradoxes, and flaws (Grant & Booth, 2009; Hedges & Cooper, 2009). Critical reviews do not integrate current knowledge and compare existing studies to one another, instead, they hold up the research work in the selected studies against a criterion. The significance of a critical review lies in its ability to identify problems, inconsistencies, and research domains in which the existing evidence and information are unreliable (Kirkevold, 1997; Paré et al., 2015). Following this, the critical reviews enable researchers to constructively develop knowledge and provide research directions on a topic (Palvia et al., 2004). Critical reviews can also employ different data analysis techniques such as positivist including content analysis techniques and interpretivist including grounded theory and meta-ethnography techniques based on the author's epistemological viewpoints (Paré et al., 2015).

The primary purpose of a critical review is to identify, analyze, and synthesize the information and knowledge from different sources and present it into a model, instead of an answer. The resulting model can be a blend of existing frameworks (or models) or the integrative analysis of the available literature (Grant & Booth, 2009). Critical reviews comprehensively examine the literature and critically assess the quality including the evaluation and conceptual innovation. The process of conceptual innovation includes the evolution of the knowledge successively accumulating in a research area; however, the critical reviews can "take stock" and assess the value of prior studies in a subject domain (Grant & Booth, 2009). Following this, the critical reviews may conclude the conflicting arguments and provide a "launch pad" for a new phase of theoretical development and conceptual innovation (Grant & Booth, 2009). Though, this review type critically analyses a wide area of research; it is selective, does not include a comprehensive search of current relevant literature (Kirkevold, 1997) and may not be able to assess the quality of studies, especially in the form of qualitative research (Paré et al., 2015). Accordingly, critical reviews lack the structured and systematic approach of literature search, analysis and synthesis in a subject domain, thus being considered subjective and lacking quality evaluation of the selected literature (Grant & Booth, 2009).

3.10 Mapping Reviews

Mapping reviews are different from scoping reviews as the outcome of this methodology is not known, thereby emphasizing further review work and primary research in a subject domain. It can contextually analyze and present comprehensive systematic literature reviews and identify the research gaps based on the evidence (Grant & Booth, 2009). Mapping reviews facilitate policymakers, researchers, and practitioners in developing policies and providing future research directions. Mapping reviews are also referred to as systematic maps and classify studies according to population groups, the setting of the study, and theoretical perspectives (Grant & Booth, 2009). Mapping reviews facilitate researchers in deciding to undertake an in-depth systematic review of all the studies or a subset of the studies. However, the mapping reviews are time-consuming and studies are selected based on the study design, therefore, lacks a quality assessment process in study selection (Grant & Booth, 2009).

3.11 Mixed Methods/Hybrid Review

Mixed method reviews include a combination of methodologies in which at least one needs to be a literature review methodology (such as systematic) accompanied by case studies or surveys. For example, Farrukh et al. (2022b) conducted a systematic literature review methodology followed by case studies performed in multiple organizations in a developing economy to examine the environmental sustainability aspects related to green-lean-six sigma enablers. Such a methodology includes the research questions of "what works" combines with "how and why does it work" (Grant & Booth, 2009) that aims to address the complex research problems of "what works under which circumstances" (Grant & Booth, 2009). Similarly, mixed/hybrid reviews may also achieve the objectives of two or more literature review methodologies. As an independent study, these reviews are well aligned with the increasing expectations of literature review (Lim et al., 2022). For instance, Chopra et al. (2021) performed a conceptual and bibliometric review to investigate studies in the research area of knowledge management for sustainability.

To this end, mixed methods reviews provide the researchers, policymakers, and practitioners with a more holistic understanding of the research issues including a combination of theoretical background with empirical findings. Despite the above potential strengths of mixed methods reviews, they may inherit the methodological challenges of evaluating and synthesizing both qualitative and quantitative research streams along with integrating the overall findings. Accordingly, this methodology includes a complicated decision regarding which research method to be used first (qualitative or quantitative) (Grant & Booth, 2009).

4. AUTHOR'S (REVIEW AUTHOR) SKILLS

Writing a quality literature review needs research expertise and knowledge of some important issues. The following discussion presents key skills and competencies necessary for scholars for conducting a high-quality literature review. First, conducting a literature review is a complex activity and requires particular skills and abilities which are learnt with experience, time, and practice as emphasized by Creswell (2012). Accordingly, the writer should have good writing skills along with logical and critical reasoning capabilities (Mohammed & Ahmed, 2019). Further, the author needs to consider some key points during a literature review process such as the relevance of the searched literature to the research question and the study context and circumstances. Additionally, the author should write a review in such a manner which familiarizes the reader with the methodology and process followed in the review (Mohammed & Ahmed, 2019). In this regard, the author needs to identify the important variables to be studied in the review, the context and specific settings in which the review is conducted, and present a clear and concise summary of the key findings from selected studies (Mohammed & Ahmed, 2019).

Second, while searching and selecting relevant literature is a challenging task, the selected studies should be critically analyzed to maintain the quality, relevance, and accuracy aligning with the research question and subject domain (Creswell, 2012). The author should also avoid any ambiguities, uncertainties, and repetition of sentences, words, and paragraphs and the tone should be constructive, polite, and logical (Mohammed & Ahmed, 2019). In addition, the author needs to follow ethical standards such as the review should be both unbiased and without any personal conflict of interest (Mohammed & Ahmed, 2019; Torraco, 2005). Further, the author needs to keep in mind that the review should be specific to a research problem, include well-defined research objectives and methodology, and cover the research gaps, key findings, and areas addressed in a subject domain followed by a good summary of the overall findings, contribution, and conclusions (Mohammed & Ahmed, 2019).

Third, Creswell (2012) also asserted a literature map to achieve the objective of a literature review which is a "figure or drawing that displays the research literature (e.g., studies, essays, books, chapters, and summaries) on a topic" (Creswell, 2012, p. 95). It also assists the review author in identifying the duplications, presenting a clear picture, and highlighting the contributions to the existing body of knowledge in a subject domain (Mohammed & Ahmed, 2019). To this end, a literature map helps in collecting data and gathering information from diverse sources relevant to a research area/subject and aims to filter, evaluate, and synthesize the relevant studies to achieve the overall objective of the literature review (Hart, 1998). After developing the literature maps, the author writes the review of the selected literature comprising methods, findings, analysis, results, and conclusions. The author organizes the selected studies, summarizes categorically the key findings based on the data analysis techniques, and identifies the gaps and discrepancies in the existing literature (Mohammed & Ahmed, 2019; Welter & Ensslin, 2021).

Fourth, along with the adequate selection of a literature review methodology, the author should hold the ability to think critically while analyzing and presenting a high-quality literature review (Mohammed & Ahmed, 2019). According to Machi and McEvoy (2021), critical thinking requires the author to be inquisitive to know more about a research area, raise questions, and think clearly and rationally (Mohammed & Ahmed, 2019). In addition, critical thinking requires the author to be determined and committed while reviewing literature and focused on finding the answer to a research problem. On the other hand, critical writing includes the author's ability to convince the target audience to recognize and agree with his/her contentions based on strong arguments (Wallace & Wray, 2021). Additionally, critical writing classifies the existing literature into different dimensions to analyze the strengths, weaknesses, consistencies, deficiencies, and research gaps in the current literature (Torraco, 2005). It focuses on the author's ability to demonstrate and present the key findings of the reviewed literature and their implications/significance for the research society (Mohammed & Ahmed, 2019). According to Torraco (2005), critical analysis of literature requires the author to carefully examine the key contributing ideas and criticize the existing body of knowledge to investigate how effectively prior literature addresses the research problem and question.

Fifth, writing a literature review is a resource-intensive activity including time and energy and requires strict ethical considerations to be followed regarding intellectual property. For example, the author needs to be unbiased, avoid any misleading information and facts, not plagiarize others' work, and cite adequately other researchers' work which aided in the review process. Furthermore, the review author should avoid grammatical and typographical errors in writing a review since these issues portray a negative image of the work and can affect the overall quality of the work. In addition to the above points, the author should maintain comprehensive records of activities followed in a review process (Murray & Moore, 2006).

Based on the above discussion, Table 1 presents the authors' skills related to different types of literature review methodologies.

Table 1. Skillset Required for Literature Review Methodologies.

Types of Literature Review	Authors' Skills
Narrative review	– Subject expert – Extensive knowledge and interpretation of the subject domain
Descriptive reviews	– Ability to perform numerical analysis – Developing logical patterns
Scoping reviews	– Expertise in conducting an in-depth analysis of the research problem – Command on content analysis – Proficiency in thematic analysis
Systematic reviews	– Transparent, standardized, and explicit approach to methodology – Ability to focus on narrow and predefined research questions
Meta-analysis	– Mastery of statistical analysis – Conversance in determining key relationship(s) between the study findings
Qualitative analysis	– Ability to summarize the findings from quantitative research studies – Theory-building competency (evaluating the emergent themes and being able to explain their inherent relationships) – Familiarity with subjective analysis
Umbrella reviews	– Experience and proficiency in accumulating knowledge from multiple types of reviews
Theoretical reviews	– Explanation building – Theory building – Expertise in framework development
Critical reviews	– Know-how of critical analysis of the extant literature
Mapping reviews	– Able to perform contextual analysis
Mixed methods/hybrid review	– Conducting literature reviews followed by empirical studies

Source: Authors.

5. QUALITY OF THE LITERATURE REVIEW

With an increasing number of published reviews and their significant contribution to a subject domain, the quality concerns of the literature review cannot be overlooked (Paré et al., 2015). Around 76.9% of reviewers emphasize the quality of a literature review as an important factor (Denney & Tewksbury, 2013). Similar to empirical research, the evaluation and assessment of literature reviews are also needed to determine their quality (Palmatier et al., 2018). The quality criteria must include depth and rigor in identifying a comprehensive/suitable strategy for selecting articles and gathering information from prior literature (Alsalami, 2022). Since all review types have their specific characteristics and limitations, the methodological quality and reporting aspects of a literature review type are the major concerns that need to be investigated. The key dimensions representing the quality of the review include the rigor and relevance of the review (Paré et al., 2015).

The term rigor includes reliability and validity. Reliability refers to the reproducibility of a review process which emphasizes the complete documentation of searching the articles, extracting the relevant information, and coding and analyzing the data from the selected studies. Following this, the author should document the stages adopted/followed in the review process (Paré et al., 2015). The primary purpose of this documentation is to enable a reader in identifying the inclusion and exclusion criteria including the search terminology, databases, years, language, and article type (such as journal paper or conference paper) (Paré et al., 2015). The validity is concerned with the appropriateness of the review process which goes beyond the documentation reflecting the decisions regarding the selection of the databases, articles, time period, keywords, and backward and forward search strategies (Brocke et al., 2009). The methodological quality of a review is also referred to as rigor which is reflected through a comprehensive search strategy, documentation, and rationality in review type selection. Accordingly, it facilitates the researchers with all the information or "enough evidence" required for replicating a review at any point (Paré et al., 2015).

The process of conducting a review and documenting the details depends on the type of review. For instance, the characteristic of flexibility is expected in narrative reviews while designing the review strategy and finding and choosing the articles (Grant & Booth, 2009; King & He, 2005). On the contrary, the descriptive review follows a structured approach in the search for relevant studies and objectively evaluates the articles (King & He, 2005). The same comprehensive approach is followed in the meta-analysis, qualitative systematic reviews, and umbrella reviews, which include structure search methodologies, a high level of rigor, and systematic analysis of the articles. On the other hand, critical reviews are subjective and follow an interpretative approach (Grant & Booth, 2009). Despite selecting any type of review methodology, the audience is interested in the evidence, process, and documentation of the review conducted (Okoli & Schabram, 2010). Following this, the information should aid the reader in understanding the relevance of the evidence and generalizing the findings of a review type.

The second dimension of quality emphasizes the relevance which answers the research questions addressed in a review for achieving the overall purpose of the review (Cooper, 1988). For example, scoping reviews explore the information, descriptive reviews discover the patterns, meta-analysis statistically evaluates the evidence, and critical reviews critically analyze the prior knowledge in a subject domain. Therefore, it is important to identify the primary purpose of a review while determining its relevance (Paré et al., 2015). In addition to the above aspects regarding the quality of a literature review, Snyder (2019) has suggested some guidelines at different stages of a literature review process of designing, conducting, data abstracting and analyzing, and structuring and writing a review which can facilitate researchers in quality assessment of literature. These guidelines are presented in Table 2:

Table 2. Guidelines for Evaluating the Quality of Literature Review, Adapted From Snyder (2019).

Phase 1: *Design stage*	Phase 2: *Conducting the review*	Phase 3: *Data abstraction and analysis*	Phase 4: *Structuring and writing the review*
– Identify the need for a literature review and its theoretical and practical contribution to the relevant field	– Determine the appropriateness of the search process in a review type	– Determine the relevance/suitability of the extracted data from the articles with the primary purpose of a review	– Coherence of the review article with the overall purpose and research question
– Clear understanding of the purpose and motivation of the literature review	– Present a clear description of the practical search process	– Clear demonstration of the data extraction process	– Clear description and documentation of conducting the literature review process
– Clarity of the overall purpose of the literature review and research questions	– Transparency of the inclusion and exclusion criteria	– Ensuring quality data extraction through proper measures	– Replicability of the study
– Description and interpretation of prior literature	– Ensuring the research quality through appropriate measures	– Alignment of the data analysis technique with the research question and extracted data/information	– Resorting the review results in an appropriate manner
– Relevance/appropriateness of literature review methodology	– Relevance of the final sample with the overall purpose of the review	– Transparency and clear description of the data analysis techniques	– Synthesis of the review findings in a clear way and significant contribution to the existing body of knowledge
– Comprehensive description and transparency of a search strategy and literature review methodology comprising the inclusion and exclusion criteria			– Usability of the review findings, and implications for the audience including researchers, practitioners, and policymakers
			– Highlighting research gaps and providing future research directions

6. CONCLUSION AND IMPLICATIONS

The objective of this chapter was to discuss the significance of the literature review, types of the literature review methodologies, author's skills, and the quality evaluation of the literature review. We have critically explicated various literature review methodologies including narrative reviews, descriptive reviews, scoping reviews, systematic reviews, mapping reviews, umbrella reviews, theoretical reviews, meta-analysis, and critical reviews along with their objectives, strengths, and limitations. Following this, the author's skills including the literature review mapping and ethical considerations have been explained. Finally, the quality aspects of the literature review are discussed which include the rigor and relevance of the selected literature aligning with the overall research topic. This chapter provides significant implications for researchers such as selecting the appropriate literature review methodology according to the nature of the research problem and research topic. In addition, this chapter assists researchers in examining the strengths and weaknesses of different types of research methodologies which can help them in conducting high-quality literature reviews. The researchers can benefit from analysing the quality criteria at different stages of a literature review including the design phase, conducting the review phase, data abstraction and analysis phase, and structuring and writing the review phase. Further, the researchers can keep in mind various important points while writing an effective literature review such as adequate documentation of the review process and critical thinking, writing, and analysis of the selected studies.

REFERENCES

Alajami, A. (2021). Critiquing the past for solidifying the future: Understanding the synthesizing facet of reviewing the social studies: Critical approach. *Current Research in Behavioral Sciences, 2.* https://doi.org/10.1016/j.crbeha.2021.100047

Alsalami, A. I. (2022). Literature review as a key step in research processes: Case study of MA dissertations written on EFL of Saudi context. *Saudi Journal of Language Studies, 2*(3), 153–169. https://doi.org/10.1108/SJLS-04-2022-0044

Arksey, H., & O'Malley, L. (2005). Scoping studies: Towards a methodological framework. *International Journal of Social Research Methodology, 8*(1), 19–32. https://doi.org/10.1080/1364557032000119616

Atkins, D., Best, D., Briss, P. A., Eccles, M., Falck-Ytter, Y., Flottorp, S., Guyatt, G., Harbour, R., Haugh, M., & Henry, D. (2004). Grading quality of evidence and strength of recommendations. *The BMJ.* https://doi.org/10.1136/bmj.328.7454.1490

Baker, M. J. (2000). Writing a literature review. *The Marketing Review, 1*(2), 219–247. https://doi.org/10.1362/1469347002529189

Bastian, H., Glasziou, P., & Chalmers, I. (2010). Seventy-five trials and eleven systematic reviews a day: How will we ever keep up? *PLoS Medicine, 7*(9), e1000326. https://doi.org/10.1371/journal.pmed.1000326

Borenstein, M., Hedges, L. V., Higgins, J. P., & Rothstein, H. R. (2021). *Introduction to meta-analysis.* John Wiley & Sons.

Brocke, J. v., Simons, A., Niehaves, B., Niehaves, B., Reimer, K., Plattfaut, R., & Cleven, A. (2009). Reconstructing the giant: On the importance of rigour in documenting the literature search process. *ECIS 2009 Proceedings, 372.* https://aisel.aisnet.org/ecis2009/372

Chivilgina, O., Elger, B. S., & Jotterand, F. (2021). Digital technologies for schizophrenia management: A descriptive review. *Science and Engineering Ethics*, *27*(2), 25. https://doi.org/10.1007/s11948-021-00302-z

Chopra, M., Saini, N., Kumar, S., Varma, A., Mangla, S. K., & Lim, W. M. (2021). Past, present, and future of knowledge management for business sustainability. *Journal of Cleaner Production*, *328*, 129592. https://doi.org/10.1016/j.jclepro.2021.129592

Collins, J. A., & Fauser, B. C. (2005). *Balancing the strengths of systematic and narrative reviews*. Oxford University Press.

Cooper, H. (1985). *Balancing the strengths of systematic and narrative reviews*. National Inst. of Education (ED), Washington, DC.

Cooper, H. M. (1988). Organizing knowledge syntheses: A taxonomy of literature reviews. *Knowledge in Society*, *1*(1), 104–126.

Creswell, J. W. (2012). *Educational research: Planning, conducting, and evaluating*. Pearson.

Daudt, H. M., van Mossel, C., & Scott, S. J. (2013). Enhancing the scoping study methodology: A large, inter-professional team's experience with Arksey and O'Malley's framework. *BMC Medical Research Methodology*, *13*(1), 1–9. http://www.biomedcentral.com/1471-2288/13/48

Davies, P. (2000). The relevance of systematic reviews to educational policy and practice. *Oxford Review of Education*, *26*(3–4), 365–378. https://doi.org/10.1080/713688543

Denney, A. S., & Tewksbury, R. (2013). How to write a literature review. *Journal of Criminal Justice Education*, *24*(2), 218–234. https://doi.org/10.1080/10511253.2012.730617

Dixon-Woods, M., Agarwal, S., Jones, D., Young, B., & Sutton, A. (2005). Synthesising qualitative and quantitative evidence: A review of possible methods. *Journal of Health Services Research & Policy*, *10*(1), 45–53.

Eakin, J. M., & Mykhalovskiy, E. (2003). Reframing the evaluation of qualitative health research: Reflections on a review of appraisal guidelines in the health sciences. *Journal of Evaluation in Clinical Practice*, *9*(2), 187–194. https://www.jstor.org/stable/26749970

Farrukh, A., Mathrani, S., & Sajjad, A. (2022a). A systematic literature review on environmental sustainability issues of flexible packaging: Potential pathways for academic research and managerial practice. *Sustainability*, *14*(8), 4737. https://www.mdpi.com/2071-1050/14/8/4737

Farrukh, A., Mathrani, S., & Sajjad, A. (2022b). Managerial perspectives on green-lean-six sigma adoption in the flexible packaging industry: Empirical evidence from an emerging economy. *Journal of Manufacturing Technology Management*. https://doi.org/10.1108/JMTM-02-2022-0080

Faulkner, G., Fagan, M. J., & Lee, J. (2021). Umbrella reviews (systematic review of reviews). *International Review of Sport and Exercise Psychology*, *15*(1), 73–90. https://doi.org/10.1080/1750984x.2021.1934888

Fink, A. (2019). *Conducting research literature reviews: From the internet to paper*. Sage Publications.

Grant, M. J., & Booth, A. (2009). A typology of reviews: An analysis of 14 review types and associated methodologies. *Health Information and Libraries Journal*, *26*(2), 91–108. https://doi.org/10.1111/j.1471-1842.2009.00848.x

Green, R. (2009). *American and Australian doctoral literature reviewing practices and pedagogies*. Deakin University.

Green, B. N., Johnson, C. D., & Adams, A. (2006). Writing narrative literature reviews for peer-reviewed journals: Secrets of the trade. *Journal of Chiropractic Medicine*, *5*(3), 101–117. https://doi.org/10.1016/S0899-3467(07)60142-6

Hart, C. (1998). *Doing a literature review: Releasing the social science research imagination*. Sage publications.

Hart, C. (2018). *Doing a literature review: Releasing the research imagination*. Sage publications.

Hart, S. L., Barney, J. B., Ketchen, D. J., Wright, M., & Dowell, G. (2010). Invited editorial: A natural-resource-based view of the firm. *Journal of Management*, *37*(5), 1464–1479. https://doi.org/10.1177/0149206310390219

Hartling, L., Chisholm, A., Thomson, D., & Dryden, D. M. (2012). A descriptive analysis of overviews of reviews published between 2000 and 2011. *PLoS One*, *7*(11), e49667. https://doi.org/10.1371/journal.pone.0049667

Hedges, L., & Cooper, H. (2009). *The handbook of research synthesis and meta-analysis*. Russell Sage Foundation.

Hedges, L. V., & Olkin, I. (1980). Vote-counting methods in research synthesis. *Psychological Bulletin*, *88*(2), 359. https://doi.org/10.1037/0033-2909.88.2.359

Higgins, J. P., Thomas, J., Chandler, J., Cumpston, M., Li, T., Page, M. J., & Welch, V. A. (2019). *Cochrane handbook for systematic reviews of interventions*. John Wiley & Sons.

Jadad, A. R., Cook, D. J., & Browman, G. P. (1997). A guide to interpreting discordant systematic reviews. *Canadian Medical Association Journal*, *156*(10), 1411–1416.

Jaidka, K., Khoo, C. S. G., & Na, J. C. (2013). Literature review writing: How information is selected and transformed. *ASLIB Proceedings*, *65*(3), 303–325. https://doi.org/10.1108/0001253 1311330665

Kamler, B. (2008). Rethinking doctoral publication practices: Writing from and beyond the thesis. *Studies in Higher Education*, *33*(3), 283–294. https://doi.org/10.1080/03075070802049236

King, W. R., & He, J. (2005). Understanding the role and methods of meta-analysis in IS research. *Communications of the Association for Information Systems*, *16*(1), 32. https://doi.org/10.17705/1CAIS.01632

Kirkevold, M. (1997). Integrative nursing research—An important strategy to further the development of nursing science and nursing practice. *Journal of Advanced Nursing*, *25*(5), 977–984. https://doi.org/10.1046/j.1365-2648.1997.1997025977.x

La Rosa, G., Bonadonna, L., Lucentini, L., Kenmoe, S., & Suffredini, E. (2020). Coronavirus in water environments: Occurrence, persistence and concentration methods – A scoping review. *Water Research*, *179*, 115899. https://doi.org/10.1016/j.watres.2020.115899

Levac, D., Colquhoun, H., & O'Brien, K. K. (2010). Scoping studies: Advancing the methodology. *Implementation Science*, *5*(1), 1–9. http://www.implementationscience.com/content/5/1/69

Lim, W. M., Kumar, S., & Ali, F. (2022). Advancing knowledge through literature reviews: 'What', 'why', and 'how to contribute'. *The Service Industries Journal*, *42*(7–8), 481–513. https://doi.org/10.1080/02642069.2022.2047941

Lorenz, H., Reinsch, T., Hess, S., & Taube, F. (2019). Is low-input dairy farming more climate friendly? A meta-analysis of the carbon footprints of different production systems. *Journal of Cleaner Production*, *211*, 161–170. https://doi.org/10.1016/j.jclepro.2018.11.113

Machi, L. A., & McEvoy, B. T. (2021). *The literature review: Six steps to success*. Sage publications.

McGauran, N., Wieseler, B., Kreis, J., Schuler, Y. B., Kolsch, H., & Kaiser, T. (2010). Reporting bias in medical research – A narrative review. *Trials*, *11*, 37. https://doi.org/10.1186/1745-6215-11-37

Mohammed, S., & Ahmed, M. (2019). Problems of academic literature review and writing: The way forward. *Journal of Management Sciences*, *16*(5), 11–26.

Murray, R., & Moore, S. (2006). *EBOOK: The handbook of academic writing: A fresh approach*. McGraw-Hill Education.

Oates, B. J., Edwards, H., & Wainwright, D. W. (2012). A model-driven method for the systematic literature review of qualitative empirical research. In *Proceedings of the International Conference on Information Systems*. Orlando, FL, United States.

Okoli, C., & Schabram, K. (2010). A guide to conducting a systematic literature review of information systems research. *Sprouts: Working Papers on Information Systems*, *10*(26). http://sprouts.aisnet.org/10-26

Palmatier, R. W., Houston, M. B., & Hulland, J. (2018). *Review articles: Purpose, process, and structure*. Springer.

Palvia, P., Leary, D., Mao, E., Midha, V., Pinjani, P., & Salam, A. F. (2004). Research methodologies in MIS: An update. *The Communications of the Association for Information Systems*, *14*(1), 58. http://aisel.aisnet.org/cais/vol14/iss1/24

Paré, G., Trudel, M.-C., Jaana, M., & Kitsiou, S. (2015). Synthesizing information systems knowledge: A typology of literature reviews. *Information & Management*, *52*(2), 183–199. https://doi.org/10.1016/j.im.2014.08.008

Paul, J., & Criado, A. R. (2020). The art of writing literature review: What do we know and what do we need to know? *International Business Review*, *29*(4). https://doi.org/10.1016/j.ibusrev.2020.101717

Pautasso, M. (2013). Ten simple rules for writing a literature review. *PLoS Computational Biology*, *9*(7), e1003149. https://doi.org/10.1371/journal.pcbi.1003149

Petticrew, M., & Roberts, H. (2006). *Systematic reviews in the social sciences: A practical guide* (Vol. 6, pp. 304–305). Blackwell Publishing CrossRef Google Scholar.

Pickering, C., & Byrne, J. (2013). The benefits of publishing systematic quantitative literature reviews for PhD candidates and other early-career researchers. *Higher Education Research & Development*, *33*(3), 534–548. https://doi.org/10.1080/07294360.2013.841651

Pickering, C., & Byrne, J. (2014). The benefits of publishing systematic quantitative literature reviews for PhD candidates and other early-career researchers. *Higher Education Research & Development*, *33*(3), 534–548.

Pickering, C., Grignon, J., Steven, R., Guitart, D., & Byrne, J. (2014). Publishing not perishing: How research students transition from novice to knowledgeable using systematic quantitative literature reviews. *Studies in Higher Education*, *40*(10), 1756–1769. https://doi.org/10.1080/03075079.2014.914907

Piedra-Cascon, W., Krishnamurthy, V. R., Att, W., & Revilla-Leon, M. (2021). 3D printing parameters, supporting structures, slicing, and post-processing procedures of vat-polymerization additive manufacturing technologies: A narrative review. *Journal of Dentistry*, *109*, 103630. https://doi.org/10.1016/j.jdent.2021.103630

Pieper, D., Buechter, R., Jerinic, P., & Eikermann, M. (2012). Overviews of reviews often have limited rigor: A systematic review. *Journal of Clinical Epidemiology*, *65*(12), 1267–1273. https://doi.org/10.1016/j.jclinepi.2012.06.015

Postholm, M. B. (2012). Teachers' professional development: A theoretical review. *Educational Research*, *54*(4), 405–429. https://doi.org/10.1080/00131881.2012.734725

Rana, S., Sakshi, & Singh, J. (2022). Presenting the POWER framework of conducting literature review. In S. Rana, Sakshi, & J. Singh (Eds.), *Exploring the latest trends in management literature (Review of management literature, Vol. 1)* (pp. 1–13). Emerald Publishing Limited. https://doi.org/10.1108/S2754-586520220000001001

Rosenthal, R., & DiMatteo, M. R. (2001). Meta-analysis: Recent developments in quantitative methods for literature reviews. *Annual Review of Psychology*, *52*(1), 59–82. https://doi.org/10.1146/annurev.psych.52.1.59

Rumrill, P. D., Fitzgerald, S. M., & Merchant, W. R. (2010). Using scoping literature reviews as a means of understanding and interpreting existing literature. *Work (Reading, Mass.)*, *35*(3), 399–404. https://doi.org/10.3233/WOR-2010-0998

Sajjad, A. (2021). The COVID-19 pandemic, social sustainability and global supply chain resilience: A review. *Corporate Governance: The International Journal of Business in Society*, *21*(6), 1142–1154. https://doi.org/10.1108/cg-12-2020-0554

Schagrin, M., Harding, J., Davis, G., & Carter, A. (2011). *Research and Innovative Technology Administration (RITA)-United States Department of Transportation*. Research and Innovative Technology Administration (RITA)-Intelligent Transportation Systems (ITS).

Seuring, S., & Müller, M. (2008). From a literature review to a conceptual framework for sustainable supply chain management. *Journal of Cleaner Production*, *16*(15), 1699–1710. https://doi.org/10.1016/j.jclepro.2008.04.020

Shea, B. J., Hamel, C., Wells, G. A., Bouter, L. M., Kristjansson, E., Grimshaw, J., Henry, D., & Boers, M. (2009). AMSTAR is a reliable and valid measurement tool to assess the methodological quality of systematic reviews. *Journal of Clinical Epidemiology*, *62*(10), 1013–1020. https://doi.org/10.1016/j.jclinepi.2008.10.009

Smith, V., Devane, D., Begley, C. M., & Clarke, M. (2011). Methodology in conducting a systematic review of systematic reviews of healthcare interventions. *BMC Medical Research Methodology*, *11*(1), 1–6. http://www.biomedcentral.com/1471-2288/11/15

Snyder, H. (2019). Literature review as a research methodology: An overview and guidelines. *Journal of Business Research*, *104*, 333–339. https://doi.org/10.1016/j.jbusres.2019.07.039

Sony, M., Antony, J., & Douglas, J. A. (2020). Essential ingredients for the implementation of Quality 4.0. *The TQM Journal*, *32*(4), 779–793. https://doi.org/10.1108/tqm-12-2019-0275

Tiwari, P., Sadeghi, J. K., & Eseonu, C. (2020). A sustainable lean production framework with a case implementation: Practice-based view theory. *Journal of Cleaner Production, 277*, 123078. https://doi.org/10.1016/j.jclepro.2020.123078

Toma, A., & Crişan, O. (2018). Green pharmacy – A narrative review. *Clujul Medical, 91*(4), 391.

Torraco, R. J. (2005). Writing integrative literature reviews: Guidelines and examples. *Human Resource Development Review, 4*(3), 356–367. https://doi.org/10.1177/1534484305527828

Wallace, M., & Wray, A. (2021). *Critical reading and writing for postgraduates.* Sage publications.

Welter, L. M., & Ensslin, S. R. (2021). How do the unintended consequences of performance evaluation systems manifest themselves? *Journal of Accounting & Organizational Change, 18*(4), 509–528. https://doi.org/10.1108/jaoc-07-2020-0087

PRISMA FOR REVIEW OF MANAGEMENT LITERATURE – METHOD, MERITS, AND LIMITATIONS – AN ACADEMIC REVIEW

Vinaytosh Mishra and Monu Pandey Mishra

ABSTRACT

Preferred Reporting Items for Systematic Reviews and Meta-Analyses (PRISMA) is a widely accepted guideline for performing a systematic review (SR) in clinical journals. It not only helps an author to improve the reporting but also assists reviewers and editors in the critical appraisal of available SR. These tools help in achieving reproducibility in research, a major concern in contemporary academic research. But there is a lack of awareness about the approach among management researchers. This chapter attempts to fill this gap using a narrative review of reliable online resources and peer-reviewed articles to discuss the PRISMA guidelines and recent amendments. The chapter further points out the limitations of PRISMA in the review of management literature and suggests measures to overcome that. This piece of literature introduces a reader to the basics of a systematic review using PRISMA as an instrument. One of the significant contributions is to delineate a seven-step strategy to attain reproducibility in the systematic review. The chapter is useful for researchers and academicians in the field of social science and management.

Keywords: Systematic review; review methods; PRISMA; PRISMA extensions; reproducibility; literature review

Advancing Methodologies of Conducting Literature Review in Management Domain
Review of Management Literature, Volume 2, 125–136
Copyright © 2024 Vinaytosh Mishra and Monu Pandey Mishra
Published under exclusive licence by Emerald Publishing Limited
ISSN: 2754-5865/doi:10.1108/S2754-586520230000002007

1. INTRODUCTION

A literature review (LR) is an integral part of academic projects. The foremost purpose of an LR is to develop a knowledge of the extant research work related to a particular topic or area of study (Knopf, 2006). Another objective of the literature review is to present insights in the form of a written report. Webster and Watson in their seminal work asserts that conducting an LR helps you in not only building your expertise in a specific area of the research field but also in identifying the research gap. An effective LR helps in the development of theory, summarizes the knowledge where an overabundance of research exists, and discovers areas where research is required (Webster & Watson, 2002). Since they wrote this paper with the roadmap of literature review 20 years back other researchers have contributed to the body of review of the literature (ROL) by defining the different types of LR (Leidner, 2018; Paré et al., 2015) or how to

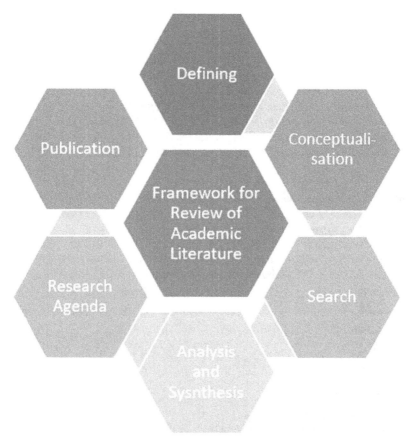

Fig. 1. Framework for Review of Academic Literature. *Source:* Adopted from (Vom Brocke et al., 2009).

make searches more inclusive and well-organized (Bandara et al., 2015; Vom Brocke et al., 2009). A general framework for the LR is depicted in Fig. 1.

Despite the recent advancement in the arena of LR, two major shortcomings persist. Foremost, the evidence synthesis fails to instill interest in the reader at the same time it lacks delineating theoretical contribution. Webster and Watson in their recent work suggests two measures for refining the procedure of LR. Firstly, they suggest systematically digitally encoding (SDE) of main knowledge contributions in the form of a graph or networks. Secondly, they propose reviewing creative literature as a source of inspiration for constructing the theoretical contributions of the paper. Fig. 2 depicts the publication data graph model suggested by Watson and Webster (2020) in their seminal work.

The task of creating a data graph model may be intimidating for a researcher who is new to the concept. The availability of Graphic User Interface (GUI) based tools for the task may result in wider acceptance of the method soon.

2. TYPES OF LITERATURE REVIEW

As discussed, in an earlier section several types of literature reviews have emerged over the years. Out of these foremost are narrative, systematic, meta-analysis, and meta-synthesis.

(1) *Narrative Literature Review:* The main objective behind the narrative LR is to examine and recapitulate an existing body of literature. To achieve this a thorough background of the literature is presented in interest to educate, identify gaps, or spot inconsistencies in the research area. Thus, the narrative review can not only assist in refining, focusing, and identifying research questions but also in proposing conceptual and theoretical frameworks

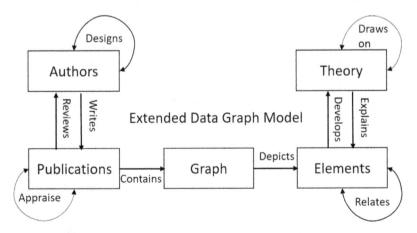

Fig. 2. Publication Data Graph Model. *Source:* Adopted from (Webster & Watson, 2020).

(Coughlan et al., 2007). Another examples can be seen as conceptual review (Rana et al., 2020, 2022).

(2) *Systematic Literature Review:* It is a more demanding method for LR. These are frequently used by researchers to get an answer to well-defined and precise research inquiries. Thus, they make the available evidence more accessible to decision-makers (Williams et al., 2021).

(3) *Meta-Analysis Literature Review:* This approach takes the results from the selected pieces of literature and analyzes these using a well-established statistical method (Coughlan et al., 2007). Polit and Beck (2006) claim that meta-analysis approaches support drawing inferences and identifying patterns and associations between results.

(4) *Meta Synthesis:* Unlike meta-analysis literature review, meta synthesis is a nonstatistical method for SLR and evidence synthesis from qualitative studies. It is an emergent technique in various fields such as medical and business research and can be used in many different methods. It aims to build on earlier conceptualizations and understandings. However, the approach must be suitable to the specific field of scientific research (Lachal et al., 2017).

Out of the methods discussed above, the dominant styles used in the review of management literature are narrative and systematic LR. The narrative review in the field of social science is suitable for pinpointing the knowledge gaps, whereas the systematic review is more focused on disseminating the existing information. Jesson et al. (2011) discuss a continuum of the diverse nuances of these two types of academic reviews (Fig. 3).

The rest of the chapter is schematized as follows. Section 2 deliberates the concerns over reproducibility in contemporary research and seven strategies to achieve it in the literature review. Section 3 discusses PRISMA guidelines and recent updates in it. The section further lists the limitations of PRISMA and its extensions of it. The chapter concludes with discussions beyond PRISMA, and frameworks used for systematic review.

3. REPRODUCIBILITY IN RESEARCH

Reproducible research ensures that if the same analysis is repeated multiple times the result obtained will be the same. It is a by-product of watchful diligence in the process of research (Alston & Rick, 2021). An article published in Nature

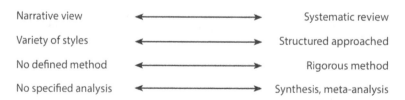

Fig. 3.   Continuum for Management LR. *Source:* Authors' compilation.

observes that more than 70% of researchers have attempted and failed to replicate the research of other academicians, while more than 50% half have been unsuccessful in replicating the findings of their research (Baker, 2016). This paints a very grim picture of the state of reproducibility in academic research. Irreproducibility of research causes grave concern in academia and the management field is no different. Moreover, irreproducibility restricts the translation of research into practice as it adversely affects the reliability of the information. Various measures to achieve reproducibility in the research listed in Table 1 (Shokraneh, 2019).

Discussion about all seven strategies is out of the scope of this chapter and needs a series of articles to discuss it adequately. The focus of the next section is to discuss PRISMA reporting guidelines and recent updates. The objective of the section is to introduce PRISMA guidelines to researchers new to this tool in a lucid manner. This chapter addresses the following three research questions:

(1) What are strategies to achieve reproducibility in management research?
(2) What are PRISMA guidelines and how to use them?
(3) What are the modifications in PRISMA 2020 statement from the 2009 version?

Table 1. Strategy to Achieve the Reproducibility Practice in Management Research.

SN	Strategy	Description
Strategy 1	Pre-registration (Stewart et al., 2012)	Researchers suggest registering the potential systematic reviews in directories such as PROSPERO. It also helps researchers in better planning their review.
Strategy 2	Open methods (Koffel & Rethlefsen, 2016)	It is suggested to share the strategies for literature search in databases and analytical codes as a part of the systematic literature review procedure.
Strategy 3	Open data (Shokraneh, 2018)	This strategy facilitates revisiting the search results. It also helps in removing duplicates and evaluating the replicability of searching, screening, and analysis.
Strategy 4	Collaboration	Teamwork among the researchers not only brings more expertise but also brings more integrity. Team members can run the procedure separately to check whether the results are reproducible.
Strategy 5	Automation (Beller et al., 2018)	Vienna principles stress the reproducibility of the automation activities and making program codes available to the research community for wider use.
Strategy 6	Reporting guidelines (Page et al., 2018)	Reporting guidelines such as PRISMA help researchers select literature. But recent guidelines emphasize more on the reproducibility of research.
Strategy 7	Post-publication review	Peer reviews are restricted to a close group while post-publication reviews provide an opportunity for an appraisal through a wider audience.

Source: Compiled by authors using mentioned resources.

(4) What are extensions of PRISMA useful in the review of the management literature?

4. RESEARCH METHODOLOGY

This study uses narrative LR to explain the PRISMA guidelines and their extensions useful in the review of the management of literature. The fundamental narrative reviews are extremely effective for obtaining a wide perspective on a subject and are often more comparable to a textbook chapter on an important topic. One of the drawbacks of this type of review is the bias of the author in the evidence synthesis. The authors of this study have tried their best to provide evidence factually and to perform narrative review. This chapter uses the approach discussed in extant literature (Contandriopoulos et al., 2010; Nasheeda et al., 2019; Rice et al., 2016).

4.1 Inclusion Criteria

Literature published in peer-reviewed journals and available online was included in the event synthesis.

4.2 Exclusion Criteria

The information available in online resources other than those mentioned on PRISMA official website was excluded. The study further excluded literature published in a language other than English. Sixty-five articles were excluded because the full text of those articles was not available, and it may result in bias.

The flow chart for the selection of literature is listed in Fig. 4.

The authors of the study (MPM) collated the information from the selected literature and presented it in a structured format for a better understanding of the readers.

5. RESULTS AND DISCUSSION

Based on the research questions of the study, the results and discussion section lists the findings in three subsections namely (1) PRISMA guidelines, (2) PRISMA 2020 additions, and (3) Extensions of PRISMA. The section is followed by the conclusion, implications, and future directions of the research.

5.1 PRISMA Guidelines

"PRISMA Statement and its extensions are an evidence-based, minimum set of recommendations designed primarily to encourage transparent and complete reporting of the systematic review. It has been developed to assist authors with appropriate reporting of diverse knowledge synthesis methods (such as SRs, scoping reviews, and review protocols) and to ensure that all aspects of this type

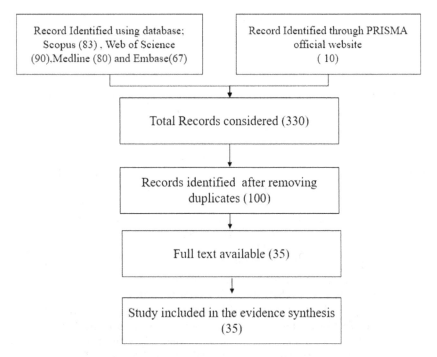

Fig. 4.   Flow Chart of Stages of Literature Search. *Source:* Authors
Compilation.

of research are accurately and transparently reported" (Sarkis-Onofre et al.,
2021). Thus, it is a guiding light to help researchers adeptly recount what was
done, what was found, and in the case of a review protocol, what they are
planning to do. "PRISMA guidelines are also helpful for reviewers and editors as
they assist them in critical appraisal of published systematic reviews. Although it
brings structure to a literature review it is not a quality assessment instrument to
judge the quality of a systematic review" (PRISMA, 2022).

PRISMA checklists help in improving the reporting quality of an SLR and
provide considerable transparency in the selection process of papers for review.
The PRISMA Statement has been recommended by various journals as one of
the publishing requirements (Page & Moher, 2017). Many journals publishing
health research refer to PRISMA in their Instructions to Authors and some
require authors to adhere to them. Similar practices can be adopted for the review
of literature in the social science and management field. In 2009, the "QUOROM
(Quality of Reporting of Meta-analyses) Statement was updated to address
several conceptual, methodological, and practical advances, and was renamed
PRISMA (Preferred Reporting Items of Systematic reviews and Meta-Analyses).
The PRISMA Group advised that PRISMA should replace QUOROM for those
journals that endorsed QUOROM in the past" (Tao et al., 2011). The next

section discusses the guidelines of PRISMA 2020 and the addition of a more than one decade-old version of it.

5.2 PRISMA 2020 Additions

"The PRISMA 2020 statement replaces the 2009 statement and includes new reporting guidance that reflects advances in methods to identify, select, appraise, and synthesize studies. The structure and presentation of the items have been modified to facilitate implementation" (PRISMA, 2022). The guidelines attempt to ensure a systematic review is valuable to users. To achieve these authors are advised to prepare a transparent, complete, and accurate account of why the review was done, what they did, and what they found. The updated guidelines reflect advances in methods to identify, select, appraise, and synthesize studies. It includes a 27-item checklist and an expanded checklist that details reporting recommendations for each item (Page et al., 2021). The new guideline also includes a revised abstract checklist, and flow diagrams for original and updated reviews. The official website of PRISMA provides tools and procedures to use guidelines in the systematic review. The key documents to be used are (1) PRISMA 2020 Checklist, and (2) PRISMA 2020 flow diagram. "The PRISMA diagram for Databases and Registers follows the same format as the previous 2009 PRISMA diagram while the diagram for Databases, Registers, and Gray Literature has an additional column on the right side of the diagram for reporting grey literature searches and results" (PRISMA, 2022). For the greater good of brevity, the authors have not included the specifics of the checklist and flow diagram. The details can be found on the official website.

The prominent additions to PRISMA 2020 guidelines are listed in 10 points as follows:

(1) The addition of the abstract writing specification within the newer guidelines.
(2) Protocol and registration items are moved from the beginning of the method section to the "Other Information" section with the addition of a sub-item suggesting authors explain changes to the information presented at the time of registration in directories such as PROSPERO.
(3) The "Search" item is modified to recommend authors present full search strategies for all databases, registers and websites searched, not just at least one database.
(4) "Study selection" items are changed to give more insight into how many reviewers screened each record and each report retrieved, whether they worked independently, and if applicable, details of automation tools used in the process.
(5) The new standard includes a subitem to the "Data items" advising authors to describe how results were defined, which of these were required, and methods for selecting a subcategory of findings from included studies.

(6) The new guideline splits the "Synthesis of results" into the "Methods" part into six sub-items and advises authors to illustrate: the processes used to determine which studies were eligible for each synthesis.

(7) The addition of a sub-item to the "Study selection" item in the Results section advises the researchers to cite studies that could appear to meet the inclusion criteria, but which were excluded, and explain why they were not included for further evidence synthesis.

(8) "Asking authors to summarize the characteristics and risk of bias among studies contributing to the synthesis; present results of all statistical syntheses conducted; present results of any investigations of possible causes of heterogeneity among study results; and present results of any sensitivity analyses" (Page et al., 2021).

(9) The inclusion of the latest items recommends researchers describe methods for results of an evaluation of conviction in the body of evidence for a result.

(10) An additional item recommends authors declare competing interests and make data, syntax, and code used in the review publicly available.

5.3 Extensions of PRISMA

Numerous extensions of the PRISMA Statement have been developed to facilitate the reporting of diverse types of SLRs. The important extensions relevant to the review of management and social science literature are (1) PRISMA-A (2) PRISMA-E (3) PRISMA-P (4) PRISMA-ScR, and (5) PRISMA-S. The details of these extensions are listed in Table 2).

Table 2. PRISMA Extensions Relevant to Review of Management Literature.

SN	Extension	Description
1	PRISMA for abstracts (PRISMA-A) Page et al. (2021)	"The 12-item checklist gives authors a framework for condensing their systematic review into the essentials for a journal or conference abstract." It is updated in PRISMA 2020 statement.
2	PRISMA equity (PRISMA-E) Welch et al. (2012)	"It guides reporting equity-focused systematic reviews to help reviewers identify, extract, and synthesize evidence on equity in systematic reviews." the PRISMA-Equity extension was published in 2012
3	PRISMA for protocols (PRISMA-P) Moher et al. (2015)	"PRISMA-P was published in 2015 aiming to facilitate the development and reporting of systematic review protocols."
4	PRISMA for scoping reviews (PRISMA-ScR) Tricco et al. (2018)	It was published in 2018 to synthesize evidence and evaluate the scope of extant articles in a research area. It also helps in assessing whether a systematic review is required of the topic at all.
5	PRISMA for searching (PRISMA-S) (Rethlefsen et al., 2021)	"The PRISMA extension for searching was published in 2021. The checklist includes 16 reporting items, each of which is detailed with exemplar reporting and Rationale."

Source: Authors compilation on basis of mentioned resources.

6. CONCLUSION

PRISMA guidelines have evolved over time and in the last decades, there have been many extensions published to cater to the specific need. The use of the PRISMA protocol not only gives structure to the review process it also helps other researchers to reproduce the findings of the systematic review. The recent updates in PRISMA go one step further and provide guidelines for result synthesis and reporting. Even then evidence synthesis is based on the selected literature deeds of the researcher performing the review. There should be a mechanism to minimize these biases. The existing guideline for PRISMA asks authors to summarize the characteristics and risk of bias among studies contributing to the synthesis. These types of majors keep a reader informed about the probable biases in the findings of the systematic review. Other tools such as the assessment of multiple systematic reviews (AMSTAR) are extensively used for examining the methodological quality of systematic reviews (SR). Again, AMSTAR is specially designed for randomized controlled trials (RCTs) and its applicability to SRs of other study designs prevalent in management literature is arguable.

PRISMA is extensively used in healthcare research but its wide use in management research is still debatable. The use of traditional narrative reviews is more common in management literature. There is a need for PRISMA extension of specific objectives review of management literature. Management researchers suggest the use of a framework for conducting a review of management literature. They argue that reviews with a framework have proven to be more acceptable as they are likely to show a more robust structure (Paul & Criado, 2020). Some of the frameworks used in the review of literature are ADO (Antecedents, Decisions, and Outcome), 6 W Framework (who, when, where, how, what, and why), and TCCM Framework (Theory, Construct, Characteristics and Methodology) (Callahan, 2014; Paul & Criado, 2020; Paul & Rosado-Serrano, 2019). Although extant literature cites the distinct advantage of using a framework for the review of management literature, there is a lack of standardization of these frameworks. Moreover, developers of these frameworks do not give a clear understanding of which framework is better in which scenario. One of the reasons behind it may be these frameworks are suggested and updated by researchers in their capacity and followed in their academic community. There is a need for a more organized effort like the PRISMA group around the review of management literature.

6.1 Implications and Future Directions

This chapter has two implications for theory. Firstly, it observes that the process of the management literature review is not standardized. Although PRISMA has useful extensions which can be adopted in the management literature the less prevalent use is strange. Secondly, the existing frameworks used in the review of literature do not highlight the method of selection of these approaches. This study again has two implications for the practices. Firstly, the study provides seven strategies to address the reproducibility crisis in management research. Secondly, it highlights the recent addition to PRISMA and the applicability of existing extensions in the review of management literature. Once management researchers start using PRISMA more extensions will come addressing specific needs. The review based on the PRISMA framework is more acceptable in interdisciplinary research involving clinicians, nursing, and allied healthcare professionals. Future research can address the mechanism to address duplicate records in literature selection. Another review article on the proprietary and open-source software available for PRISMA will be helpful for the readers.

REFERENCES

Alston, J. M., & Rick, J. A. (2021). A beginner's guide to conducting reproducible research. *The Bulletin of the Ecological Society of America, 102*(2), 1–14.

Baker, M. (2016). 1,500 scientists lift the lid on reproducibility. *Nature, 533*(7604), 452–454.

Bandara, W., Furtmueller, E., Gorbacheva, E., Miskon, S., & Beekhuyzen, J. (2015). Achieving rigor in literature reviews: Insights from qualitative data analysis and tool support. *Communications of the Association for Information Systems, 37*(1), 8.

Beller, E., Clark, J., Tsafnat, G., Adams, C., Diehl, H., Lund, H., Ouzzani M, Thayer, K., Thomas, J., Turner, T., Xia, J., Robinson, K., & Glasziou, P. (2018). Making progress with the automation of systematic reviews: Principles of the International Collaboration for the Automation of Systematic Reviews (ICASR). *Systematic Reviews, 7*(1), 1–7.

Brocke, J. V., Simons, A., Niehaves, B., Niehaves, B., Reimer, K., Plattfaut, R., & Cleven, A. (2009). *Reconstructing the giant: On the importance of rigor in documenting the literature search process.* CIS 2009 Proceedings Paper 161.

Callahan, J. L. (2014). *Writing literature reviews: A reprise and update.* https://doi.org/10.1177/1534484314536705

Contandriopoulos, D., Lemire, M., Denis, J. L., & Tremblay, É. (2010). Knowledge exchange processes in organizations and policy arenas: A narrative systematic review of the literature. *The Milbank Quarterly, 88*(4), 444–483.

Coughlan, M., Cronin, P., & Ryan, F. (2007). Step-by-step guide to critiquing research. Part 1: Quantitative research. *British Journal of Nursing, 16*(11), 658–663.

Jesson, J., Matheson, L., & Lacey, F. M. (2011). *Doing your literature review: Traditional and systematic techniques.* Sage Publications Ltd.

Knopf, J. W. (2006). Doing a literature review. *PS: Political Science & Politics, 39*(1), 127–132.

Koffel, J. B., & Rethlefsen, M. L. (2016). Reproducibility of search strategies is poor in systematic reviews published in high-impact pediatrics, cardiology, and surgery journals: A cross-sectional study. *PLoS One, 11*(9), e0163309.

Lachal, J., Revah-Levy, A., Orri, M., & Moro, M. R. (2017). Meta-synthesis: An original method to synthesize qualitative literature in psychiatry. *Frontiers in Psychiatry, 8*, 269.

Leidner, D. E. (2018). Review and theory symbiosis: An introspective retrospective. *Journal of the Association for Information Systems, 19*(6), 1.

Moher, D., Liberati, A., Tetzlaff, J., Altman, D. G., Altman, D., Antes, G., Atkins, D., Barbour, V., Barrowman, N., Berlin, J. A., Clark, J., Clarke, M., Cook, D., D'Amico, R., Deeks, J. J., Devereaux, P. J., Dickersin, K., Egger, M., Ernst, E.,... Tugwell, P. (2015). Preferred Reporting Items for Systematic Review and Meta-Analysis Protocols (PRISMA-P) 2015 statement. *Systematic Reviews, 4*(1), 1. https://doi.org/10.1186/2046-4053-4-1

Nasheeda, A., Abdullah, H. B., Krauss, S. E., & Ahmed, N. B. (2019). A narrative systematic review of life skills education: Effectiveness, research gaps, and priorities. *International Journal of Adolescence and Youth, 24*(3), 362–379.

Page, M. J., Altman, D. G., Shamseer, L., McKenzie, J. E., Ahmadzai, N., Wolfe, D., Yazdi, F., Catalá-López, F., Tricco, A. C., & Moher, D. (2018). Reproducible research practices are underused in systematic reviews of biomedical interventions. *Journal of Clinical Epidemiology, 94*, 8–18.

Page, M. J., McKenzie, J. E., Bossuyt, P. M., Boutron, I., Hoffmann, T. C., Mulrow, C. D., Shamseer, L., Tetzlaff, J. M., Akl, E. A., Brennan, S. E., Chou, R., Glanville, J., Grimshaw, J. M., Hróbjartsson, A., Lalu, M. M., Li, T., Loder, E. W., Mayo- Wilson, E., McDonald, S.,... Moher, D. (2021). The PRISMA 2020 statement: An updated guideline for reporting systematic reviews. *Systematic Reviews, 10*(1), 1–11.

Page, M. J., & Moher, D. (2017). Evaluations of the uptake and impact of the Preferred Reporting Items for Systematic reviews and Meta-Analyses (PRISMA) Statement and extensions: A scoping review. *Systematic Reviews, 6*(1), 1–14.

Paré, G., Trudel, M. C., Jaana, M., & Kitsiou, S. (2015). Synthesizing information systems knowledge: A typology of literature reviews. *Information & Management, 52*(2), 183–199.

Paul, J., & Criado, A. R. (2020). The art of writing a literature review: What do we know and what do we need to know? *International Business Review, 29*(4), 101717.

Paul, J., & Rosado-Serrano, A. (2019). Gradual Internationalization vs Born-Global/International new venture models: A review and research agenda. *International Marketing Review, 36*(6), 830–858.

Polit, D. F., & Beck, C. T. (2006). The content validity index: Are you sure you know what's being reported? Critique and recommendations. *Research in Nursing & Health, 29*(5), 489–497.

PRISMA. (2022). *The PRISMA 2020 Checklist and flow diagram.* https://prisma-statement.org/

Rana, S., Raut, S. K., Prashar, S., & Hamid, A. B. A. (2020). Promoting through consumer nostalgia: A conceptual framework and future research agenda. *Journal of Promotion Management, 27*(2), 211–249.

Rana, S., Raut, S. K., Prashar, S., & Quttainah, M. A. (2022). The transversal of nostalgia from psychology to marketing: What does it portend for future research? *International Journal of Organizational Analysis, 30*(4), 899–932.

Rethlefsen M. L., Kirtley S., Waffenschmidt S., Ayala, A. P., Moher, D., Page, M. J., Koffel, J. B., & PRISMA-S Group. (2021). PRISMA-S: An extension to the PRISMA statement for reporting literature searches in systematic reviews. *Systematic Reviews, 10*(1), 39. https://doi.org/10.1186/s13643-020-01542-z

Rice, S. M., Purcell, R., De Silva, S., Mawren, D., McGorry, P. D., & Parker, A. G. (2016). The mental health of elite athletes: A narrative systematic review. *Sports Medicine, 46*(9), 1333–1353.

Sarkis-Onofre, R., Catalá-López, F., Aromataris, E., & Lockwood, C. (2021). How to properly use the PRISMA Statement. *Systematic Reviews, 10*(1), 1–3.

Shokraneh F. (2018, November 26). *Reproducible and Replicable Search for Research Methods in Systematic Reviews.* Search Solutions.

Shokraneh, F. (2019). Reproducibility and replicability of systematic reviews. *World Journal Meta-Analysis, 7*(3), 66–71.

Stewart, L., Moher, D., & Shekelle, P. (2012). Why prospective registration of systematic reviews makes sense. *Systematic Reviews, 1*(1), 1–4.

Tao, K. M., Li, X. Q., Zhou, Q. H., Moher, D., Ling, C. Q., & Yu, W. F. (2011). From QUOROM to PRISMA: A survey of high-impact medical journals' instructions to authors and a review of systematic reviews in anesthesia literature. *PLoS One, 6*(11), e27611.

Tricco, A. C., Lillie, E., Zarin, W., O'Brien, K. K., Colquhoun, H., Levac, D., Moher, D., Peters, M. D. J., Horsley, T., Weeks, L., Hempel, S., Chang, C., Elie, A., McGowan, J., Stewart, L., Hartling, L., Aldcroft, A., Wilson, M. G., Garritty, C.,... Straus, S. E. (2018). PRISMA extension for scoping reviews (PRISMA-ScR): Checklist and explanation. *Annals of Internal Medicine, 169*(7), 467–473. https://doi.org/10.7326/M18-0850

Watson, R. T., & Webster, J. (2020). Analyzing the past to prepare for the future: Writing a literature review on a roadmap for release 2.0. *Journal of Decision Systems, 29*(3), 129–147.

Webster, J., & Watson, R. T. (2002). Analyzing the past to prepare for the future: Writing a literature review. *MIS Quarterly, 26*(2), 13–23.

Welch, V., Petticrew, M., Tugwell, P., Moher, D., O'Neill, J., Waters, E., & White, H. (2012). Guidelines and guidance-PRISMA-equity 2012 extension: Reporting guidelines for systematic reviews with a focus on health equity. *PLoS Medicine, 9*(10), 1487.

Williams, R. I., Jr., Clark, L. A., Clark, W. R., & Raffo, D. M. (2021). Re-examining systematic literature review in management research: Additional benefits and execution protocols. *European Management Journal, 39*(4), 521–533.

REALIST SYNTHESIS: AN INNOVATIVE APPROACH TO LITERATURE REVIEW FOR COMPLEX MANAGEMENT PHENOMENA

Ellen Pittman

ABSTRACT

Common literature review methods such as systematic review and narrative review are poorly suited to the investigation of complex management phenomena. Systematic reviews are highly driven by protocol and procedure, and are oft-criticized as reductive and poorly equipped to examine the interaction between phenomena and context, nonlinear processes, and empirical outcomes that are less predictable. Narrative reviews, on the other hand, are pluralistic and iterative and thus better suited to descriptions of the complex and unpredictable; however, they tend to lack methodological transparency, trustworthiness, and pragmatism in application. The "realist synthesis" approach to literature review can be seen as the middle-ground between these two common methods, offering both methodological rigor alongside flexibility and nuance. Realist synthesis takes an explanatory frame, with a focus on unearthing the theorized causal mechanisms at play beneath a phenomenon of interest.

Keywords: Realist synthesis; realist review; literature review; complexity; wicked problems; review methods

Advancing Methodologies of Conducting Literature Review in Management Domain
Review of Management Literature, Volume 2, 137–159
Copyright © 2024 Ellen Pittman
Published under exclusive licence by Emerald Publishing Limited
ISSN: 2754-5865/doi:10.1108/S2754-586520230000002008

1. BACKGROUND

1.1 What Is Realist Synthesis?

Realist synthesis (also known as "realist review") was developed as an alternative method to systematic review, offering a more context-sensitive and iterative approach to reviewing and integrating scholarly information, and drawing conclusions about complex social phenomena (Pawson et al., 2004). Realist synthesis seeks to identify and critically examine the various theories and hypotheses that exist about phenomena of interest, and to develop a pragmatic explanation as to why a specific outcome may manifest "for whom, in what circumstances, in what respects, and why?" (Pawson et al., 2004). The approach does this by identifying theory-oriented (rather than empirically-oriented) configurations of: "context," "mechanism," and "outcome" (Jagosh, 2019).

As a method, realist synthesis was built upon the principles of critical realism (Bhaskar, 1979) – a viewpoint from the philosophy of science that is positioned between logical positivism (traditionally associated with the natural sciences and "the scientific method") and interpretivism (linked to social research which seeks to derive, describe and construct meaning/s by exploring and comparing multiple perspectives and experiences). Realist synthesis has been applied in diverse social research fields, such as sociology (Quinlan et al., 2019), psychology (Roodbari et al., 2022), environmental studies (Nilsson et al., 2016) and, to a very small extent, management (Armstrong, 2019).

Realist synthesis provides a method for both analyzing and synthesizing research evidence with an explanatory rather than judgmental or categorical focus (Pawson et al., 2004). The method seeks to unpack the mechanisms at play beneath an empirical outcome and how these mechanisms have unfolded in particular contexts, enabling decision-makers to gain a better understanding of how to ensure a strategy, change, or policy will work in new contexts (Pawson et al., 2004).

As an approach to literature review, realist synthesis was developed by social researchers most familiar with health and social service contexts, with an interest in the evaluation of specific healthcare or human service "interventions" (e.g. health policy, clinical trial, evidence-based procedure etc.) (Jagosh, 2019). For this reason, the documented method for realist synthesis (e.g. RAMESES protocol and reporting guidelines (Wong et al., 2013)) requires re-framing and small adjustments for use by management scholars. In particular, the level of analysis must be broadened from a small project/intervention level of analysis or a policy reform, to be suitable for the investigation of research questions relevant to the discipline of management – from the unit or project level (e.g. human resource strategies), to whole-of-organization (e.g. leadership approaches), to the institutional or cross-organization context (e.g. broader trends or theories, such institutional theory). This chapter presents the documented realist synthesis method, with minor adaptations to suit the theoretical and practical requirements of management scholars.

1.2 Realist Synthesis Compared With Other Review Methods

As introduced earlier, many of the major literature review methods such as systematic review and narrative review, have emerged from (or roughly belong to) distinct ontological and epistemological viewpoints. For this reason, we can distinguish fundamental differences between literature review methods - in assumption, underlying logic, purpose/aim and approach (see Table 1). A comprehensive explanation and comparison of prominent literature review methods and their epistemic roots, is available elsewhere (Pawson & Bellamy, 2006; Pawson et al., 2004), with a very brief overview provided here.

As presented in Table 1, at one end of the spectrum sits logical positivism/ empiricism upon which systematic review is based, and at the other, there is interpretivism/constructivism – the underlying logic for many narrative reviews.[1] Systematic review favors a reductive logic and high levels of procedural standardization (Grant & Booth, 2009). The primary aim is to determine the best evidence (through comparison of effect size) in order to predict, generalize and replicate the findings in new empirical settings. This approach to literature review is highly structured and planned, with little emphasis on theory or comparison of competing theories, and no room to adapt the literature search or screening process during the review (Grant & Booth, 2009). The high degree of structure assists with procedural transparency and replicability, but does not allow for a genuine process of discovery, which (seemingly) runs counter to the aims of a review; that is, to represent a reliable, valid and trustworthy summary on a particular topic. For example, as a reviewer gathers more information and knowledge on a topic through the citation search and selection process, a more adaptive and iterative search approach may lead to the discovery of unexpected conceptual linkages, new terminology and concepts (including alternate or additional key search terms that require new searches), alternative methodologies, and parallel fragments of discipline-specific commentary and theoretical development. Systematic review does not allow for procedural variance from the protocol, thus risking gross omissions in theory and evidence. This omission is particularly relevant (and detrimental) to research on social rather than laboratory settings – as scholarship on social phenomena is more commonly fragmented, discursive, and overlapping (Pawson et al., 2004).

Narrative review, on the other hand, is exploratory in nature and tends to value a plurality of viewpoints, methods, study setting and findings (Greenhalgh et al., 2018). Knowledge is generated through interpretation and sense-making across case/study comparisons, relying heavily on the reviewer's expertise and discernment as they seek to generate new theoretical insights, through rich description and synthesis across several studies (Greenhalgh et al., 2018). The

---

[1]It is worth noting that narrative review is less distinct in its ontological/epistemological origins, as the decision to use narrative review may also be reflective of a "default position" where there is little to no consideration of the underlying assumptions and where the method may be chosen somewhat casually or without regard for the need for consistency between assumption and method.

Table 1. A Comparison of Realist Synthesis With Systematic and Narrative Review Methods.

	Systematic Review	Realist Synthesis	Narrative Review
Epistemic tradition	Logical positivism Empiricism	Critical realism	Interpretivism Constructivism
Key assumptions	Objective truth Reductionism	Pragmatism Pluralism Open systems Nonlinearity Equifinality	Subjective and relative truth Pluralism
Logic	Deductive Empirical	Abductive Explanatory	Inductive Exploratory
Aim of approach	To determine the best evidence (effect size) for prediction, generalization and replication	To determine, establish and/or integrate which theory, for best application, within which circumstances	Holistic comparison to construct a theory-driven "recipe" for a particular empirical outcome, which may be used to upscale or spread
Key focus	Method-driven analysis of effect sizes	Theory-driven synthesis of mixed outcomes in various settings and contexts	Theory-driven holistic comparison through description
Unit of analysis	Empirical unit (e.g. an individual, organization, country) containing independent variable of interest	Mechanism (e.g. cultural norms, human interpretation, agency)	Theoretical unit (e.g. a project, policy, intervention)
Method	Predetermined by protocol, methodological transparency/ reproducibility	Planned and iterative, but with methodological transparency/auditability	Iterative and often low transparency in method
Approach to generalizability	Empirical generalizability	Theoretical generalizability	Identification of proximal similarity derived from exemplary cases
Degree of difficulty in use of method	Simple but laborious	Difficult, requiring continual discernment and expert knowledge	Simple but highly reliant on discernment
Key strengths	Standardized and reproducible	Logical and structured Pluralist and flexible Sensitive to context and complexity Theory-building and integrating	Pluralist and flexible Sensitive to context and complexity Theory-building and integrating
Key limitations	Judgmental Seeks a "one-size-fits-all" conclusion Evidence-base is often weak/contested Retrospective	Not standardizable or reproducible	Not standardizable or reproducible Poor transparency of method Poor treatment of dissimilarity between included studies Poor trustworthiness

Source: Author derived from Pawson et al. (2004), Pawson and Bellamy (2006) and Jagosh (2019).

approach to literature searching is inductive and unstructured allowing for organic discovery and lateral connections across the literature/s; however, this flexibility in search strategy and review method is often very poorly documented, relatively unplanned, and it is not replicable or verifiable. For this reason, narrative review is often considered low on trustworthiness (Pawson & Bellamy, 2006). That is, it is difficult to establish the degree to which the results of a narrative review accurately represent or approximate the body of knowledge on a topic or question. There is risk of cherry-picking, and the introduction of other biases or issues of reliability. Also, procedurally, there are concerns over the validity of integrated findings, whereby studies with diverse viewpoints, aims, methods, instruments, quality standards etc., are compared and synthesized without adequate consideration for the risks involved in isolating findings from their epistemic and methodological contexts (Pawson & Bellamy, 2006). In short, the practice of narrative review is diverse, creative and unstructured, which can act as both a conceptual blessing and a reliability curse.

The realist synthesis approach to literature review was developed from the critical realist viewpoint – a relatively complicated ontological and epistemological stance - often seen as the "middle-ground" between logical positivism and interpretivism (see Wynn and Williams (2012) for an accessible yet detailed description). In grossly simplified terms, the "realism" relates to an alignment with logical positivism, which favors a degree of ordering, structuring and categorization of knowledge through an analytical process, while the "critical" corresponds to an attempt to go beyond the categorical, to capture complexity in the hidden mechanisms that prompt or cause an outcome (Lönngren & van Poeck, 2021).

1.3 Why and When to Select Realist Synthesis?

Given its position within the epistemic "middle ground" between logical positivism and interpretivism, realist synthesis is suitable for the exploration of a broad sweep of management topics and research questions (arguably: all and any topics and questions); however, the method has *particular* advantage for the analysis of complex management phenomena (Pawson et al., 2004). I will argue that reductive methods of literature review, such as systematic review, are fundamentally incompatible with key tenets of systems and complexity theories and are therefore insufficient as a method of investigation. Further, I argue that while interpretivist methods, such as narrative review, may offer descriptive value on topics of complexity, they are less useful when attempting to *explain* phenomena. Rather, the most appropriate review method for complex phenomena strikes a balance between analysis (e.g. classification or categorization) and synthesis (e.g. theory-building, through an examination of the interconnections between categories of factors and how they interact) (Greenhalgh & Manzano, 2022). I will examine key concepts from the "complex problems" and "wicked problems" literature to illustrate this point, though it is important to note that realist synthesis is not limited to the examination of "problems" alone.

Complex problems and wicked problems are parallel but related concepts that emerged from a common conceptual source: systems theory (Peters, 2017). Proponents of both concepts seek to reject the reductionist orthodoxy which assumes that social problems can be defined, understood, broken down and rationally solved through precise planning and controlled remediation (Head & Alford, 2013). Management and policy practitioners have readily adopted the wickedness notion to explain and explore persistent and seemingly intractable challenges – ranging from poverty and climate change to health care financing and organizational turnaround (Peters & Tarpey, 2019). Complex problems are viewed as distinct from merely "complicated" and "simple" problems, and wicked problems are distinguished from "tame" problems (Peters, 2018).

Wicked problems are defined in relation to a set of categorical criteria linked to the nature of the problem itself, whereas complex problems are defined by patterns of attributes or descriptive features with relational, temporal or other dynamic characteristics (see Table 2). For the purpose of this chapter, it is useful to examine both concepts in tandem, as they provide a broad basis upon which to examine the literature reviewer's task when faced with complex management phenomena.

In simplified terms, a wicked problem is: difficult to define and is unique; potential solutions to the problem are both difficult to define and to apply; and there are inevitable unintended consequences or "ripple effects" that arise from efforts to solve a wicked problem (Xiang, 2013). Complex problems have several features, including the presence of: multiple causes which may impede transparency and problem identification; multiple agents (people/groups) with diverse goals which may be in conflict; patterns of interaction between these multiple factors and agents that are difficult to predict; cascading effects across multiple factors or agents due to changes initially observed with only one factor or agent; a tendency for rapid change and dynamism in the contextual environment; and the potential for delayed or protracted effects in response to changes (Funke, 1991). These two nonreductive approaches to framing problems remain largely compatible with one another, with one key difference: wicked problems do not recognize nonlinearity, whereas this is a key feature of the complexity viewpoint (see Table 2).

"Wicked problems," by definition, evade the sorts of classifications and simplifications that characterize systematic review methods. For example, reductive methods are not equipped to explore problems that are unique, difficult to define, or where unexpected and irreversible "ripple effects" may stem from a single policy or intervention (Head, 2019). Similar difficulties arise with "complex problems": one-track systematization cannot grapple with the presence of multiple factors, multiple conflicting goals, and unexpected interactions between factors or actions where changes may occur rapidly or with time-delayed effects (Petticrew et al., 2013). Systematic literature reviews require clear definition and operationalization of terms, they favor the use of protocols where a search strategy is planned in advance with no capacity for adaptation during the process of review, and their underlying logic is virtually context-free (Grant & Booth, 2009; Pawson & Bellamy, 2006).

Table 2. Defining Criteria for "Wicked Problems" and Defining Features of "Complex Problems".

Summarized Criteria for Problem "Wickedness"	Attributes of Complex Problems
Indeterminacy in problem formation – problem definition (with a set of unique and determinate criteria) is not possible due to high levels of diversity, conflict, and change over time	*Intransparency* – multiple factors involved, and only the symptoms rather than causes may be readily identifiable
Nondefinitiveness in problem solution – the design of a rigorous and ultimate solution, with definitive results, is not possible due to the inability to determine the problem and to determine the full scope of repercussions arising from the problem	*Polytely* – the existence of multiple and possibly conflicting goals held by multiple agents or groups
Nonsolubility – resulting from the first two criteria, wicked problems cannot be "solved" (eliminated) with a tendency for recurrence. This is in contrast to "tame problems," which are amenable to solutions because their characteristics can be adequately determined within defined goals and rules	*Situational complexity* – complex patterns of interaction between multiple factors, with low predictability regarding their interaction
Irreversible consequentiality – all attempts to solve a wicked problem have their own consequences, leading to a cascade of associated "ripple effects" that are nonreversible and nonstoppable	*Connectivity of factors* – a change in one factor may have consequences for multiple other factors, impeding predictability of outcomes
Individual uniqueness of problem – the presence of one or more distinguishing characteristics resulting in the problem (and measures taken to resolve it) being essentially "one-of-a-kind" resulting in wicked problems not fitting to classifications or "classes" or being amenable to transferable solutions	*Dynamic developments* – a context of rapid and unpredictable change *Time-delayed effects* – timing of factor interactions and their effects may be delayed and unfold in nonlinear ways

Source: Author derived from Xiang (2013), Rittel and Webber (1973) and Funke (1991).

The persistent use of reductive literature review methods to investigate highly complex phenomena and settings often leads to inconclusive or contested findings or explanations that splinter into silos of single-factor theories (Petticrew et al., 2013). In response to mixed or conflicting evidence surrounding complex phenomena, "context" may be invoked as a catch-all explanation; however, the notion of context is rarely defined or operationalized (Greenhalgh & Manzano, 2022) and research investigations into context have tended to produce "shopping lists" of context variables (Pettigrew, 1985, p. 23) without adequate reflection or guidance as to how these variables might interact and coalesce to produce an empirical outcome (Bate, 2014).

On the other hand, narrative review methods are often criticized as lacking rigor and replicability, with low levels of utility for management practitioners and policy-makers – two primary consumers of literature reviews (Pawson & Bellamy, 2006). Narrative reviews tend to be heavy on theory and light on data, with poorer capacity for measured comparison and insufficient reflection on issues of generalizability (Greenhalgh et al., 2018). Due to methodological fuzziness, it may be difficult to establish the degree to which narrative descriptions adequately represent the scope and spectrum of scholarship on a topic (Grant & Booth, 2009); and although narrative reviews may be well-placed to *describe* a complex or wicked problem, given the lack of focus on causation, they often neglect to canvas the mechanisms that underlie a problem. This is a weighty omission, given the need to understand the root causes in order to develop a sustainable solution to a problem (Peters & Tarpey, 2019).

As detailed in the next section, the realist synthesis approach retains the strengths and at least partially addresses the weaknesses of both interpretivist and logical approaches. As an abductive method, realist synthesis facilitates analysis and simplification of the literature (e.g. through classification of theory or data) as well as taking a synthetic approach (e.g. through theory-building and refinement). Tactically, realist synthesis combines systematic and adaptive techniques, providing both rigor as well as the capacity to examine lateral connections between factors and their combined effects (Pawson & Bellamy, 2006).

2. HOW TO CONDUCT A REALIST SYNTHESIS

This section outlines the steps and considerations involved in conducting a realist synthesis. "Considerations" is apt here, given that the realist synthesis method is abductive and iterative and the reviewer/s need to continually use discernment when applying the principles and structure, outlined. This section includes a procedural comparison with traditional systematic review; and provides examples of realist synthesis steps that have been "worked through" (drawing on hospital performance improvement as the sample complex management phenomena of interest – as adapted from Pittman (2020)). Table 3 provides a brief overview of the realist synthesis process, with detailed commentary thereafter.

2.1 Scoping

A systematic review (as opposed to realist synthesis) begins with the identification of a research question to set the purpose and scope boundaries for the review and to operationalize the key concepts and terms to guide the review, throughout (Grant & Booth, 2009). Additionally, it is essential that a systematic review be developed in such a way as to ensure that the review "compares apples with apples" – drawing cross-study conclusions only where there are reasonable equivalencies in aim and empirical factors (study design, population, independent variable, dependent variable/outcome measure, etc.) (Pawson et al., 2004).

A realist synthesis, on the other hand, engages with this initial scoping process at a deeper conceptual level, is more pluralistic in its approach, and also continues to return to and refine scoping parameters (as needed) throughout early stages of the review process (Pawson et al., 2004). Like systematic review, realist review begins with the development of an initial research question; however, at this early stage of the review the research question remains provisional and is likely to be modified at later stages in response to the discovery of new information. At the initial stage of the review, it is also important that a realist review

Table 3. Steps Involved in Planning and Conducting a Realist Synthesis.

Step	Description
1 Scoping the literature	An exploratory process to initially scope the literature from a theoretical rather than empirical perspective. This step is designed to: • Help identify and refine the research question, • Clarify the purpose of the review, and • Establish the theoretical landscape for the review.A theoretical framework is adopted or established for the specific purposes of the review
2 Searching	A systematized approach, using a purposive sampling strategy and clearly defined decisions relating to: search sources (e.g. databases or journals), search terms, search methods, and how to deal with "saturation" of search results. So long as changes to method are well-documented, the search strategy may vary during the search process, including adding new search sources and new search terms, potentially identified through the process of "snowball" searching or other lateral methods of searching
3 Selection and appraisal of documents	Use of inclusion and exclusion criteria to ensure that the evidence included in the review is both relevant and rigorous
4 Data extraction	Use of data extraction instrument/s (forms or templates) to assist with a comparison of findings across included studies, and appraisal of study quality
5 Synthesis of empirical data/findings	Comparison of findings from included studies, in order to address the aims and questions of the review. This includes the examination of findings that both confirm and contradict the theoretical framework guiding the review
Theoretical synthesis	Refinement of the theoretical framework based on the empirical evidence, new theoretical information, identification of contradictions, conceptual synthesis and integration of data sources
6 Drawing conclusions and reporting findings	The use of "retroductive reasoning" to develop findings on the generative causal mechanisms underlying an empirical outcome of interest, and a standardized approach to report findings from realist synthesis, assisting with consistency, transparency, and comparability between reviews

Source: Derived from Wong et al. (2013).

be grounded by a defined purpose – a statement about what the review intends to explain (Jagosh, 2019; Pawson et al., 2004). This requires a difference in perspective compared with a traditional systematic review, where the primary focus of systematic review is verification of efficacy ("what works") and the potential to make predictions based on conclusions of efficacy (Pawson & Bellamy, 2006). For realist synthesis, the primary purpose is *explanation* (the "how and why" of the phenomena) (Jagosh, 2019).

Finally, the scoping stage of a realist review requires that the reviewer artic-ulate the key theories to be explored in the review. This may be achieved through any combination of: consultation with experts in the field (e.g. Delphi study) and/or with field practitioners (e.g. industry leaders, policy-makers); identification and review of seminal theoretical papers, chapters and sources; and/or a process of literature searching on the topic – with a particular focus on identifying the scope and nature of key theories. A conceptual framework may be adopted (if it already exists), adapted, or developed by the reviewer (Pawson et al., 2004).

Box 1: Step 1. Scoping – An Example of the Realist Synthesis Approach

Objective

This realist synthesis seeks to assess the range, quality and convergence of theoretical and empirical explanations for hospital performance, and from this, to offer practical advice to decision-makers and researchers. The review is conducted as a review of reviews, otherwise known as an "umbrella review."

Research Questions

The review is guided by five research questions:

(1) What is the spectrum of explanations, hypotheses and theories relating to hospital performance and performance improvement?
(2) What credible evidence exists for each of these explanations, hypotheses and theories?
(3) How has the literature discussed the relationship between various explanations, theories and hypotheses for hospital performance, including multifactor explanations, and the interactive or cumulative effect of multiple explanations, hypotheses or theories operating together?
(4) What context-mechanism-outcome relationships are evident within the existing literature?
(5) Based on the aims and findings of this literature review, what guidance can be offered to decision-makers and researchers?

Conceptual Framework

The Ashworth et al. (2010) triad of theoretical determinants for public service performance ("environment + attribute + strategy = performance") was used as a conceptual guide for the development of an adapted conceptual framework for this review (as per Pittman (2020), see Fig. 1). "Environment" theoretical explanations refer to the external context (e.g. patient demographics, or national funding, regulatory and performance monitoring schemes). "Attribute" theoretical explanations refer to the internal organizational context (e.g. organizational structure, culture, leadership). "Strategy" explanations refer to active interventions or programs employed to bring about an improvement or desired outcome (e.g. quality improvement programs, strategic planning, innovations).

(Continued)

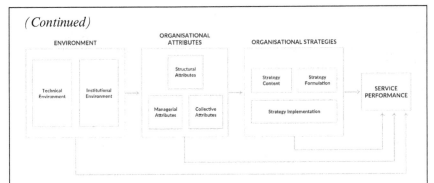

Fig. 1. Triad of Theoretical Determinants for Public Service Performance. *Source:* Pittman (2020) as adapted from Ashworth et al. (2010).

Scoping Procedure

Alongside a review of seminal papers, a preliminary rapid scoping search was conducted in order to identify the spectrum of explanations for hospital performance that sit beneath the overarching "environment-attribute-strategy" theoretical frame. The initial scoping process also helped to develop the search strategy used within the review. 210 citations were identified within the Scopus database using broad search terms on the topic of "hospital performance." 123 citations were screened by abstract and 63 articles were included by full-text. An appraisal of these relevant articles resulted in the development of 18 search categories, representing four multifactor and 14 single-factor explanations/theories for hospital performance. Search categories were altered and refined at later stages of the review.

Environment	Attribute	Strategy	Multifactor
• Financial reimbursement • Demography • Regulation • Reputation	• Structure & governance • Leadership & management • Organizational culture	• Planning • Financial strategy • Quality improvement • Innovation & IT • Human resources • Learning • Capabilities	• Contingency/configuration • Complexity • Corporatization • Turbulence

2.2 Searching

The next step involves searching for relevant literature. This is achieved by scouring research databases, hand-searching target journals, "snowball" searching, and looking for relevant gray literature in specific policy repositories or on government websites. For systematic literature reviews, this is a highly detailed and methodical process – led by a rigid protocol, which relies heavily and somewhat exclusively on research database searches and a set of key search terms determined prior to searching (Grant & Booth, 2009). For a realist synthesis, the process is both planned and adaptive, and grey literature sources are valued alongside peer-reviewed academic sources (Pawson et al., 2004). In particular, grey literature sources are seen to offer important conceptual and theoretical value, and may include a pragmatic commentary on possible causal mechanisms, which may be less empirically relevant, but help to deepen lateral thinking, beyond the constraints of academic justification. Thorough record-keeping of the realist synthesis search process is paramount (Wong et al., 2013), and it is advisable to keep a record of all searches, including the "search string", the information source, how many citations were found, how many citations were screened, and any additional snowball searches that arose etc.

For realist synthesis, searching may take a number of different approaches. Initially it might involve performing several background searches to get a "feel" for the literature (Pawson et al., 2004). More specific searches may then be used to target a deeper understanding of the theoretical landscape. Akin to traditional systematic review searching, literature databases may be systematically scoured with key search terms, for empirical evidence on the topic (Pawson & Bellamy, 2006). Search terms may evolve over time. "Snowball searching" may also be interspersed with these methods, where a researcher may find new sources by reviewing the reference lists of articles deemed relevant, or where research databases and their "relevance" algorithms may be used to "suggest" a related article (Wong et al., 2013).

For realist synthesis, the search process is both systematized (through the use of search terms and inclusion/exclusion criteria) and iterative/recursive, where the primary purpose is knowledge saturation (Glaser & Strauss, 1967) – on both theoretical and conceptual levels. Unlike systematic approaches, a realist synthesis reviewer must use a degree of discernment in order to determine when saturation has occurred, which underlines the level of mastery required in performing reviews from the realist viewpoint.

Box 2: Step 2. Searching – An Example of the Realist Synthesis Approach

Eighteen discrete search strategies were devised to correspond with the 18 categories of explanation for hospital performance identified and developed in the initial scoping stage. These 18 search strategies were used to query Scopus, PubMed, Cochrane and Google Scholar databases, with key term adjustments made between databases, as necessary. A gray literature search was also conducted spanning seven key grey literature databases and industry websites.

Common across each search strategy were the key words "hospital" AND "performance", which were used in conjunction with words specific to the

(Continued)

particular category of explanation, for instance, for the "leadership" category, the key words "leaders*" OR "senior management" OR "top management" OR "CEO" were added. New search terms were trialled or adopted throughout the process. A total of 112 separate searches were conducted – each recorded in a spreadsheet for future review and replication.

Database results were limited to peer-reviewed review articles published between January 2000 and June 2017, filtered by "Title/Abstract/Keyword" for Scopus and Cochrane databases and "Title/Abstract" for PubMed. It was not possible to limit the search by field or for peer-reviewed review articles in Google Scholar and so "literature review" was manually added to the search string.

Recognizing the well-documented limitations of electronic database searching for complex or contested social science research topics (Greenhalgh, 2004) a "relevance and saturation protocol" was devised to manage the high volume of (often irrelevant) citation returns. The protocol functioned to reduce the number of search results that were screened by title. This was achieved by applying the "relevance" or "best match" sorting feature within Scopus and PubMed, respectively, and abandoning discrete database searches after a minimum of 100 citations were screened with no relevant result (here a "result" is defined as a citation download by screened abstract). This was taken to indicate a saturation point for the particular search.

In addition to this, "snowball searching" was conducted, including a review of the reference lists of included articles and citation tracking through the algorithmic "related articles" suggestions provided by research databases and in Google Scholar.

2.3 Selection and Appraisal

Selecting and appraising evidence involves an assessment of both relevance and rigor (Pawson et al., 2004). Systematic review achieves this by applying a set of rigid criteria: - inclusion and exclusion criteria are used to screen for "relevance" or other pragmatic boundaries such as language and publication dates; and checklists for assessing methodological quality screen for "rigor" (Grant & Booth, 2009). Realist synthesis uses defined inclusion and exclusion criteria and may use quality checklists, but the process is less reliant on the checklist or tool itself, and includes a higher degree of judgment and discernment. This is particular so, as the primary focus for realist synthesis is *theoretical* relevance, rather than empirical or methodological rigor (Pawson et al., 2004). For example, an article of moderate trustworthiness may contain highly relevant material of theoretical significance (e.g. as is often the case with qualitative research). This disparity would not be grounds for exclusion, but may alter the way the article is treated in later stages of literature analysis and synthesis. This is further described under Sections 2.4 and 2.5.

Box 3: Step 3. Selection and Appraisal – An Example of the Realist Synthesis Approach

Papers were screened for inclusion in three phases: by title, by abstract and by full-text. The following selection criteria was applied during all three stages of review, with increasing granularity at each screening: (i) paper relates to hospital performance as a dependent variable or outcome, (ii) paper is a review article or publication reporting a systematized search and selection strategy, and (iii) paper was published in any language, between January 2000 and June 2017.

Although included papers were later screened for quality, methodological and reporting quality was not used as a criterion for exclusion, thus retaining explanations and theories that might otherwise have been missed. Similarly, articles whose primary focus was not hospital performance per se, but did meet the criteria of "relevance" to hospital performance (for instance, publications on healthcare performance including hospitals), were included. The issue of "relevance" was also treated later in the analysis process through a graded assessment of each article's relatedness to hospital performance.

All included papers were subject to an assessment of rigor. The Critical Appraisal Skills Program (CASP) checklist for systematic review was adapted to suit the objectives of the current study, using prior modifications made by Black et al. (2011) as a basis. Each paper was scored (0 = no or can't tell, 1 = somewhat, 2 = clearly) across 13 equally weighted criteria, with a maximum score of 26. A second reviewer moderated the results of the quality appraisal. Assessment of risk of bias was not suitable given the aims of the review. The assessed quality of the paper was not used as a basis for exclusion, but informed how the paper was treated later in the review.

2.4 Data Extraction

For systematic review, data extraction involves locating discrete information across each included article and inserting extracts into a table, in order to facilitate a comparison of "like for like" information across studies. For instance, a data extraction table/form may include fields such as "author," "year," "population," "sample," "type of treatment," "effect size," "spread of impact" etc. The importance here is equivalence and comparability of included studies – requiring high levels of homogeneity across studies.

For realist syntheses, however, ensuring homogeneity and equivalence across included studies is less important. Comparisons and syntheses can be made on theoretical as well as methodological grounds, and there is more room for identifying contrasted elements between included studies – so long as this is done knowingly and transparently. There is also the capacity to extract relevant elements that may be unique to one study or a smaller selection of studies. Alongside data extraction tables, realist synthesis draws heavily on note-taking and annotation during this stage of the process. Evidence is sifted and sorted iteratively and relevant information extracted and recorded methodically and diligently.

The research aims, research questions and conceptual framework should be used as the driving force for the extraction process – helping to focus extraction efforts on information that sheds light on key questions of the review.

Box 4: Step 4. Data Extraction – An Example of the Realist Synthesis Approach

A tailored data extraction form was used to record and collate data. Each included article was provided with an ID number and data extracted under the following headings: author, year, type (of publication), journal/publisher, discipline, review method, dates (of included studies), setting, explanation code, explanation description, outcome variable, linked factor/s, key findings, quality appraisal (by authors of the included study). Some categories of data extraction were added during the process. It was at this stage that the categories of hospital performance explanation (i.e. "Regulation," "Leadership," or "Quality Improvement") were finalized, through a recursive process of conceptual framework-testing, theory-building and theory refinement.

2.5 Data Synthesis

2.5.1 Empirical Synthesis

Systematic reviews tend to favor (wherever possible) a meta-synthetic approach, in which data from comparable studies is combined and reanalyzed statistically. The synthesis of empirical information for a realist review, however, is treated narratively. This is not to imply that the "narrative" process is unstructured, intuitive or lacking in transparency; rather, narrative synthesis of empirical information is methodical, but relies on *text* as the unit of analysis rather than numeric data (Popay et al., 2006). This approach applies to both empirical synthesis and theoretical synthesis (treated separately, under 2.5.2).

The narrative synthesis process involves returning to information extracted in the previous step, and drawing higher-order conclusions about the broader body of evidence. Findings may be organized in new ways, to trace new patterns in the data, including directions of effects, effect sizes, barriers or facilitators or other explanatory factors that may contribute to certain outcomes, and importantly, the strength of evidence for dimensions of the theoretical framework. Popay et al. (2006) outlines seven tools and techniques for narrative synthesis: textual descriptions, groupings and clusters, tabulation, transforming data into a common rubric, vote counting as a descriptive tool, translating data through thematic analysis, and translating data through content analysis. This process may continue to challenge, stretch, and refine the conceptual framework, in response to empirical findings.

It is advisable that this stage include an appraisal of the characteristics of studies included within each conceptual category (in order to manage issues of nonhomogeneity between studies, or weaknesses in relevance or rigor) as well as an assessment of the strength of evidence for a particular category of theory. This can be achieved by using "vote counting" as a descriptive tool, following the technique outlined by Popay et al. (2006).

Box 5: Step 5a. Empirical Synthesis – An Example of the Realist Synthesis Approach

Data was synthesized in several stages, corresponding with each of the research questions underpinning the review. Vote counting tactics outlined by Popay et al. (2006) were used as a broad guide throughout the synthesis. First, data was grouped by category of explanation, and then each explanatory grouping (with the exception of the "multifactor" articles) was subject to a coding procedure with explicit decision-rules, using "low," "moderate," and "high" classifications to determine: (i) the relative volume of evidence; (ii) the homogeneity (of study aims) and consistency (of evidence and conclusions); (iii) the relevance of the literature (relatedness to the hospital setting); and (iv) the methodological rigor and quality of the studies. This process helped to characterize the evidence for each category of explanation. A sample table is included (Table 4) for theories/explanations belonging to the "environment" category. This process was repeated for each category of the theoretical framework.

Table 4. Sample Findings From a Vote Counting Synthesis of the Characteristics of Included Studies (Following Popay et al. (2006)).

Explanation	Characteristics of Evidence			
	Volume	Homogeneity	Relevance	Rigor
Environment				
Funding model (*n* = 13)	✔✔	✔✔	×	✔
Demography (*n* = 3)	✔	✔✔	✔	✔
Regulation (*n* = 6)	✔✔	✔✔	✔✔	✔
Reputation (*n* = 9)	✔✔	✔✔	✔	✔
Continued...				

Source: Author adapted from Pittman (2020).
Note: Characteristics of the evidence: ✔✔ high, ✔ moderate, × low, N/A not applicable.

The key findings of each article within each grouping were then assessed and allocated to one of five categories relating to the strength of evidence: "moderate positive," "weak positive," "no effect/mixed," "weak negative," or "moderate negative." This was done for each of the five aspects of hospital performance included in this review: accessibility, effectiveness, efficiency, safety and quality, and performance (not specified). A "vote count" tally helped to draw conclusions about the direction and strength of the evidence for each category of explanation. Explicit decision rules for coding, category allocation and "vote tallying" were used. A sample table is included (Table 5) for theories/explanations belonging to the "attribute" category. This was process was repeated for each category of the theoretical framework.

(Continued)

Table 5. Sample Findings From a Vote Counting Synthesis of Evidence (Following Popay et al. (2006)).

Explanation	Evidence for Impact on Hospital Performance			
	Hospital Access	Hospital Effectiveness	Hospital Efficiency	Hospital Safety
Environment				
Funding model (*n* = 13)	−/+	−/+	−/+	−/+
Demography (*n* = 3)	N/A	N/A	+	+ +
Regulation (*n* = 6)	N/A	−/+	−/+	−/+
Reputation (*n* = 9)	+	+	+	−/+
Continued...				

Source: Author adapted from Pittman (2020).

Note: Evidence for impact upon hospital performance: + + moderate positive evidence, + weak positive evidence, −/+ no effect/mixed, N/A not applicable (no evidence).

Following this, an overall summary and assessment of the evidence was conducted for each explanation/theory, taking into consideration both the characteristics of the evidence (e.g. relevance, rigor etc.) and the evidence of impact on hospital performance. Evidence was classified as: "positive," "weak positive," or "inconclusive" overall.

2.5.2 Theoretical Synthesis

A more theory-driven synthesis can be undertaken following (or in parallel with) a synthesis of empirical information. This is a stark departure from systematic review, and may rely more heavily on Popay and Colleague's (2006) thematic tools and techniques, such as textual descriptions, groupings and clusters, and thematic analysis. In particular, this part of the process supports deeper analysis of the mechanisms that may have brought about the various empirical outcomes revealed, and an attempt to identify causal links between context, mechanism and outcome configurations. This also helps to unearth interactions between factors or theoretical constructs.

Box 6: Step 5b. Theoretical Synthesis – An Example of the Realist Synthesis Approach

Having discovered that the strength of empirical evidence for each of the theoretical explanations for hospital performance was relatively weak, a more qualitative approach was taken in order to synthesize evidence.

A theory-driven narrative synthesis was performed drawing on guidance from Greenhalgh (2004) and Greenhalgh (2014), and following an abductive approach. The discussion and conclusion sections of each included article were imported into NVivo 11, a computer-assisted qualitative data analysis

(Continued)

software package. Initially, a number of preliminary (deductive) text queries were performed across the entire dataset to highlight key data related to "context" and "mechanisms" (and associated key words).

Second, articles were regrouped according to what (if any) testing or discussion occurred within the article about the interactions between the broad categories of explanation: environment, attribute and strategy. Each article was allocated to either a single explanation grouping: "environment," "attribute," "strategy" (and then discounted from this stage of the analysis); or a grouping that characterized interaction between the primary category or focus of explanation, and another category: "environment-attribute," "environment-strategy," "attribute-strategy," or "environment-attribute-strategy." The Venn Diagram shown in Fig. 2 illustrates how each of the 98 included articles were divided.

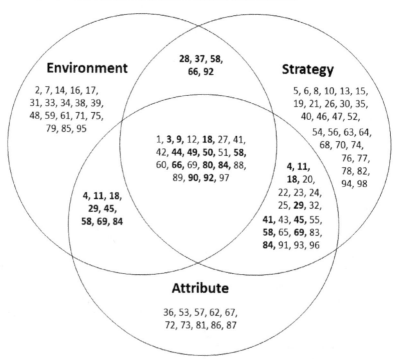

Fig. 2.   Venn Diagram Describing the Scope of What Is Known From the Literature on the Interactions Between Environment, Attribute and Strategic Factors and Their Influence on Hospital Performance (*n* = 98). *Source:* Author adapted from Pittman (2020).

The discussion and conclusion sections of the articles within these latter four groups then underwent a thematic analysis (following Braun and Clarke (2006)) to identify how the hospital performance literature has discussed the relationships between various explanations, theories and hypotheses, and the potentially cumulative or interactive effects of factors spanning multiple explanation categories.

2.6 Drawing Conclusions and Reporting Findings

Having extracted and synthesized review data, this final stage of literature review involves drawing conclusions – as aligned to the aims and research questions that prompted the review, and in relation to what is already known to scholars and management practitioners. Critical realist researchers use a mode of reasoning called "retroduction" to form these conclusions, drawing on both inductive and deductive logics, as well as valuing the researcher's expertise and capacity to form "hunches" worthy of intellectual pursuit (Olsen, 2010). The objective is to build and interrogate theories about the possible causal processes, properties, and patterns that may underpin a particular phenomenon. It is a theory-furthering pursuit, which may involve creative conceptual leaps for future testing and research.

Box 7: Step 6. Drawing Conclusions – An Example of the Realist Synthesis Approach

A prominent observation within the literature was that there is no simple answer, "silver bullet," or "one correct way" to bring about hospital performance improvement. Rather, the factors that surround, embed and operate within a hospital, appear to be interconnected, interdependent and mutually reinforcing, and collectively give rise to performance outcomes that are specific to local circumstances and cumulative actions.

Five themes emerged from the thematic analysis (as previously described in Box 6), which help shed light on the nature of factor interactions between the hospital environment, organizational attributes and strategy factors. These themes were used to refine the initial conceptual framework – illustrating several (possible) causal relationships operating between factors (Fig. 3).

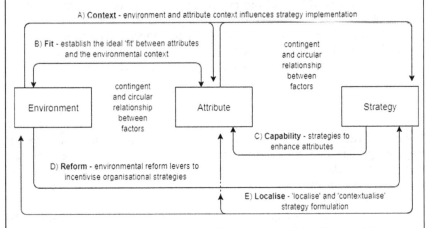

Fig. 3.   Interactions Between Hospital Environment, Attribute and Strategy Factors, as Currently Discussed Within the Literature. *Source:* Author adapted from Pittman (2020).

Finally, there is an expectation among scholars that realist syntheses be reported and written up with consistency and rigor. Realist synthesis reporting standards have been published elsewhere (Wong et al., 2013), and very little adaptation is needed for use by management scholars.

3. DISCUSSION AND CONCLUSION

3.1 Implications for Policy and Practice

Realist synthesis is not strictly a method, but a logic of inquiry and a broad approach to a specific task. Should the underpinning philosophy and logic suit the scholar and the scholarly task – particularly in instances of high complexity – it may offer great benefit. Realist synthesis comes from a research tradition built upon principles of pragmatism (Wynn & Williams, 2012), and the approach is therefore well suited to the aims of policymaker/practitioner as well as academic scholar. Complexity, turbulence, rapid change, unpredictability – each of these elements are commonplace in managerial and policy settings, and there is often an intuitive alignment between the realist viewpoint and those who wish to bring about tangible change in real world settings. The rapid adoption of the "wicked problems" paradigm in policy settings attests to this (Peters & Tarpey, 2019).

Realist synthesis addresses many of the common criticisms leveled against systematic review and narrative review approaches (Pawson & Bellamy, 2006). Philosophically situated between these two viewpoints – realist synthesis offers scholars both a methodical and adaptive approach, straddling a desire for procedural rigor and transparency alongside depth in discovery, creative problem solving, and theory-development (Wong et al., 2013).

It is worthwhile remembering that the viewpoint and purpose of realist synthesis is distinct from other approaches. The focus is on *explanation*, as opposed to narrative review which seeks to explore and describe, and systematic review which seeks to verify and predict. In comparing these approaches, it may be best to think of them as complementary rather than in competition (Greenhalgh et al., 2018). A researcher ought to select the right approach to match the set of assumption they bring to the research, and the research query they seek to illuminate.

3.2 Limitations

The realist synthesis approach has three major shortcomings. First, the approach may be rigorous and transparent, but it is not standardizable or reproducible (Pawson et al., 2004). Although a clear record of key decisions, turning points and adaptations ought to be kept by the researcher, replication is not the aim (Wong et al., 2013). The second shortcoming relates to this – procedural flexibility and adaptation relies upon a researcher's capacity for discernment, and the approach is therefore not as suitable for students, novice researchers, or researchers who do not feel confident breaking away from more prescriptive methods (Pawson et al., 2004). Finally, realist synthesis may produce more questions than answers. The objective is to further our collective capacity to explain complex phenomena, but this rarely brings about a simple or straightforward solution (Greenhalgh, 2014). The examination of nonlinear processes, context-dependent phenomena, and unique interactions between factors, requires a scholarly willingness to embrace the discomfort that may arise from complexity and the almost inevitable cognitive dissonance that this entails.

Critiqued from another perspective, some scholars of critical realism – the philosophical origins for realist synthesis – have argued that the realist synthesis method is overly influenced by logical positivism, and that the emphasis on procedural rigor detracts from the capacity for researches to explicate hidden causal mechanisms (Hinds & Dickson, 2021). This may indeed be a valid criticism, reflecting: (i) an overarching bias toward positivist research within the discipline that developed the realist synthesis method – health services research; and (ii) an opportunity for future scholars to further develop the realist synthesis approach, possibly with greater emphasis on how researchers may be guided to develop skills in retroductive reasoning and problem-solving, rather focusing on technical aspects of the method.

3.3 Conclusion

This chapter has sought to offer scholars an overview and introduction to the realist synthesis approach to literature review. The chapter began with a comparison between realist synthesis and other prominent literature review methods, and described in detail, the circumstances in which realist synthesis offers particular value over and above other methods. In the latter sections of the chapter, a summary of the steps required to conduct a realist synthesis was provided, followed by a brief overview of the approach overall.

4. ACKNOWLEDGEMENTS

I would like to acknowledge the contributions of the following scholars to the conceptual refinement of this paper: Distinguished Professor Gregory Peterson (University of Tasmania), Associate Professor Nuttaneeya Torugsa (Mahidol University), Doctor Karen Ford (University of Tasmania) and Mr Craig Quarmby (University of Tasmania).

REFERENCES

Armstrong, R. (2019). Revisiting strategy mapping for performance management: A realist synthesis. *International Journal of Productivity and Performance Management, 68*(4), 721–752. https://doi.org/10.1108/IJPPM-08-2017-0192

Ashworth, R. E., Boyne, G. A., & Entwistle, T. (2010). *Public service improvement: Theories and evidence.* Oxford University Press.

Bate, P. (2014). Context is everything. In *Perspectives on context.* Health Foundation.

Bhaskar, R. (1979). *The possibility of naturalism: A philosophical critique of the contemporary human sciences.* Harvester Press.

Black, A. D., Car, J., Pagliari, C., Anandan, C., Cresswell, K., Bokun, T., McKinstry, B., Procter, R., Majeed, A., & Sheikh, A. (2011). The impact of eHealth on the quality and safety of health care: A systematic overview. *PLoS Medicine, 8*(1), e1000387. https://doi.org/10.1371/journal. pmed.1000387

Braun, V., & Clarke, V. (2006). Using thematic analysis in psychology. *Qualitative Research in Psychology, 3*(2), 77–101.

Funke, J. (1991). Solving complex problems: Exploration and control of complex systems. In R. Sternberg & P. Frensch (Eds.), *Complex problem solving: Principles and mechanisms* (Vol. 4, pp. 185–222). Lawrence Erlbaum Associates.

Glaser, B., & Strauss, A. L. (1967). *The discovery of grounded theory*. de Gruyter.

Grant, M. J., & Booth, A. (2009). A typology of reviews: An analysis of 14 review types and associated methodologies. *Health Information & Libraries Journal, 26*(2), 91–108. https://doi.org/10.1111/j. 1471-1842.2009.00848.x

Greenhalgh, T. (2004). Meta-narrative mapping: A new approach to the systematic review of complex evidence. In *Narrative research in health and illness* (pp. 349–381). Blackwell Publishing.

Greenhalgh, J. (2014). Realist synthesis. In P. K. Edwards, J. O'Mahoney, & S. Vincent (Eds.), *Studying organizations using critical realism: A practical guide* (pp. 264–281). Oxford University Press.

Greenhalgh, J., & Manzano, A. (2022). Understanding 'context' in realist evaluation and synthesis. *International Journal of Social Research Methodology, 25*(5), 583–595. https://doi.org/10.1080/ 13645579.2021.1918484

Greenhalgh, T., Thorne, S., & Malterud, K. (2018). Time to challenge the spurious hierarchy of systematic over narrative reviews? *European Journal of Clinical Investigation, 48*(6), e12931. https://doi.org/10.1111/eci.12931

Head, B. W. (2019). Forty years of wicked problems literature: Forging closer links to policy studies. *Policy and Society, 38*(2), 180–197. https://doi.org/10.1080/14494035.2018.1488797

Head, B. W., & Alford, J. (2013). Wicked problems: Implications for public policy and management. *Administration & Society, 47*(6), 711–739. https://doi.org/10.1177/0095399713481601

Hinds, K., & Dickson, K. (2021). Realist synthesis: A critique and an alternative. *Journal of Critical Realism, 20*(1), 1–17. https://doi.org/10.1080/14767430.2020.1860425

Jagosh, J. (2019). Realist synthesis for public health: Building an ontologically deep understanding of how programs work, for whom, and in which contexts. *Annual Review of Public Health, 40*(1), 361–372. https://doi.org/10.1146/annurev-publhealth-031816-044451

Lönngren, J., & van Poeck, K. (2021). Wicked problems: A mapping review of the literature. *International Journal of Sustainable Development & World Ecology, 28*(6), 481–502. https://doi. org/10.1080/13504509.2020.1859415

Nilsson, D., Baxter, G., Butler, J. R. A., & McAlpine, C. A. (2016). How do community-based conservation programs in developing countries change human behaviour? A realist synthesis. *Biological Conservation, 200*, 93–103. https://doi.org/10.1016/j.biocon.2016.05.020

Olsen, W. (2010). Editor's introduction: Realist methodology – A review. In W. Olsen (Ed.), *Realist methodology: Benchmarks in social research methods series* (Vol. 1, pp. xix–xlvi). Sage Publications.

Pawson, R., & Bellamy, J. L. (2006). Realist synthesis: An explanatory focus for systematic review. In J. Popay (Ed.), *Moving beyond effectiveness in evidence synthesis: Methodological issues in the synthesis of diverse sources of evidence* (pp. 83–94). National Institute for Health and Clinical Excellence.

Pawson, R., Greenhalgh, T., Harvey, G., & Walshe, K. (2004). *Realist synthesis: An introduction*. ESRC Research Methods Programme.

Peters, B. G. (2017). What is so wicked about wicked problems? A conceptual analysis and a research program. *Policy and Society, 36*(3), 385–396. https://doi.org/10.1080/14494035.2017.1361633

Peters, B. G. (2018). Wicked, complex, or just difficult problems. In *Policy problems and policy design*. Edward Elgar Publishing.

Peters, B. G., & Tarpey, M. (2019). Are wicked problems really so wicked? Perceptions of policy problems. *Policy and Society, 38*(2), 218–236. https://doi.org/10.1080/14494035.2019.1626595

Petticrew, M., Rehfuess, E., Noyes, J., Higgins, J. P. T., Mayhew, A., Pantoja, T., Shemilt, I., & Sowden, A. (2013). Synthesizing evidence on complex interventions: How meta-analytical, qualitative, and mixed-method approaches can contribute. *Journal of Clinical Epidemiology, 66*(11), 1230–1243. https://doi.org/10.1016/j.jclinepi.2013.06.005

Pettigrew, A. (1985). *The awakening giant: Continuity and change in ICI.* Basil Blackwell.

Pittman, E. (2020). *A hospital hive mind?: A critical realist analysis of a high performing hospital.* University of Tasmania.

Popay, J., Roberts, H., Sowden, A., Petticrew, M., Arai, L., Rodgers, M., Britten, N., Roen, K., & Duffy, S. (2006). Guidance on the conduct of narrative synthesis in systematic reviews. *A Product from the ESRC Methods Programme Version, 1*(1), b92.

Quinlan, E., Robertson, S., Carr, T., & Gerrard, A. (2019). Workplace harassment interventions and labour process theory: A critical realist synthesis of the literature. *Sociological Research Online, 25*(1), 3–22. https://doi.org/10.1177/1360780419846567

Rittel, H. W. J., & Webber, M. M. (1973). Dilemmas in a general theory of planning. *Policy Sciences, 4*(2), 155–169. https://doi.org/10.1007/BF01405730

Roodbari, H., Axtell, C., Nielsen, K., & Sorensen, G. (2022). Organisational interventions to improve employees' health and wellbeing: A realist synthesis. *Applied Psychology, 71*(3), 1058–1081. https://doi.org/10.1111/apps.12346

Wong, G., Greenhalgh, T., Westhorp, G., Buckingham, J., & Pawson, R. (2013). RAMESES publication standards: Realist syntheses. *BMC Medicine, 11*(1), 21. https://doi.org/10.1186/1741-7015-11-21

Wynn, D., & Williams, C. K. (2012). Principles for conducting critical realist case study research in information systems. *MIS Quarterly, 36*(3), 787–810. https://doi.org/10.2307/41703481

Xiang, W.-N. (2013). Working with wicked problems in socio-ecological systems: Awareness, acceptance, and adaptation. *Landscape and Urban Planning, 110*, 1–4.

INDEX

Printed in the USA
CPSIA information can be obtained
at www.ICGtesting.com
JSHW011733210324
59678JS00004B/74